JESUS CHRIST AND THE SOCIAL QUESTION

AN EXAMINATION OF THE TEACHING OF JESUS IN ITS RELATION TO SOME OF THE PROBLEMS OF MODERN SOCIAL LIFE

BY

FRANCIS GREENWOOD PEABODY

PLUMMER PROFESSOR OF CHRISTIAN MORALS
IN HARVARD UNIVERSITY

New York
THE MACMILLAN COMPANY
LONDON: MACMILLAN & CO., LTD.
1908

Norwood Press
J. S. Cushing & Co. — Berwick & Smith
Norwood Mass. U.S.A.

THROUGH SUNNY DAYS AND ON THROUGH STORMY WEATHER,
  YET EVER HAND IN HAND, BELOVED WIFE,
WE TWO HAVE WALKED OUR QUIET WAY TOGETHER
  ALONG THE DUSTY ROAD OF COMMON LIFE.

BRIGHT WERE THE VISTAS ON OUR JOURNEY SEEN,
  AND DARK THE VALLEYS OF THE SHADOW LAY,
BUT YOUR DEAR LOVE, LIKE ISRAEL'S GOD, HAS BEEN
  MY LIGHT IN DARKNESS AND MY SHADE BY DAY.

I CANNOT GIVE YOU WHAT A SCHOLAR OUGHT,
  LEARNING OR WIT OR INSIGHT FOR THE TRUE;
I BUT TRANSCRIBE WHAT YOU HAVE DAILY TAUGHT, —
  THE SPIRIT OF THE MASTER SEEN IN YOU.

CONTENTS

CHAPTER I

PAGE

THE COMPREHENSIVENESS OF THE TEACHING OF JESUS . 1

CHAPTER II

THE SOCIAL PRINCIPLES OF THE TEACHING OF JESUS . 76

CHAPTER III

THE TEACHING OF JESUS CONCERNING THE FAMILY . . 129

CHAPTER IV

THE TEACHING OF JESUS CONCERNING THE RICH . . 183

CHAPTER V

THE TEACHING OF JESUS CONCERNING THE CARE OF THE
POOR 226

CHAPTER VI

THE TEACHING OF JESUS CONCERNING THE INDUSTRIAL
ORDER 267

CHAPTER VII

THE CORRELATION OF THE SOCIAL QUESTIONS . . . 327

JESUS CHRIST AND THE SOCIAL QUESTION

CHAPTER I

THE COMPREHENSIVENESS OF THE TEACHING OF JESUS

The life was the light of men.

THERE are many periods in history which, as one looks back on them, seem marked by distinct and central problems or achievements, as if to each such time there had been committed a special work to do. Their characteristics stand out clearly against the past, as a distant range of mountains stands out against an evening sky. We speak with confidence of the mission of Greece to civilization, of the place of Rome in history, of the vocation of the Hebrews, of the period of the Reformation, of the epoch of Napoleon. By one lesson at a time, — through types of beauty or strength or righteousness, through instructions in intellectual liberty, or warnings of the lust for power, — the Master of the ages seems to have directed the education of the human race. Sometimes this mission of an age or race is recognized by those who are fulfilling it; sometimes it is discerned when one stands at a distance, where the crowded details of life melt into a general view. The Hebrews, on the one hand, were sustained throughout their history by the conviction of their sacred and special calling, and that conviction gave to their career its sombre, strenuous, self-examining character; in Greek life, on the other hand, it was the very unconsciousness of a didactic mission which made possible the prevailing serenity and charm. If Greek art had stood consciously before the glass of the future, it might have been the teacher, but could not have been the joy, of the world.

The present age belongs, without question, to the former class. There is not only given to it a mission, but there is added a distinct consciousness of that mission. We do not have to wait for the philosophical historian of some remote future to discern the characteristic problem of the present time. Behind all the extraordinary achievements of modern civilization, its transformations of business methods, its miracles of scientific discovery, its mighty combinations of political forces, there lies at the heart of the present time a burdening sense of social mal-adjustment which creates what we call the social question. "The social question," remarks Professor Wagner, "comes of the consciousness of a contradiction between economic development and the social ideal of liberty and equality which is being realized in political life."[1] This is what gives its fundamental character to the present age. The consciousness of contradiction between economic progress and spiritual ideals may use the language of social philosophy, or may take the form of social service, or may be organized in social legislation, or may simply utter itself in the passionate cry of indignation or hate which comes from the hungry or despairing, or from those who sympathize with them. In all these varied, and often unreasonable or extravagant, ways the characteristic emotion of the time expresses itself. It is the age of the social question. Never were so many people, learned and ignorant, rich and poor, philosophers and agitators, men and women, so stirred by this recognition of inequality in social opportunity, by the call to social service, by dreams of a better social world.

There is, of course, a huge, inert mass of unobservant humanity, with no perception of this new region of hope and faith into which the present generation is entering. These persons live their lives of business or of pleasure, as Jesus, with splendid satire, said of such persons in his own age, with just enough power of observation to tell the signs of to-morrow's weather, but without the

[1] A. Wagner, " Lehrbuch der politischen Oekonomie," 2. Aufl., 1876, s. 36. So also Bebel, " Die Frau und der Sozialismus," 10. Aufl., 1891, s. 240: " Society, in its form of wealth, has grown far more aristocratic than in any earlier age, . . . in its ideals and its legislation it has grown far more democratic."

capacity to discern the signs of their own times.[1]
No one, however, who lifts his eyes from his own
private life can mistake these signs of the times.
The literature of the present age is saturated with
the desire for social amelioration or social revolution; workmen with grimy hands and women
with eager eyes are turning the pages of the
economists in search of practical guidance; social
panaceas are confidently offered on every hand;
organization on an unprecedented scale is con-
solidating the fighting force of the hand-working
class; legislation is freely advocated which practically revolutionizes the earlier conception of the
function of government; and, finally, the party of
revolution, with its millions of voters in European
countries, officially announces that all other issues
are to be subordinated to the social question, and
that all other parties are to be regarded as "a
mere reactionary mass."[2]   It is the age of the
social question; and to pretend that social life is
undisturbed, or is but superficially agitated, is simply to confess that one has been caught in an
eddy of the age and does not feel the sweep of its
main current.

It is, however, not enough to say that among
human interests the social question is just now

---

[1] Matt. xvi. 2, 3; Luke xii. 54–56.

[2] "Die Befreiung der Arbeit muss das Werk der Arbeiterklasse
sein, der gegenüber alle anderen Klassen nur eine reaktionäre Masse
sind," Programm der sozialdemokratischen Partei Deutschlands,
Gotha, 1878.

central and commanding. There are, it must be added, two characteristics of the modern temper which make of the social question of the present time something quite different from the economic and social agitations of the past. In the first place, we are now confronted by a degree of radicalism and a scope of reconstructive purpose which practically create a new situation. Social and industrial reforms in the past have been for the most part ameliorative or philanthropic measures, accepting the existing order of things, and mitigating its harsher effects. Now and then a sudden wave of indignation has risen out of the depths of human nature and has swept away some special abuse like American slavery, or some special form of social relationship like the *ancien régime* of France; but for the most part the desire to relieve the unfortunate and improve the condition of the hand-worker has satisfied itself with deeds of charity and with industrial expedients which calm the surface of social life. A wholly different state of mind prevails to-day. Beneath all the tranquillizing arrangements of philanthropy or industry which are being applied to social disorder, there is a vast and rising tide of discontent, stirring to its very bottom the stream of social life. The social question of the present age is not a question of mitigating the evils of the existing order, but a question whether the existing order itself shall last. It is not so much a problem of social amelioration which occupies the modern mind, as a problem of social transformation and reconstruction. The new social interest is concerned not so much with effects as causes; not with social therapeutics, but with social bacteriology and social hygiene. Indeed, in this frame of mind there is often to be discerned a violent reaction from traditional ways of charity and from moderate measures of reform. The time is wasted, it is urged, which is given to lopping off occasional branches of social wrong, when the real social question cuts at the root from which these branches grow. Instead of inquiring what ways of charity are wise, let us rather, it is urged, inquire why charity is necessary and why poverty exists. Instead of reforming the adjustments of industry, let us rather ask why the effects of industry are so cruel, debasing, and unjust. Not a merciful use of things as they are, but a state of things where mercy will not be necessary; not patronage, but justice; not the generous distribution of superfluous wealth, but the righteous restitution of wealth to those who have created it, — such are the demands to which our ears have of late become accustomed, and which indicate the character of the modern social question. "The number of relief- and charity-panaceas for poverty," said an English agitator, "are of no more value than a poultice to a wooden leg. What we want is economic revolution, and not pious and heroic resolutions." [1]

---

[1] Ben Tillett, in *London Times*, January 1, 1895.

This unflinching radicalism proceeds to examine the very pillars of social life, and to consider whether they are worth what it costs to buttress and maintain them.   Three such social institutions appear to support the fabric of modern civilization — the family, private property, and the State ; and there is not one of these institutions whose continued existence in its present form is not now a matter of active discussion, or whose abolition is not confidently prophesied.   Is not the institution of the family to be regarded as a passing incident in the course of social evolution, the end of whose social service has nearly arrived?   Is not the institution of private property a mere symbol of social oppression, so that, as the earlier revolutionists cried, "Property is robbery," their modern followers may now add, "It is right to rob the robbers"?   Is not the institution of the State, in its present form, a mere instrument of the privileged class, and must it not be supplanted by a coöperative commonwealth of collective ownership?   Questions like these, freely agitated in our day by all sorts and conditions of people, indicate how fundamental and thoroughgoing the social problem of which they are a part must be.   They propose a revolution, not only in the outward conditions of social life, but in the very instincts and habits of mind which adjust themselves to the present social order.

Such possibilities of social change are viewed by many persons with grave apprehension, and by many with jubilant hope. To one class of observ-ers, we appear to be threatened by social disaster, industrial chaos, a new slavery; to the opposite class, we appear to be at the dawn of a happy era of brotherhood and justice, and Mr. William Morris sings:—

> "Come hither, lads, and hearken, for there is a tale to tell,
>   Of the wonderful days a-coming when all shall be better
>   than well."[1]

From either point of view, however, the social question is seen to have a quality of comprehen-siveness and radicalism which makes it practically a new issue, and it is important at the outset of the present inquiry to recognize how large a ques-tion it is with which we have to do. A generation ago Mr. Lowell touched the note of the social question of his time in his "Vision of Sir Launfal." Social duty seemed then fulfilled in deeds of benev-olence and self-sacrificing love; and a whole gen-eration learned to repeat his lines as the summary of social service:—

> "Not what we give, but what we share,
>   For the gift without the giver is bare.
>   Who giveth himself with his alms feeds three, —
>   Himself, his hungering neighbor, and Me."

The temper of the present age is no longer com-prehended by such a statement of the social ques-tion. Instead of generosity, men ask for justice; instead of alms, they demand work. Thus the le-

---

[1] "Chants for Socialists," London, 1885.

gend of the search for holiness, if written for present-day readers, must be translated from the language of charity into the language of industrial life, and the new Sir Launfal finds his Holy Grail through productive labor rather than through pitying love.

" They who tread the path of labor, follow where Christ's feet have trod,
  They who work without complaining, do the holy will of God.
  Where the weary toil together, there am I among my own,
  Where the tired workman sleepeth, there am I with him alone.

      *   *   *   *   *   *   *

  This is the Gospel of labor — ring it, ye bells of the kirk,
  The Lord of Love came down from above to live with the men who work." [1]

A second characteristic of the modern social question is quite as unmistakable and significant. Whatever aspect of it we approach, we find the discussion and agitation of the present time turning in a quite unprecedented degree to moral issues, and using the language and weapons of a moral reform. The social question of the present time is an ethical question. Selfishness enough exists, it is true, among advocates of social change; class hatred is also there, and the lust for power, and the primitive instincts which, as Hobbes said, make each man a wolf to his neighbor; but the power and the pathos of the modern social movement reside in the passionate demand, now heard

[1] Henry Van Dyke, "The Toiling of Felix," 1898.

on every hand, for justice, brotherhood, liberty, the chance for a human way of life. In his "Progress and Poverty" Mr. Henry George remarks, "If our inquiry into the cause which makes low wages and pauperism the accompaniments of material progress has any value, it will bear translation from the language of economics into that of ethics, and, as the source of social evils, show a wrong."[1] That is the note of the present situation. The social question, which on its surface is an economic question, issues in reality from a sense of wrong. This ethical note is struck by the new philanthropy, in its unprecedented sense of social obligation, its call for personal devotion, its demand for self-discipline and wisdom; and the same note is heard in the harsher tone of the labor agitation, declaring against the iniquity of the employer and the inconsistency of private ownership with the brotherhood of man. Behind many an economic fallacy which would seem to have no right to permanent influence lies this force of moral feeling, which supports the irrational creed, as a building supports the scaffolding which leans against it.

Here is a quality of the modern social question which one immediately perceives to be a sign of promise. Misdirected, passionate, inarticulate, the cry for social righteousness may be; but after all

---

[1] "Progress and Poverty," Book VII, Ch. I. See also, Preface to fourth edition: "The inquiry passes into the field of ethics. . . . It also identifies the law of social life with the great moral law of justice."

it is an unmistakable sign of social progress, when millions of people, in all lands and of all conditions, are trying, however blindly, to discover what is right and what is wrong in social conduct, and to reach some consistency between their social condition and their social ideals.   "The real solution of this problem," said Professor Ingram to a Trades-Union Congress in Dublin, "can be effected only by such reorganization of ideas and renovation of sentiment as will rise to the dimensions of an intellectual and moral reform."[1]   It is not by accident, then, that the social question is most conspicuous in the most prosperous and best educated countries.   It is one expression of prosperity and education.   There is no social question in Turkey or Egypt.   The problem of social justice does not grow out of the worst social conditions, but out of the best.   It is not a mark of social decadence, but of social vitality.   It is one expression of popular education, intellectual liberty, and quickened sentiments of sympathy and love, and there can be nothing but good in the end to come of an agitation which fundamentally represents a renaissance of moral responsibility.

It is its ethical quality, moreover, which gives to the social question of the present day its commanding interest for generous minds.   Great numbers of men and women are lavishing their time and thought on social service, without precisely defining to themselves why such occupations

[1] Kaufmann, "Christian Socialism," 1888, p. 12.

open, as they are pursued, into a peculiar peace and joy. There is nothing intrinsically picturesque or noble about the poor or degraded; there is little romance in the administration of details in industrial or social life. Why is it, then, that time, ability, money, and sympathy are in such abundance offered for such service? It is because, through these channels of activity, the moral life of the time finds its natural outlet. It is a great source of happiness to be associated with people who are trying, however imperfectly, to make a better world. Many a life emerges through such association from an experience of narrowness and emptiness into one of breadth, fulness, and satisfaction. It is like a journey from one's own village to a foreign land, from which one returns with a new sense of human kinship, a more comprehensive sympathy, and a profounder gratitude for his own blessings. The advent of the social question in its present form has brought with it a great and happy revival of ethical confidence. The older ethics was individual, introspective, self-examining, and its stream grew narrow and uninviting and dry; but into its bed there has broken this new flood of social interests, like a spring freshet filling the channel to its banks; and now a score of outlets can hardly contain the stream of philanthropic service which sweeps on to the refreshing of the world.[1]

[1] The ethical character of the social question is observed not by the social reformers only, but by the philosophers of history: Th.

In the light, then, of these two characteristics of the modern social question, its radical intention and its ethical passion, a further quality which one observes in the present situation may appear at first sight surprising. It would seem as if there were an obvious kinship between the spirit of this

Ziegler, "Die soziale Frage eine sittliche Frage," 1891, a stirring attempt "to examine critically the conditions which exist, and to consider how they may be brought to an issue in which our highest good shall not be lost," s. 8. See also: Jodl, "Volkswirtschafts-lehre und Ethik, Deutsche Zeit- und Streitfragen," 1886; F. Hasler (from the Roman Catholic standpoint), "Ueber das Ver-hältniss der Volkswirtschaft und Moral," 1887; Bonar, "Philosophy and Political Economy in some of their Relations," 1893, Bk. V; *International Journal of Ethics*, January, 1897, p. 191, C. S. Devas, "The Restoration of Economics to Ethics," "All [these sciences] move in an ethical atmosphere; . . . all have principally to do with what is right and wrong"; L. Ragaz, "Evangelium und Moderne Moral," 1898; and for the history of this "socialization of ideals," Stein, "Die soziale Frage im Lichte der Philosophie," 1897, especially s. 660 ff., "Die Sozialisierung der Religion." Compare also the evidence of the economists : A. T. Hadley, "Economics," p. 23, "The modern economist . . . would say that nothing was economically beneficent which was ethically bad ; he would insist with equal force that nothing could be ethically good which was economically disastrous"; C. D. Wright, "The Relation of Political Economy to the Labor Question," 1882 ; F. A. Lange, "Die Arbeiterfrage," 1879. Note also the remarkable expansion of systematic ethics into the sphere of the social question: Wundt, "Ethik," 1886, ss. 159 ff., 498 ff., 529 ff.; Paulsen, "System der Ethik," 1889, s. 698 ff.; and his paper before the 10ter Evang.-soz. Kongress, 1899, s. 95, "Wandlungen des Bildungsideals in ihrem Zusammenhang mit der sozialen Entwickelung"; Runze, "Prak-tische Ethik," 1891, s. 65 ff., with much bibliographical material ; H. S. Nash, "Genesis of the Social Conscience," 1897, p. 223 ff.; Newman Smyth, "Christian Ethics," Ch. IV; "The Social Prob-lem and Christian Duties."

new philanthropy and the spirit of the Christian religion. In both there is the same sense of value in the humblest human soul, the same desire for a spiritual democracy, the same call for self-sacrifice, the same readiness to overthrow existing traditions and institutions for the sake of righteousness. The social question, one might anticipate, would be at heart not only an ethical question but a religious question also. "The religious element," said Mazzini, "is universal, immortal. . . . Every great revolution has borne its stamp and revealed it in its origin or in its aim. . . . The instinctive philosophy of the people is faith in God."[1] "Socialism," it has been remarked, "in its most explicit and absolute form, has a great attraction for the masses, by reason of that quality which it possesses in common with the gospels. . . . It is this factor which has lent to those who profess and propagate it the illusion of an apostolate, and has inspired in those who are its objects an enthusiasm extending to fanaticism, to crime devoid of personal motive, to the scaffold itself."[2] Yet, nothing is in fact more conspicuous than the lack of practical coöperation, and in many instances the distrust and hostility, which prevail between these two ways of social service. Sometimes there is a candid dread of theological complications, as when scientific charity lays down the

[1] " Faith and the Future," 1835.

[2] "Nuova Antologia," 16 November, 1898, p. 269. F. Nobili-Vitelleschi, " Il Socialismo di Stato."

principle of abstinence from proselytizing. Some
times there is a sheer disappointment with the
social effectiveness of the Christian Church, such
as forced one of the most judicious labor leaders in
England to say that he saw no place for religion in
the working-man's programme. Sometimes, again,
there is a genuine reproduction of Christian principles of conduct without formal recognition of the
Christian Church, as in the extraordinary growth
of the coöperative system in Great Britain.   In
many such ways of social activity the instincts
which in other centuries would have drawn
people toward religion are finding their satisfaction
without religion ; or, rather, are finding in philanthropy or labor unions or coöperative societies or
kindred social interests practical equivalents for
religion, satisfying hearts with generous emotions
and offering strong persuasions to loyalty and
fellowship.   When, further, we turn to the more
radical expressions of social discontent, the prevailing attitude toward religion becomes even less
friendly.   It is not necessary to notice the merely
vulgar talk of agitators who make it a part of
their stock in trade to ridicule and vilify the
religious life.[1]   It should also be observed that in

[1] A collection of such coarser utterances may be found in Kaufmann, "Christian Socialism," 1888, Ch. IX; and in profusion in
Köhler, "Sozialistische Irrlehren von der Entstehung des Christentums," 1899, s. 21 ff. "To suppress religion which provides an
illusory happiness is to establish the claim of real happiness,"
"Nouveau Parti," 1884 (Kaufmann, p. 195). "The cross, once a
symbol of suffering, is now a symbol of slavery," *To-day*, January,

the official programmes of social revolution religion is, as a rule, declared to be a matter of personal decision, toward which neutrality may be maintained.[1] The expositors of revolutionary principles, however, do not hesitate to teach that with the overthrow of capitalism will crumble the institutions of religion. "Religion," said Bebel, "will not be abolished; God will not be dethroned. . . . Without violent assault, and without suppression of opinions of any kind, religion will of itself gradually disappear."[2] "It is useless," writes Mr. Belfort Bax, "blinking the fact that the Christian doctrine is more revolting to the higher moral sense of to-day than the Saturnalia of the cult of Proserpina could have been to the conscience of the early Christians;"[3] and in another place he says: "In what sense socialism

1894 (Kaufmann, p. 3). "We are all, I take it, disciples of the materialist philosophy of history derived from Marx," Remarks at Stuttgart Congress (Köhler, s. 7).

[1] "Erklärung der Religion zur Privatsache," Programm der sozialdemokratischen Partei Deutschlands. See also, *Nation*, Nov. 12, 1891, "German Socialists in Council," an account of the Erfurt Congress of 1891, F. G. Peabody.

[2] "Die Frau und der Sozialismus," 10te Aufl., s. 313. Through a curious similarity in names a citation derived from Wilhelm Marr, "Das junge Deutschland in der Schweiz," Leipzig, 1846, was, in earlier editions of this book, erroneously assigned to Marx, and the mistake is now tardily acknowledged. The view of Marx concerning the future of religion was not that of destructivism, but rather the more radical faith that religion, as a reflection of the present industrial order, will share the fate of that order, and with it be transformed or disappear.

[3] Quoted, *Pall Mall Magazine*, April, 1895.

is not religion will be now clear. It utterly despises 'the other world,' with all its stage properties, — that is, the present objects of religion. In what sense it is not irreligious will be also, I think, tolerably clear; it brings back religion from heaven to earth. . . ." " It is in the hope and struggle for the higher social life that . . . the socialist finds his ideal, his religion." " The socialist requires no transformed Christian rites to aid him in keeping his ideal before him. . . ." "It is only natural that the socialist should resent with some indignation the continual reference of ideal perfection to a semi-mythical Syrian of the first century, when he sees higher types even in some men walking this upper earth."[1] In short, as the eloquent Pastor Naumann concludes, "Social democracy turns against Christ and the Church because it sees in them only the means of providing a religious foundation for the existing economic order."[2]

[1] Bax, "The Religion of Socialism," 1886, pp. 52, 96.

[2] F. Naumann, "Das soziale Programm der evangelischen Kirche," 1891, s. 49. The attitude of scientific socialism to the Christian religion is sufficiently indicated by : "Geschichte des Sozialismus in Einzeldarstellungen," 1895, 3ter Band, F. Mehring, "Geschichte der deutschen Sozialdemokratie," 1897, 2ter Teil, s. 387 ff., Die Christlich-soziale Agitation; Engels, "Zur Geschichte des Urchristentums, Neue Zeit," 1894–1895; Lütgenau, "Natürliche und sozialistische Religion," 1894 ; Stein, "Die Soziale Frage im Lichte der Philosophie," s. 660 ff., "Die Sozialisierung der Religion." The popular acceptance of this view is illustrated by Rade, "Die sittlich-religiöse Gedankenwelt unserer Industriearbeiter," 9ter Evang.-soz. Kongress, 1898, s. 66; and by P. Göhre, "Drei Monate

C

Here we come upon one of the most curious
and important facts of the revolutionary movement.
At first sight it is difficult to understand why a
movement which appears to propose simply an
economic change should be colored by this antipa-
thy to spiritual ideals. The truth is, however, that
this characteristic of social radicalism proceeds,
in the main, not from an economic necessity, but
from the philosophy of history with which the
German school of scientific socialism happens to
be associated. Marx and Lassalle, the apostles of
the German socialist gospel, though of very different types of character, were both of Jewish extrac-
tion, and both had been swept into the current of
the Hegelian philosophy, in its more radical interpretation. To this way of thought the universe
presented itself as a self-unfolding process of
material forces, one result of which was expressed
in the shifting opinions and beliefs of men. These
doctrines and ideals were, to the left wing of Hegel-
ianism, not glimpses of reality, but effects of social
conditions. Spiritual ideals were the result of

Fabrikarbeiter," 1891, s. 142 ff. Adequate criticism of this position
is offered by: Herrmann, " Religion und Sozialdemokratie," 2ter
Evang.-soz. Kongress, 1891; A. Wagner, " Das neue sozialdemokratische Programm," 3ter Evang.-soz. Kongress, 1892. See also
the less important discussion in Flint, " Socialism," 1894, Ch. IX,
" Socialism and Religion." The whole subject is treated in elaborate detail by H. Köhler (op. cit.). So Uhland: —

" Ich ging zur Tempelhalle zu hören christlich Recht,
Hier innen Brüder alle, dort draussen Herr und Knecht !
Der Festesrede Giebel war : Duck dich, schweig dabei !
Als ob die ganze Bibel ein Buch der Könige sei."

economic circumstances, not revelations of absolute truth. Given a certain range of economic condition, and there would ensue a certain quality of spiritual belief or of religious fellowship. "Every man," said Bebel, "is a product of his time and an instrument of circumstances. Christianity, then, the prevailing spiritual expression of the present economic order, must pass away as a better social order arrives. Indeed, the wise reformer should apply himself to economic revolution exclusively, because he is sure that the evanescent imaginations which capitalism has suggested will disappear like dew when the morning of socialism arrives." It would not at first seem as if such a philosophy of the universe could have had great significance for a parliamentary party of plain working-people; yet the fact is that it tinges a great portion of the talk of labor agitators, falls in with many lower impulses, becomes the justification of many natural prejudices, and contributes greatly to the consolidation of the working-class against the privileged and the pious. It is not enough to say that the socialist programme is indifferent to religion. It undertakes to provide a substitute for religion. It is a religion, so far as religion is represented by a philosophy of life, to which men give themselves with passionate attachment. It sets itself against Christianity because, as Liebknecht said, "That is the religion of private property and of the respectable classes." It offers itself as an alternative to the Christian religion.

It is, as a distinguished critic has remarked, not merely a new economic and social programme, but proposes to compete with Christianity in offering a comprehensive creed.[1]

We find, then, a gulf of alienation and misinterpretation lying between the social movement and the Christian religion, — a gulf so wide and deep as to recall the judgment of Schopenhauer, that Christianity, in its real attitude toward the world, is absolutely remote from the spirit of the modern age. Yet, from the time when the social question began to take its present form, there have not failed to be heard a series of protests against this alienation of the new movement from the organization of the Christian life. To any one, indeed, who has once recognized the ethical quality of the modern social question, the interpretation of it in terms of sheer philosophical materialism must appear a perversion of its characteristic aim, which can have occurred only through an unfortunate historical accident. What reason has the Christian Church for existing, many persons are now asking, if it is not to have a part in that shaping of a better world which at the same time is the aim of the social movement ? What was the gospel of Jesus if it was not, as he himself called it, a gospel for the poor, the blind,

[1] H. Holtzmann, "Die ersten Christen und die soziale Frage" ("Wiss. Vorträge über rel. Fragen," 1880), s. 55. So Nathusius, "Die Mitarbeit der Kirche an der Lösung der sozialen Frage," 1897, s. 115 ff., "Radical socialism must be in opposition to prevailing religion, because it is itself a religion."

the prisoners, and the broken-hearted? Is it not possible that the social movement, which so often seems remote from, or even hostile to, the work of the Christian religion, may be in reality nothing else than a modern expansion of that religion? May it not come to pass that the solution of the social question shall be found in the principles of the Christian religion? And is it not, on the other hand, evident that the only test of the Christian religion which the modern world will regard as adequate is its applicability to the solution of the social question? Must we not, as Maurice said, either socialize Christianity or Christianize socialism? Such considerations have prompted a great number of propositions,— experimental and philosophical, reactionary and radical,— looking to the reconciliation of economic needs with Christian ideals. They range all the way from the most obvious and practical undertakings to the most visionary and speculative schemes. Each plan creates strange companionships,— Catholics with Protestants, scholars with hand-workers,— yet all are at one in the desire to find a place for the Christian life in the modern world; and while a complete history of such schemes is quite beyond our present purpose, it may be instructive to indicate briefly a few of the ways in which this reconciliation has been sought.

The first and most elementary scheme thus proposed is that of a literal reproduction of the economic life of primitive Christianity.   The disciples, we read in the book of Acts, "had all things com-mon"; and "sold their possessions and goods, and parted them to all, according as any man had need"; "and not one of them said that aught of the things which he possessed was his own."[1] These passages have given encouragement to a long series of experiments in Christian communism, sometimes monastic in form, sometimes ascetic in bond of union, but always inspired by the hope of practically establishing a Christian way of life in the midst of an unchristianized world.   No one can recall these tranquil communities of pious and self-effacing souls without a touch of admiration. It is reassuring to see the lusts of the world, which dominate so many lives, powerless to disquiet or control.   The lingering communities which still attempt, in unambitious seclusion, this reproduc-tion of apostolic life are to our time what the best of monastic life was in its own age — spots of calm in the centre of the cyclonic activity of the world.

Yet these conscientious attempts to revive the industrial life of the first disciples have no substan-tial justification, either in economics or in Christian history.   On the one hand, they do not meet the modern problem of economic life ; they simply run away from it.   It is impossible for such communi-ties to enter on a large scale into direct competi-tion with the methods of the great industry ; and it

[1] Acts ii. 44; iv. 32.

is equally impossible for the needs of the world
— or, for that matter, of the community itself —
to be supplied by these primitive ways of production. Communism, while it rejects the economic order surrounding it, still rests on that
order. The factories, railways, great cities, and
exchanges of commerce provide the very conditions which make it possible for the privileged
few to retreat to a life of calm. It was the
same with the monastic system. It could not be
for the many, still less for all. The world's work
had to go on, and the unproductive saints had to
be, in large part, supported by the toiling and
unsanctified world which lay about the monastery's
walls. Christian communism then, even at its
best, is not an advance, but a retreat. Its disciples deceive themselves with the impression that
they have subdued the world, when in reality they
have fled from the world. The only way out of
economic disorders and imperfections is through
them; and the Christian life in the present age
must be sought, not in reversion to an impossible
past, but in the creation of a better future.

To these considerations must be added the fact
that these supposed reproductions of primitive
Christian economics have no adequate justification
even in the Scriptural passages on which they
appear to rest. The social life of the first disciples, when more closely scrutinized, is seen to have
been something quite different from the rule of a
monastic order with its vow of poverty, or of a

modern society with its communal control of productive industry and family life. Indeed, it is
quite contrary to the spirit of those first days of
Christian discipleship to think of them as devoted
to the establishing of any economic system or the
prescribing of any fixed rule of social life. There
is, in the first place, no evidence that what is reported of the little company at Jerusalem became
in any degree a general practice, as though enjoined
by the teaching of Jesus. No other instance of
communal ownership is cited in the book of Acts;
but, on the other hand, the mother of Mark continues to own her home in Jerusalem,[1] and voluntary relief is sent from Antioch by "every man
according to his ability." [2] The apostle Paul knows
nothing of such communistic regulations. "Let each
man," he says, "do according as he hath purposed in
his heart; not grudgingly, or of necessity."[3] "Upon
the first day of the week let each one of you lay by
him in store, as he may prosper." [4] "We command
and exhort in the Lord Jesus Christ, that with
quietness they work, and eat their own bread." [5]
In short, the communism of the day of Pentecost,
like the gift of tongues described in the same
chapter, was a spontaneous, unique, and unrepeated
manifestation of that elevation and unity of spirit
which possessed the little company in the first
glow of their new faith. Still further, this sharing of each other's possessions, which was thus

---

[1] Acts xii. 12.   [2] Acts xi. 29.   [3] 2 Cor. ix. 7.
[4] 1 Cor. xvi. 2.   [5] 2 Thess. iii. 12.

for the moment a sign of their perfect brotherhood, was even then no formal or compulsory system.   The narrative immediately goes on to say
that one disciple, Barnabas, "having a field, sold
it, and brought the money, and laid it at the
apostles' feet,"[1]— singling this man out, it would
appear, as unusually munificent.   In the case of
Ananias and Sapphira,[2] it is not the keeping back
part of the price of the land, but the lie to the
Holy Ghost which is condemned.   "Whiles it remained, did it not remain thine own? and after it
was sold, was it not in thy power?"[3]   This man
and woman wanted to appear to have made the
same exceptional sacrifice which had been praised
in the case of Barnabas, and it was their fraudulent virtue, not the reserving of their private property, which made their sin so base.

Thus the so-called communism of primitive Christianity was simply a glad, free, domestic relationship
of generous aid and service, such as any modern
Christian congregation might legitimately strive to
imitate.   It did not abolish distinctions of rich and
poor, still less did it enter the sphere of productive
industry.   Its economics were those of a loving
family.   Each man might keep his own possessions, but "not one of them said that aught of the
things which he possessed was his own."   The
hearts of the first believers were stirred to self-for-
getful and self-sacrificing service, and the church
at Jerusalem soon became in such a degree a

[1] Acts iv. 37.   [2] Acts v. 1–10.   [3] Acts v. 4.

refuge for the poor that it was in need of missionary help from Gentile congregations. In all this,
however, there is no warrant for identifying Christian faith with a single system of economic distribution. Gladly as Jesus would have welcomed that
new glow of loyalty which had "all things common," and certainly as he would recognize the
same self-effacing love in many an uncompetitive
and unambitious community to-day, it is both impracticable and unhistorical to regard communism
as that solution of the social question to which
the New Testament is committed. Fortunately
for the Christian life, Jesus does not shut it within
the limits of any single social scheme, still less of
a programme which can have no important place
in the organization of the modern world.[1]

[1] It is as a rule assumed by interpreters of the New Testament
with socialist sympathies that the communism of the book of Acts
is a genuine anticipation of the modern protest against capitalism.
Nitti, "Catholic Socialism," London, 1895, p. 62, " It is certain that
the early Christians practised communism or community of goods.
. . . The first Christians did not seek to acquire wealth; like
Christ, they sought to annihilate it. . . . Christianity was a
vast economic revolution more than anything else." Herron, "Between Cæsar and Jesus," p. 109, "Apostolic Christianity took
seriously the economic facts of the spiritual life. Men understood
that in becoming Jesus's disciples it was incumbent upon them to
surrender private interests." Renan, "The Apostles" (tr. J. H.
Allen, 1898), "The account in Acts is in perfect accord with what
we know of the other ascetic religions, — Buddhism, for example, —
which always begin with cenobitic (or communistic) life, the first
adepts being a host of mendicant monks." Todt, "Der radikale
deutsche Sozialismus und die christliche Gesellschaft," 2. Aufl., s. 70,
"The first Christian community was penetrated by the thought of

A second and more familiar way of applying the Christian spirit to the social question is the way of Christian philanthropy. The work of

the unity of interests. Each strove for all and all for each. In this striving they were communists as our socialists are to-day." Yet Todt later, s. 188 ff., admits that this was no fixed or invariable rule. "The New Testament represents human liberty and accepts any form of property-holding which fulfils this condition, whether it be private property in real estate or communal ownership in the socialist sense." For the prevailing teaching of scientific socialists, see the abundant literature cited and the criticism offered in Köhler, "Sozialistische Irrlehren von der Entstehung des Christentums," 1899, s. 85 ff.

On the other hand, New Testament critics of the first rank are practically agreed in recognizing that no real analogy exists between the modern situation and the early Christian practice: Pfleiderer, "Urchristentum," 1887, s. 24; Weizsäcker, "Apost. Zeitalter," 2. Aufl., 1892, s. 47; and the conclusive discussion of Wendt (Meyer's "Kommentar, Apostelgesch.," s. 102 and 120). See also, Rogge, "Der irdische Besitz im Neuen Testament," 1899, s. 73, "The κοινωνία of the first Christians is not an institution like the communism of the Essenes or Therapeutes, rather a condition marked, as Uhlhorn fittingly says, 'by absence of institutions.'" Uhlhorn, "Charity in the Early Church," p. 74, "We might as well speak of the institution of a community of goods in a family . . . the thought with which we are dealing is not an institution of a community of goods, but noble almsgiving." M. von Nathusius, "Die Mitarbeit der Kirche an der Lösung der sozialen Frage," 2. Aufl., 1897, s. 403, "The communism of the first congregation in Jerusalem consisted essentially in a point of view. No one said of those things which were his own that they were his own; but it must be recognized that the basis of this moral duty lay in the right to private property. The Christian must spend his private property for the general good." H. Holtzmann, in his elaborate study of this subject, "Die ersten Christen und die soziale Frage," 1882, goes still farther, concluding not only that (s. 30), "No compulsory abandonment of property relations or legally introduced commu-

religion in a world of social needs is here held
to be, not the impracticable imitation of primitive social life, but the illumination of the world
as it is with works of mercy and service. " By
this shall all men know that ye are my disciples,
if ye have love one to another." [1]   This way
of service has come to be a self-evident Christian
duty. Never before was there so clear a recognition of the social responsibility of Christian believers; never was there such multiplication of
philanthropic agencies in the name of Christianity,
or such general agreement that the test of religion
in the present age must be its capacity to inspire
deeds of love. In 1849 Pastor Wichern, the founder

nism is suggested. Of such an institution the book of Acts speaks
not a word ; " but going on to suggest that (s. 49), "The picture
offered by the book of Acts of communism in Jerusalem represents
the social ideal of the author, described as realized in the sacred
days of the beginnings of Christianity ;" a view which Rogge
(s. 69) regards as "a complete contradiction of the method in
which the author of the third gospel and the book of Acts elsewhere deals with his sources."   Even a critic of avowed sympathy
with the socialist programme, like O. Holtzmann, " Jesus Christus
und das Gemeinschaftsleben der Menschen," 1893, candidly remarks: " What the book of Acts describes is free offerings of
Christian brotherhood; . . . of industry in common, of the estimating of each individual according to his work, of any levelling of
possessions or of labor, there is not a sign. No likeness is to be
found between the conditions of the first Christian community and
the programme proposed by socialism." Compare also: G. Adler,
"Geschichte des Sozialismus und Communismus von Plato bis zur
Gegenwart," Erster Teil, 1899, s. 69 ff.; Stein, " Die soziale Frage
im Lichte der Philosophie," s. 232 ff.; " Das Urchristentum und die
soziale Frage."

[1] John xiii. 35.

of the *Innere Mission* in Germany, addressed his
Letter to the Nation, urging Christian believers to
enter "into the ferment and questioning of the time,
. . . and give the only indisputable proof that Christianity . . . can accomplish what is possible to
no power or wisdom without the gospel;"[1] and
this proving of Christian faith by Christian works
has become the special mark of modern Christianity. A hundred ways of service, visitation, and
relief, the advocacy of temperance and of recreation, the provision of the social settlement and of
the institutional church, illustrate the expansion
of the work of religion into the sphere of the social
movement. Yet these Christian activities, beautiful and fruitful as they are, and testifying as they
do to the vitality of the Christian religion, cannot
be regarded as presenting in themselves a solution
of the modern social question. This question, as
we have already seen, cuts quite beneath the whole
problem of philanthropy, and cannot be summed
up in terms of pity for the unfortunate or of almsgiving for the poor. It inquires for the causes of
ill fortune, and demands justice for the poor. It
applies itself to changing the conditions which make
people poor, rather than to pitying the poverty which
evil conditions have made. However legitimate

---

[1] Wichern, "Die innere Mission der deutschen evangelischen
Kirche," 3. Aufl., 1889 ; Göhre, "Die evangelisch-soziale Bewegung," 1896, s. 3 ff. ; Schäfer, "Leitfaden der inneren Mission,"
1889, s. 52 ff. ; Uhlhorn, "Die christliche Liebesthätigkeit seit der
Reformation," 1890, s. 347 ff.

and beneficent, then, the progress of Christian sympathy and charity may be, it does not satisfy the
demand of the time.   It is the work of a practising
physician, dealing with special cases of disease, while
beneath his mitigation of results lie profounder
inquiries concerning the causes and prevention of
disease.   To meet the social question as it now presents itself, religion must be more than merciful
and generous; it must find a place for itself in that
search for better economic conditions and better
social organization which absorbs the attention of
the present time.

Here, then, we come upon many schemes and
dreams which, in the name of the Christian religion, concern themselves directly with the disorder
and incompleteness of the industrial world.   They
may be roughly classified in a few general types.
First, and on the outskirts of these definite propositions and programmes, there is what may be
called the work of prophecy.   The prophet, in
the social question, as in religion, is not the sys-
tem-maker, or even the foreteller of the future.
He is the advocate of righteousness; he lays bare
the sins of his people, and pronounces judgment on
their transgression; he pictures the rule of equity
and peace, and promises to justice its reward.   Here
is at least one legitimate work of the Christian
preacher.   It does not need a training in political
economy to make one sensitive to social sins.   The
same passion for righteousness which made the
burden of Hebrew prophecy finds its place in an

effective Christian ministry to-day. The prophet may not know precisely what form the better future is to assume; and when he depicts the details of that future, he may become only an impracticable visionary. His place is to proclaim the eternal law of righteousness and the retribution which, for a nation as for an individual, is sure to follow wrong. "The prophet that hath a dream," he says. "Is not my word like as fire? saith the Lord; and like a hammer that breaketh the rock in pieces?"[1] "Behold, I am against them that prophesy lying dreams, saith the Lord; . . . I will cast you off, and the city that I gave unto you;"[2] and again, of the faithful he says, "I will give them an heart to know me, that I am the Lord: and they shall be my people." "I will set mine eyes upon them for good, and I will bring them again to this land."[3]

Among such prophets of the modern social question, two have had extraordinary influence on the consciences of Christians.[4] Carlyle attacked

[1] Jer. xxiii. 28, 29.   [2] Jer. xxiii. 32, 39.   [3] Jer. xxiv. 7, 6.
[4] Of Carlyle's own writings the most significant are: "Chartism," 1840; "Past and Present," 1843; "Latter Day Pamphlets," 1880. See also: Schulze-Gävernitz, "Zum sozialen Frieden," 1890, I, ss. 77-290; "Thomas Carlyle als Sozialtheoretiker und Sozialpolitiker"; Garnett, "Life of Thomas Carlyle" (with bibliography), Gibbins, "English Social Reformers," 1892, p. 181 ff.; and the unsparing criticism of Robertson, "Modern Humanists," 1891, p. 11 ff. Of Ruskin the most significant writings are: "Unto this Last," 1862; "Crown of Wild Olive," 1866; "Time and Tide," 1867; "Fors Clavigera" (passim). See also the warm advocacy of J. A. Hobson, "John Ruskin, Social Reformer," 1898; the critical

with splendid satire the mammonism and dilettant-
ism of modern life, and pictured a revival of the
ancient ways of social stability and peace; Ruskin
arraigned the prevailing political economy as unreal and illusory, and substituted for it, in what he
held was his most important work, a political
economy whose roots should be honor, and whose
veins of wealth should be "the purple veins of
happy-hearted human creatures." Both of these
great teachers were of the prophetic order. No
one can read their arraignment of social unrighteousness without a glow of sympathy and of self-
reproach. To many a mind, sunk in an Egyptian
self-content of commercialism, the summons of
Carlyle has been as if a new Moses were calling
his people into the sterner region of the moral ideal;
to many a mind which has been stupefied by the
ugliness and squalor of modern civilization, Ruskin
has restored the hope of beauty and peace. Instead
of an England of cruel traders and chattering politicians, Carlyle conceives an England of heroes and
captains of industry, fit to lead a holy war. Instead
of wealth which sinks a man, as a belt of gold pieces
would sink him in the sea, Ruskin calls for a new
definition of riches. The only wealth is life; all
else is not wealth, but "ill-th." "I can even imagine that England may cast all thoughts of posses-
sive wealth back to the barbaric nations among

estimate of F. J. Stimson, *Quarterly Journal of Economics,* 1888;
and the less sympathetic treatment of Robertson (*ut supra*), p.
184 ff.; and of Politicus, "New Social Teachings," 1886, Ch. I. and II.

whom they first arose, — and be able to lead forth her sons, saying, 'These are my jewels.' " [1]

Yet these teachers of duty and of beauty, when they abandon the path of spiritual inspiration, and undertake that of economic instruction, warn us of the limits of the prophetic office. Carlyle proposes a reversion of industrial life from liberty of contract to the bondage of feudalism. " I am for permanence in all things." "Gurth, the serf of Cedric, with a brass collar round his neck, is not what I call an exemplar of human felicity, but Gurth to me seems happy in comparison with many a man of these days, not born thrall of anybody." " Liberty when it becomes the liberty to die by starvation is not so divine." [2]   Ruskin proposes a principle of exchange which shall abolish all distinctions of ability or fidelity, and which assumes an equality of service, the possibility of which Ruskin himself denies.[3]   Nothing, indeed, is more curious in literary history than the place which both Carlyle and Ruskin have come at last to occupy in the history of social reform.   Both were completely opposed to the democratic tendency of modern politics and industry.   Both were at heart aristocrats and reactionaries.   Neither had any fundamental sympathy with the socialist pro-

[1] " Unto this Last," Essay II, Conclusion.

[2] " Past and Present," Book III, Ch. XIII.

[3] Compare, " Unto this Last," Essay III, with " Fors Clavigera," Letter V: " No liberty, but instant obedience to known law and appointed persons; no equality, but recognition of every betterness and reprobation of every worseness."

D

gramme.   Both stood for authority, order, obedience.   Ruskin speaks of himself as an "old Tory"
and as an "Illiberal." [1] Carlyle pours contempt
on the antislavery agitation of a "long-sounding,
long-eared Exeter Hall." [2] Both found in mediæ-
valism an escape from modern social ills.   Carlyle
would heal the economic evils of the nineteenth
century by a reversion to feudalism ; Ruskin would
redeem the ugliness of modern civilization by a revival of primitive simplicity.   Both distrusted the
spirit of democracy and the rule of the majority.
"I hate your Clutterbuck republics," said Carlyle,
of the United States ; and Ruskin, in his splendid
rhetoric, coincides in this view : "This I say, because the Americans as a nation set their trust in
liberty and in equality, of which I detest the one
and deny the possibility of the other ; and because,
also, as a nation, they are wholly undesirous of
rest, and incapable of it ; irreverent of themselves
both in the present and in the future ; discontented
with what they are, having no ideal of anything
which they desire to become, as the tide of the
troubled sea when it cannot rest." [3]   Yet, by a
strange perversion of the main intention of Carlyle
and Ruskin, their prophetic denunciations have
outlived their positive teachings ; their invectives
against the world as it is have been heard, while
their pictures of the world as it ought to be have

[1] Hobson, p. 203.
[2] "Past and Present," Book IX, Ch. V.
[3] "Time and Tide," p. 152.

been forgotten. Carlyle's "Past" would be absolutely intolerable to the radical reformers who still
delight in his arraignment of the "Present." Ruskin's "Unto this Last," in its economic doctrine,
may be so impracticable as to justify the jest that
its title should be "Beyond his Last," but the visionary quality of Ruskin's economics does not
diminish the effectiveness of his splendid satire or
of his moral exhortation. The prophetic quality
in both these literary masters outlives their advocacy of feudal authority, and both have been swept
into the movement of radical socialism from which
they would have instinctively recoiled, and find
themselves at last cited as leading authorities in
the text-books of social revolution.[1] Few lessons
are of more importance for teachers of righteousness to learn than the natural limitations of the
prophetic office which even these distinguished
cases illustrate, and which are much more obvious
in less gifted men. Many a Christian preacher,
stirred by the recognition of social wrong, — and
not infrequently by the burning message of Carlyle
or of Ruskin, — is called to be a prophetic voice,
crying in the wilderness of the social question;
but many a prophet mistakes his office for that
of the economist, and gives a passionate devotion to industrial programmes which are sure to
fail. Neither ethical passion nor rhetorical genius
equip a preacher for economic judgments. It is

[1] *E.g.* Morris, "Art and Socialism," 1884, appendix, with passages
from Carlyle and Ruskin.

for the prophet of righteousness to exhort and warn, rather than to administer and organize. A different temper and training are required for wisdom in industrial affairs.

Reasonable, however, as such criticism may be concerning the function of prophecy, it does not fix a limit for Christian thought concerning the social question. On the contrary, it may happen that those who desire to apply the religious motive to social life shall frankly dismiss the function of prophecy, and enter, like other people, into the region of economic discussion and research. While it is true that there is nothing in Christian piety which of itself fits one for social wisdom, it is certainly not true that there is anything in such a sentiment which disqualifies one from prudent and patient inquiry or from intelligent decision. Beyond the position of the prophet, therefore, lie various phases of direct and practical service through which it is proposed to utilize religion as a social force, and to give it a definite place in economic life.

The most usual and the most moderate type of the social utilization of religion is in what may be called — if the title may be used as one of appreciation and honor — the method of Christian opportunism. The opportunist is not necessarily a time-server; he may be simply a reformer who uses each opportunity as it arrives. The opportunist has no definite or final programme, but is ready to use any means which for the moment appears practicable. He feels his way through what is immediately possible toward the end which he desires. This is the frame of mind of the great majority of those who are attempting to apply the spirit of Christianity to the social question.   The "Social Congresses" of Catholics and Protestants held each year in European countries, urge on their adherents, not specific enterprises in the name of religion, but observation, research, and readiness to apply the motives of religion to social life wherever the way may open.   They represent an alert, awakened, opportunist spirit, stirring great communions of Christians, — a spirit which is often led by new circumstances into quite unanticipated ways of usefulness.[1]   Of this direction of the Christian impulse into unforeseen channels one of the most notable illustrations is to be found in the devoted service of Maurice and his friends in England.[2]

[1] "Verhandlungen des Evang.-soz. Kongresses," I–XI, 1890–1900 ; L. Grégoire (pseudonym), "Le Pape, les Catholiques et la question sociale," 1895 (p. 313, "Programme du Congrès Catholique de Cologne," 1894).

[2] The story of the Maurice-Kingsley movement is delightfully told in the "Life of Frederic Denison Maurice, Chiefly in his Own Letters," 4th ed., 1885, especially Vol. II, Ch. I (a bibliography is prefixed to Vol. I) ; and in Brentano, "Die christlich-soziale Bewegung in England," 1883 (with bibliography). Of Maurice's own writings, the most significant are : "Dialogue between Somebody (a person of respectability) and Nobody (the author)," 1890 ; "Reasons for Coöperation," 1891 ; and of Kingsley: "Message of the Church to Laboring Men," 1891 ; "Alton Locke," 1880; "Yeast," 1891 ; "Literary and General Lectures," 1880. See also Kaufmann, "Christian Socialism," 1888, p. 57 ff. The true relation of Kingsley to Maurice is recorded in a conversation reported by E. Yarnall, "Reminiscences," 1899, p. 190: "'I owe all that I am to

The only economic principle which seemed at first clear to these brave men was their conviction of the unchristian character of the prevailing economic system. It was, as Kingsley said, a "narrow, conceited, hypocritical, anarchic, and atheistic view of the universe." Of positive teaching they had little to offer. "I do not see my way," said Maurice, "farther than this: Competition is put forth as the law of the universe; that is a lie." Thus, the original position of this group was one of expectant opportunism. By a fortunate coincidence, however, the English coöperative movement — devised, as must always be proudly remembered, by the humblest of hand-workers, without the counsel of the learned — was just beginning its history of extraordinary expansion, and in the spirit of this industrial enterprise Maurice found an expression for his social Christianity. "Competition," said Kingsley, "means death; coöperation means life." The English opportunists gave the strength of their leadership to the coöperative movement, and found satisfaction for their Christian socialism in a practical scheme which they themselves had not devised.

Sympathetic opportunism, however, does not exhaust the resources of Christian thought concerning the social question. Beyond the readiness to use whatever way of service may offer itself lie many deliberate attempts to give to the social question a systematic interpretation in terms

Maurice,' said Kingsley. 'I aim only to teach to others what I get from him.' 'I live to interpret him to the people of England.'"

of Christianity. They may proceed either by
denying the extreme revolutionary doctrine, or by
accepting it; in either case there is a distinct
meeting of the economic issue and a definite inter-
vention, in the name of religion, in the affairs of
the industrial life. On the one hand is what may
be called the scientific reaction, — the renewed
examination, that is to say, of the facts which
create the social question, and the interpretation
of them as facts of the moral and personal life
rather than of the economic and social order. Of
this direction of research an important illustration
may be recalled in the work of the French engineer,
Le Play.[1] This distinguished inquirer was not
only of the first rank in his scientific calling, but
was also a devout Catholic. No sooner had the
storm of revolution in France spent its force than
Le Play applied to the facts of social disorder the
same scientific examination which he had already
given to the geology of Europe. With amazing

[1] Le Play, "Les Ouvriers Européens," 2e ed., 1879; "La Réforme Sociale," 3 vols., 1872; C. de Ribbe, "Le Play d'après sa
correspondance," 1884; Curzon, "Frédéric le Play, sa méthode, sa
doctrine, son œuvre, son esprit," 1899; *Quarterly Journal of Economics*, IV, 408, H. Higgs (and Appendix); "La Réforme Sociale,
Bulletin des Unions de la Paix Sociale, fondée par F. le Play." The
Musée Social, founded in 1895 by the Comte de Chambrun, and
occupying his palace, 5 Rue las Casas, Paris, perpetuates in its
library and its varied investigations the methods of Le Play. See
Bödicker, "Le Comte de Chambrun et le Musée Social, Paris,"
1896; "Statuts du Musée Social," 1896; "Chronique du Musée
Social, Paris," Arthur Rousseau, 14 Rue Soufflot. See also C.
Jannet, "Le Socialisme d'état et la réforme sociale," 2e ed., 1890.

industry and unprecedented range of observation he studied the conditions of domestic and industrial life, in many countries and under many phases of civilization, and tabulated in minute detail the budget of income and expenditure which represented the economic condition of typical lives. His results were in undisguised opposition to the revolutionary dogmas which had already become conspicuous in France. The social question, he concluded, was not fundamentally one of economic transformation or of the abolition of privileges, but one of domestic integrity, industrial thrift, moral education, and living religion. The issue was ethical rather than economic ; the security of a country like France was to lie in the vitality of its family stocks, in greater prudence in expenditure, in productive skill, and in faith in the moral order of the world. The scientific liberalism of Le Play gained at once large hearing. It approved itself to the instinctive conservatism of the Church, and it has been perpetuated, with much statistical and historical learning, by many distinguished disciples.

Yet even in France, and within the Catholic Church itself, this reactionary opposition to the collectivist creed has of late given way to a more sympathetic view. Whatever may be said of domestic virtues and moral education, there has seemed to many Christians no possibility of defining the social question in these terms alone. The specific problem of industrial change, it has been felt, must be met, and met in the name of the

Christian Church. The Church must have a social programme; there must be a Christian doctrine of economics; the revolutionary social movement must be tempered and deepened by the spirit of Christian faith. These are the convictions which have expressed themselves in the general type of thought known as Christian socialism, and which have united, in unanticipated fellowship, Catholics and Protestants, Germans and Frenchmen, conservative ecclesiastics and radical preachers.

The first determined note of the new Christian programme was struck in Germany; not, as might be anticipated, by a Protestant reformer, but by a Catholic prelate. Several reasons may be suggested for this interesting historical fact. The Catholic Church has maintained throughout its history a continuous tradition of organic responsibility, and in this respect was peculiarly prepared to receive and interpret the conception of industrial unity which marks the modern social question. The Catholic Church, moreover, was in Germany the party of protest; and its exclusion from political control gave it a freer hand for social agitation than was permitted to an Established Church. Even before the revolution of 1848, the French Abbé Lamennais[1] had announced a

[1] Nitti, "Catholic Socialism," p. 99 ff.; Nathusius, "Die Mitarbeit der Kirche an der Lösung der sozialen Frage," 1897, s. 121; Kaufmann, "Christian Socialism," 1888, p. 35 ff.; Mazzini's "Essays" (Camelot edition, 1887), p. 73: " Wherefore, thought Lamennais, — the mission of the Peoples, and their disposition toward order and justice, being recognized — wherefore should the Church refuse

new mission for his religion, and had found in the alarming watchwords, "Liberty, Fraternity, Equality," not merely the signs of social revolution, but the summons to a revival of Christianity. His voice, however, was of one crying in a wilderness of conservative tradition, and his teaching was condemned by Gregory XVI. As the social question grew more distinct in form and the working-people of Germany were won to the socialist cause, the Catholic Church renewed its sympathetic intere. t. At the very beginning of the new period, Lassalle, always more of an idealist than Marx, had proposed his scheme of working-men's productive associations, subsidized by the State, — a scheme at first welcomed by the German Social Democracy, but soon supplanted by more comprehensive plans of revolution. Lassalle's suggestion, however, was a seed which took root in strange soil. Baron von Ketteler,[1] Archbishop of Mayence, a gallant prince of the Church, found in Lassalle's proposal the suggestion of an economic programme for the Church itself. In his notable book, "The Labour Question and Christianity," he accepted the principle, and often the language, of the socialist scheme. The self-help proposed by the Liberals of his day for poverty

to regulate their movements, to preside over the action of this providential instinct of the multitudes?"

[1] Ketteler, "Die Arbeiterfrage und das Christentum," 4. Aufl., 1890; Girard, "Ketteler et la Question Ouvrière," 1896; Kaufmann, "Christian Socialism," 1888, p. 108; Rae, "Contemporary Socialism," p. 224; Nitti, "Catholic Socialism," p. 100 ff.

is, to von Ketteler, in the working-man's present
condition, a mere mockery. Associated production, in the hands of the working-class itself, is
to be its redemption from capitalism. While
Lassalle, however, had turned to the State for
the endowment of such productive industry, von
Ketteler turned to the Church. Let Christians,
he proposed, voluntarily supply the means for
this industrial emancipation. What is this, indeed, but the renewal of that earlier spirit in
which monasteries were endowed and cathedrals
built? The new age calls for Christian munificence like that which enriched France and England with the splendors of Gothic art. "May
God in his goodness quickly raise up men who
will sow the fruitful idea of the association of
production in the soil of Christianity."

It was a bold and noble conception of the
social duty of a living Church, and, though the
conditions of Germany were unpropitious and
the scheme of von Ketteler was soon lost in
larger plans of revolutionary socialism, it has had of
late, at the centre of Catholic authority, a most
interesting revival. No sooner had the social
chaos of 1871 in France given way to some degree of order, than a group of Catholic Legiti-
mists set themselves to the reorganizing of labor
under the principles of religion. The principal
representative of the French Catholic labor party,
the soldierly and eloquent Count de Mun, found
in the programme of industry suggested by von

Ketteler, and modified by the later German Catholic Socialists, a key to the situation.[1] There must be revived that system of industry which the Middle Ages knew as guilds. Economic liberty is a modern illusion; the demand of the socialist for the reconstruction of industry under common ownership is legitimate and inevitable; but that common ownership should be religious in spirit and Catholic in administration. Religion must reorganize the old order, and must utilize legislation to that end. The State may strengthen the hands of the Church, but it is the Church which must reconstruct, — under the tutelage of religion, — the productive associations which Lassalle had vainly dreamed could be maintained by the working-men alone.

Should this picturesque revival of industrial feudalism, it may be asked, be a compulsory system, or a voluntary organization? The Comte de Mun and his allies urge the necessity of State authority and control; and their political demands coincide in the main with the programme of the Social Democratic party. On the other hand, there have sprung up in France a few voluntary associations which actually illustrate the practical direction of productive industry by the spirit of religion. Few more idyllic scenes are to be witnessed in the modern world than that presented

[1] Nitti, "Catholic Socialism," p. 273 ff., p. 292 ff., with further references; *Fortnightly Review*, January, 1896, "An Object-lesson in Christian Democracy" (Val-des-Bois).

by the famous factory of Léon Harmel at Val-des-Bois, — a contented, secluded, homogeneous population, a "*famille ouvrière*," a picture of what the world of industry might be if only all working-people were French Catholics, and all employers were as devout and judicious as Harmel. Meantime the Church itself, while it has not authoritatively committed itself to either method of control, has given the highest approval to the general plan of a Catholic organization of industry. When the present Pope, in his remarkable Encyclical of May 15, 1891, enumerated the direct ways of economic relief which commended themselves to him, he began with these words : " First in order come the guilds of arts and trades. The increasing requirements of daily life render it necessary that these guilds be adapted to present conditions." Such suggestions, carefully guarded though they are, indicate the profound interest which has been awakened by enterprises like that of Harmel, and by parliamentary propositions like those of the Comte de Mun. A revival of guild life may indeed be impracticable except within the narrow limits of a homogeneous community ; but it is at least one way of direct acceptance by the Christian Church of the economic issue, and it appears to have received the formal commendation of that remarkable man who, it is said, desires to be remembered as the Pope of the working-classes.[1]

[1] The social doctrine of the Roman Catholic Church cannot be inferred from the view of Nitti's " Catholic Socialism," 1899. Indeed,

When we turn to the parallel development of Christian socialism in Protestant Germany, we find. as might be expected, less continuity and definiteness in social schemes, though not less determination to find a place for religion in the social movement. The history of such efforts begins with the work of a most interesting, though now half-forgotten, personality, the learned and devout Victor Huber.[1] This diligent scholar had become acquainted, during his visits in England, with the work of Maurice, while, on the other hand, he had maintained a sympathetic correspondence with von Ketteler. Thus he was in some degree a link, uniting the Christian Socialist movement in Great Britain with that of Catholic Germany. From

one of the most curious features of this learned book is the reiterated criticism of its author by its translator. For authorized exposition of Catholic teaching see: Encyclical of May 15, 1891 (tr. Nitti, p. 404 ff.); *American Catholic Quarterly Review,* July, 1891, (a commentary on the Encyclical by Bishop Keane); *Forum,* January, 1897, De Vogué, "Pope Leo XIII"; and the very noteworthy book of Léon Gregoire (pseudonym), "Le Pape, les Catholiques, et la Question Sociale," 2e ed., 1895. Of a more general nature are: Soderini, "Socialism and Catholicism," with a preface by Cardinal Vaughan, 1896; Winterstein, "Die christliche Lehre vom Erdengut," 1898; see also J. G. Brooks, *International Journal of Ethics,* "The Social Question in the Catholic Congresses"; and American Economic Association, 1894, "The Papal Encyclical on the Labor Question."

[1] R. Elvers, "V. A. Huber, sein Werden und Wirken," 1879; Göhre, "Die evangelisch-soziale Bewegung," 1896, s. 6 ff.; Kaufmann, "Christian Socialism," 1888, p. 137. See also the references to Huber in England, in Maurice, "Life and Letters," 4th ed., 1885, Vol. II, p. 2 ff.

the one he derived his faith in industrial coöperation, applying the principle not only to production
and consumption, but to building societies, loan
associations, and even, under the title of "Home
Colonization," to the organization of German village life; from the other he derived a confidence
in the Christian organization of industry, which
led him to establish his "Associations for Christian Order and Liberty." Huber, however, was a
man born out of due time; he was politically a
Liberal of the earlier school, equally opposed to
the governmental paternalism which had already
begun to dominate Germany, and to the revolutionary socialism which was formulating its first
programme. There was no natural constituency
for his scheme. He would have no governmental
aid for his coöperative societies, nor, on the other
hand, would he deliver them over to the Social
Democracy. He put his confidence in private
initiative and free Christian feeling. He had seen,
in England, a few Christian scholars devoted to
a working-class movement, and he fancied that
there might be in Germany a similar leadership.
He had not realized, however, the violence of the
working-class reaction in Germany from all alliance with the prosperous. He was also, it is said,
by temperament, lacking in conciliatory wisdom,
and had something of that isolation of spirit which
marks what the Germans call an "*Einspänner.*"
His career was one of disappointment; he withdrew from the academic circles of Berlin in 1851,

for eighteen years lived in seclusion among the Harz Mountains, and the direct results of his generous efforts were transient and meagre. He is to be remembered, however, as the first German Protestant who, in the name of the Christian religion, proposed a definite social programme. Christian philanthropy, he maintained, was not to be satisfied with almsgiving and help for the helpless, but was called to contribute to the new industrial issue the forces of organization and self-help. The social climate of England favored the efforts of Maurice, while that of Germany blighted the plans of von Ketteler and Huber, and the socialism of the State and of the Revolution left, between them, little room for Christian liberalism; but it is not impossible that, when the full effect of prosperity secured by legislation comes to be observed in Germany, there may be a renewal of interest in enterprises of personal and spiritual initiative; and if that time arrives, there is likely to be a renewed recognition of this early believer in the free activity of a living Church.

Much more in accord with the tumultuous and shifting character of the modern social movement is the career of a second German Protestant leader, the eloquent and masterful Pastor Stöcker.[1] For twenty-five years this brilliant orator has been

[1] A. Stöcker, "Christlich-soziale Reden und Aufsätze," 1885; Göhre, "Die evangelisch-soziale Bewegung," 1896, s. 41 ff.; Rae, "Contemporary Socialism," 1891, p. 234; Kaufmann, "Christian Socialism," 1888, p. 159.

among the most conspicuous and the most criticised of Germans. Few critics would question
the motives of his intense and varied activity, but
no one can recall the changeful policies of his
stormy life without a pathetic impression of wasted
power.   As early as 1878, being then Court
Preacher in Berlin, he organized his " Christian
Socialist Labor Party," " on the basis of the
Christian faith," to " lessen the division between
rich and poor, and to bring in a greater economic
security." He dismissed the Social Democracy
as " impracticable, unchristian, unpatriotic," and set
forth a Christian programme as its substitute.   It
is not, he says, " in the name of the Church that
the programme is proposed "; " the Church is not
called to make an economic programme."   His
organization was not to be one of the clergy to
help the working-men, but one of the working-men
to help themselves.   It was impossible, however,
for a Court Preacher, with a mind essentially conservative and a following of the cultivated class, to
command the genuine confidence of German hand-
workers.   Stöcker's original ambition was thwarted
also by legislation introduced by the government
against the Socialists, — an attack which only
served to consolidate their forces and to shut out
the labor party of Stöcker from consideration.
His zeal turned, therefore, to a new and less noble
crusade.   The sympathy which was coldly received
by the working-men found a warmer welcome in
the ranks of tradespeople of the humbler type,

E

whose industrial welfare was seriously threatened by an extraordinary increase in power and prosperity among the Jews. The social interest of Stöcker joined with his orthodox theology in converting his original Christian socialism into anti-Semitism, and he became much more widely known as a Jew-hater than as a working-man's friend. Finally, in 1895, as if conscious that a working-class movement was impossible, Stöcker and his friends turned to a more comprehensive but more conservative scheme. There was organized at Eisenach a "Christian Social Party," for the purpose of uniting "under the principles of Christianity and patriotism persons of all classes and occupations who are moved by the Christian social spirit." "While its special attention is to be given to the elevation of the working-class as the present problem of the time, it will with equal gladness serve the needs of all productive interests in city and country, in agriculture, factory life, and menial labor." It opposes "all unchristian and un-German schemes of spurious liberalism, oppressive capitalism, rapacious Hebraism, and revolutionary socialism." Thus Stöcker's new platform combined in one programme all the various ends for which in turn he had already contended. It has failed, however, of wide effect through its comprehensiveness, as the first programme failed through its limitations. Supported though Stöcker has been by persons of importance, the distinction between his political ideals and those of the conservative

party has not been such as to detach votes, while
he has been a special object of the attack against
clerical influence in politics. The legislation of
Bismarck concerning socialism cut the ground
from under Stöcker's feet, and in 1890 he withdrew from his position as Court Preacher. He
has since remained a striking and solitary figure in
parliamentary life, regarded by many persons with
hesitating admiration and by some persons with
special animosity; yet he is, none the less, to be
counted as the most eloquent and persistent of
German Protestants in maintaining that social
organization is an essential duty of the Christian
Church in the modern world.

Genuine and devout, then, as the Christian
socialism of German Protestants has been, it cannot be said to have produced a definite industrial programme, or to have had a profound effect.
It has found itself between two fires, the distrust
of the government, and the undisguised contempt
of the Social Democracy. On the one hand, it
is met by the emperor's dictum that the clergy
should leave politics alone; on the other hand, it
is confronted by the Socialist belief that religion
is a superstition maintained in the interest of the
confiscating class. In this state of things, the
last proposition of the Protestant Socialists of
Germany, while it is certainly heroic, would seem
to be Quixotic, if not suicidal, in its character.
The rebuke of the emperor, it is said by the
eloquent preacher Naumann and his friends, is

not without justification. A clergyman in a State Church may not hope at the same time to main. tain his clerical office and to establish a friendly relation with the working-class movement. Either his freedom of speech will cost him his place, or he will address property holders alone. His only escape from such a dilemma is to abandon the ministry as a profession, and, in the name of a new parliamentary party, to throw himself into political life. Christian socialism must be regarded as a political alternative, to be presented to German hand-workers in place of the Social Democracy which now commands their votes. It accepts the economic programme of the Socialist, but interprets and maintains that programme as a witness of the Christian religion. Gallant and self-sacrificing as this programme is, it cannot be regarded as a hopeful phase of practical effort. To abandon the Church for the sake of religion; to see in politics the field for a religious revival; to ally one's self with the Socialist party for the sake of supplanting them, — this will seem to most observers like the charge at Balaklava, magnificent, but not war; and the withdrawal of these Christian preachers from their prophetic office does not, at present, appear likely to carry with it the assurance of a corresponding influence and leadership in the political world.

It is not essential for our purpose to cite further instances of the Christian protest against the aliena·

tion of the social question from the Christian religion. By many ways of utterance, by attempted imitation of New Testament economics, by works of philanthropy, by words of prophecy, by research, by organization, and by political methods, the Christian life of the modern world has maintained its right to interpret and direct the social agitations of the time. When one recalls, however, all these varied expressions of Christian responsibility, he cannot help remarking that one form of inquiry, which would seem to be of fundamental importance, has had but meagre attention. Behind all that may be urged of the duty of the Christian Church, and all that may be demanded of social life in the name of Christianity, there lies, for all followers of Jesus Christ, the preliminary question concerning his personal teaching. What did Jesus himself have to say of the various.spheres of social duty ? What is the social doctrine of the gospel ? By the answers to such questions the practical conduct of a loyal disciple of Jesus must be largely determined. It is most surprising, therefore, that in a period of such extraordinary social interest on the part of Christian believers, and in a time when the watchword "Back to Christ!" has become so familiar, there should have been undertaken so few systematic or scientific inquiries concerning the nature of his social teaching. Incidental treatment of the relation of Jesus to problems of social life may be found, of course, in the elaborate studies of the life of Christ, of which,

since the days of Strauss and Renan, there has
been such an abundance; and chapters also in
the text-books of Christian ethics; but in few such
instances is disclosed any appreciation of the intense
eagerness with which the present age desires to
learn the social teaching of the gospel. The
theological and philosophical interest of the life
of Jesus has for the most part quite overshadowed his human and social significance. It has
seemed more important to determine the relation
of the person of Christ to the mystery of the
Godhead than to determine his attitude toward
the secular problems of the modern world. In
fact, to many minds the personality of Jesus bears
so wholly a superhuman and other-worldly aspect
that there appears to be something like impiety in
discussing his social doctrine at all. It is a striking fact that the creed which to millions sums up
the essence of Christian discipleship devotes its
attention so exclusively to the supernatural aspects
of the drama of redemption that it makes no allu-
sion whatever to any incident of the human life of
Jesus; as though, for the essentials of a Christian
faith, it were unimportant to recall anything that
happened between the miraculous birth and the suffering death of Christ.[1]   Even so profoundly reverent and appreciative a study of the life of Jesus as
was presented in the epoch-making book known as

[1] See the striking article in *New World*, June, 1899, p. 299 ff.,
F. A. Christie, " The Influence of the Social Question on the Genesis
of Christianity."

" Ecce Homo," was regarded by many of its earlier
critics, because of its emphasis on the human and
ethical aspects of the life of Jesus, as bringing grave
dishonor on his nature and mission, and was described by the excellent Lord Shaftesbury as "the
most pestilential book that has ever been vomited
forth from the jaws of hell." A German theologian
of the highest rank, being lately asked to explain
this dearth of literature concerning the relation of
Jesus to the social question, gave it as his opinion
that it was the risks of ecclesiastical discipline
which had driven German theologians to think of
safer themes.[1] It would probably be more just to
refer the phenomenon to the habits of isolation and
traditionalism which beset the theological mind.
The interest of theological studies is so independent of the shifting issues of the world, and tends
so often to detach the mind from the passing
incidents of social life, that the theologian may
find himself at last thinking of one series of questions while the world about him is interested in
quite another series, and there may come to be
hardly any contact between his professional researches and the human needs of modern life.
This, at least, is the impression made on multitudes
of plain minds by the discussions which to the theologians appear most vitally interesting.   These

[1] Compare, however, the new expression of responsibility in
"Verhandlungen des 10ten Evang.-soz. Kongresses," 1899, s. 12 ff.,
"Das Verhältniss der lutherischen Kirche zur sozialen Frage," by
Professor Kaftan; and remarks by Professor Harnack, s. 32.

subtle distinctions and acrimonious ecclesiastical differences are simply without interest to persons who are struggling with the tragic problems of modern poverty, social service, and political morality; and to such persons the Christian Church takes on a look of unreality and misdirected energy, as though it were concerning itself with little more than what Coleridge called the problem of "superhuman ventriloquism," and existed only to exercise the ingenuity of its ministers and occupy the leisure of its adherents.

Nor is this all that is likely to happen when a Christianity of dogma is confronted by an intensely practical and ethical age. The person of Jesus Christ, it is soon discovered, cannot be thus excluded, even by the preoccupation of the theological mind, from the world of the social question. No sooner does one open his New Testament than he finds Jesus teaching of social duty with the same authority with which he discourses of Divine love. The story of the life of Jesus moves through a world of human relationships, and he scatters on either side of his path words of refreshing and deeds of blessing for the poor, the humble, the weary and the heavy laden, the burdened and blind and sad. His gospel, as he expressly says, is twofold, and one half of it is a social message, " Thou shalt love thy neighbour as thyself." [1] What wonder is it then, that, when attention is recalled to the neglected aspect

[1] Matt. xxii. 39.

of the person of Jesus, this unmetaphysical, un-
ecclesiastical, human, pitying friend of man, —
stooping to serve the lowly and quick to rebuke
the proud, — there should be a quick swing of the
pendulum of opinion, and, instead of the Christ of
the creeds, there should seem to be discovered a
new Messiah, the Saviour of the toiling and destitute masses of men? What was the young man
Jesus, it is asked, but a carpenter at his bench?
Who were his companions but men of what is now
called the proletariat? What words were oftener
on his lips than, "Woe unto you that are rich,"[1]
"Blessed are ye poor"?[2] What, then, is the
teaching of Jesus, when it is stripped of the theological interpretations which have obscured it,
but the gospel of a working-man's movement,
the language of a social agitator, the historical
anticipation of the modern programme of social
democracy? Here is the inevitable reaction from a
metaphysical Christology. The new time recalls
such words as "How hardly shall they that have
riches enter into the kingdom of God!"[3] "Sell all
that thou hast, and distribute unto the poor";[4] the
attack upon the property-holding classes is fortified by the thought of Dives in hell and of Lazarus contented; and instead of a supernatural
Christ, sitting at the right hand of the Father in
another world, the figure which wins fresh loyalty
is that of the Carpenter, the poor man's Advocate,

[1] Luke vi. 24.   [3] Luke xviii. 24.
[2] Luke vi. 20.   [4] Luke xviii. 22.

the greatest of socialists, or, as he has been lately called, "Jesus the Demagogue." [1]

The first of the modern biographers of Jesus to emphasize this view of his person and office was Renan.[2] It was a part of his general modernization of the gospel to picture Jesus as having kinship with the modern labor agitator, attacking on the one hand the government and on the other hand the prosperous. "Jesus," Renan says, "was in one view an anarchist; for he had no idea of civil government, which appeared to him an abuse pure and simple." "Pure Ebionism — that is to say, the doctrine that the poor (ebionim) alone can be saved . . . was accordingly the doctrine of Jesus." "He pardoned the rich man only when the rich man, because of some prejudice, was disliked by society." "He openly preferred people of questionable lives." His conception of the world was "socialist with a Galilean coloring." "A vast social revolution in which rank should be leveled and all authority brought low was his dream." The Jesus of Renan was, in short, a forerunner of the modern revolutionist, limited in the radicalism of his programme by the conditions of his social environment; and it is not surprising that this interpretation of the gospel in terms of the modern social question has appeared to many socialist writers the final word of New Testament criticism.

[1] *Contemporary Review*, March, 1896, p. 427 ff., W. Walsh, "Jesus the Demagogue."

[2] "Life of Jesus," 23d ed. (tr. J. H. Allen, 1896), pp. 170, 212, 215, 171.

The same interpretation, however, may be utilized, not to enforce the teaching of Jesus, but to condemn it. A distinguished English philosopher, accepting the gospel as a revolutionary tract, finds that characteristic not a reason for obeying the teaching of Jesus, but a reason for rejecting that teaching as impracticable and visionary. To assume that Jesus was a pious anarchist, is to dismiss his gospel as inapplicable to modern life.[1] The Christian theory of self-sacrifice is, it is said, self-destructive. "If Christianity is to mean the taking the gospels as our rule of life, then we none of us are Christians, and, no matter what we say, we all know we ought not to be." "There is not one of our great moral institutions which it [the New Testament] does not ignore or condemn. The rights of property are denied or suspected, the ties of family are broken, there is no longer any nation or patriotism. . . . The morality of the primitive Christians is homeless, sexless, and nationless." "We have lived a long time now the professors of a creed which no one consistently can practise, and which, if practised would be as immoral as it is unreal."

A much more sober and cautious approach to

[1] *International Journal of Ethics*, October, 1894, F. H. Bradley, "The Limits of Individual and National Self-sacrifice." So also L. Stein, "Die soziale Frage im Lichte der Philosophie," 1897, s. 244, "Christianity is stamped with an ascetic and pessimistic character." "It has a dark and monastic quality (etwas mönchisch Finsteres), unfavorable to social and philosophical inquiries which assume a confidence in human capacity."

the social teaching of Jesus was made, somewhat
before the picturesque romanticism of Renan, by a
now largely forgotten, but most devoted and painstaking, German scholar, who anticipated by more
than thirty years the importance which the New
Testament would have in the social movement.
Rudolf Todt [1] was an undistinguished pastor, who
was stirred by a passing suggestion of the more
famous Stöcker [2] to examine with systematic care
the teaching of the New Testament in its relation
to the socialist programme. He found, as he
believed, in the gospels, not only general principles, but " positive and concrete judgments for the
solution of social questions." The doctrine of the
New Testament deals, he affirms, " with the problem of the State, the rich and the poor." "Who-
ever would understand the social question," he
writes on his first page, " and would contribute to
its solution, must have on his right hand the works
of political economy, on his left those of scientific
socialism, and before him must keep open the New
Testament." Todt proceeds to set forth in detail
the various articles of the socialist creed, and confronts each in turn with the teaching of the New

[1] Todt, " Der radikale deutsche Sozialismus und die christliche
Gesellschaft," 2. Aufl., 1878; " Recapitulation of the Social Doctrine
of the New Testament," p. 396 ff. See also Göhre, " Die evange-
lisch-soziale Bewegung," s. 10 ff.; and compare the criticism in
Holtzmann " Die ersten Christen und die soziale Frage " (" Wiss.
Vorträge über rel. Fragen," s. 21).

[2] In the *Neue evangelische Kirchenzeitung* for 1873. See Todt,
p. 1, " Die Frage ging mir durch's Herz."

Testament; and concludes that "with the exception of its atheism . . . the theory of socialism cannot be opposed from the point of view of the gospel. Its principles not only conform to the tests of the New Testament, but contain evangelical and Divine truths." The special form of faith assumed by the Social Democracy of Germany, appeared to Todt "unevangelical and unnecessary." Every Christian must be a Socialist, but need not be a Social Democrat. Against atheistic socialism, therefore, a Christian socialism must be organized. Todt thereupon, with Stöcker and other friends, began the organization of a "Central Association for Social Reform on Religious and Constitutional Principles," a movement which through various vicissitudes and transitions has been perpetuated in the Evangelical Social Congress and the Christian Socialist party, and whose vitality has proceeded in very large degree from the painstaking study of the gospels with which it began.

Finally, as the present outcome of this interpretation of the New Testament, we reach a most stimulating and noble personality, whose teaching reverts with special emphasis to the personal influence of Jesus Christ. Pastor Naumann[1] of Frankfort was one of the few genuine orators of the

---

[1] Naumann, "Das soziale Programm der evangelischen Kirche," 1891; "Was heisst Christlich-Sozial?" 1894, s. 9 ff. ; "Jesus als Volksmann," Göttingen, *Arbeiterbibliothek I*, I, 1896, ss. 5, 13; "Soziale Briefe an reiche Leute," 1899 ; Göhre, "Die evangelisch-soziale Bewegung," 1896, s. 163 ff.

German pulpit, and through all his preaching runs a strain of such masculine piety that his enforced withdrawal and his unpromising ventures in political life excite most natural regret. It must not be supposed that Naumann sees in Jesus nothing more than a social reformer. On the contrary, he enters profoundly into the personal relationships of Christian faith. "Lord Jesus," he says, "we would sit at thy feet and feel what Christianity really is." Jesus Christ is "neither a philosopher nor statesman, neither physicist nor economist, . . . he brings neither conclusions nor methods. He lives, and his life is the revelation of God." Yet to Naumann the social question, with its tragedies of want and suffering, is so overwhelmingly absorbing that he dwells with constant emphasis on the social teaching of the gospel. "Jesus is," he says, "a man of the people"; his talk is "with constant reiteration of the rich and poor." "To save men's souls he is the enemy of wealth." "Jesus loves the rich, but he knows that their souls are free only when they are ready to throw their wealth away." He is "on moral grounds a radical enemy of capital." "What are to be the tests of the Last Judgment? Not dogmas or confessions, but one's relation to human need." "An age which does not feed the hungry, care for the naked, and visit the sick and the prisoners belongs in the everlasting fire." "Christianity is to help the poor." To these passionate utterances of Naumann it is hardly necessary to add the more exaggerated statements of other modern students. " Christianity," says the Italian economist Nitti, "was a vast economic revolution more than anything else." " Poverty was an indispensable condition for gaining admission to the kingdom of heaven." [1] With still less self-restraint an American writer advances to more sweeping generalizations. "The Sermon on the Mount," he writes, "is the science of society. It is a treatise on political economy." " The rejection of his [Christ's] social ideal was the crucifixion he carried in his heart." " An industrial democracy would be the social actualization of Christianity. It is the logic of the Sermon on the Mount." [2] These extravagances of exegesis indicate how sharply the pendulum of interest has swung from a Christology which ignored the social question to one which finds the social question the centre of the gospel.

[1] Nitti, "Catholic Socialism," 1895, pp. 58, 64.

[2] Herron, "The New Redemption," pp. 30, 34, 80 ; compare p. 143, " The worst charge that can be made against a Christian is that he attempts to justify the existing social order." See also the other writings of this self-sacrificing advocate of revolution, *e.g.* : "The Larger Christianity ; " " A Plea for the Gospel ; " " Between Cæsar and Jesus." " No man can read the Gospel himself without seeing that Jesus regarded industrial wealth as a moral fall and a social violence." "The Church as a whole does not know what Jesus taught, and so far as it knows does not believe his teaching practicable," "Between Cæsar and Jesus," p. 107. " I dread nothing more than the influence upon the social movement of existing organizations of religion," Boston Address, 1895. "If we would follow Jesus in the social redemption, it will be by storming the citadel of monopoly." " We can only save the people from being ground to profit by capturing the 'machine,'" *The Industrialist*, July, 1899.

Indeed, as has been lately suggested, it would not be difficult, under these principles of interpretation, to re-edit the New Testament as a socialist tract.[1] Jesus drove, we may suppose, the swine into the sea in order to testify his indifference to the institution of private property. When meeting the multitude his first care is to feed them, in order to indicate the precedence of economic problems over spiritual questions. He scourges the money-changers from the temple in order to bear public witness against capitalism and its sins.

However unfounded in history such a conception of the person of Christ may be, it is welcomed with enthusiasm by great numbers of plain people. For the Church and the theologians, the modern revolutionist has, as we have already seen, scant respect. The Church is to him the bulwark of the property-holding class, and the theologians are distracting the minds of the unfortunate by promises of prosperity elsewhere. "We'll give them back some of their heaven," said Felix Holt, "and take it out in something for us and our children in this world." For the person of Jesus, on the other hand, regarded as a working-man, a friend of the poor, an outcast, a preacher of condemnation against scribes and Pharisees, the working-class movement offers fresh reverence and homage. The real Jesus seems indeed, to many hand-workers, to have been rediscovered by them, as though beneath some mediæval fresco of an unreal and mystical Christ there

[1] *Contemporary Review*, March, 1896.

had been freshly laid bare the features of the man of Nazareth. "Christ," answered one German working-man to an inquirer, "was a true friend of the working-people, not in his words alone, like his followers, but in his deeds. He was hated and persecuted as is the modern socialist, and if he lived to-day he would, without doubt, be one of us."[1] "Christ," wrote another, "was a great revolutionist; if any one now preached as he did, he would be arrested." "He would have accomplished more," adds a third, "if he had given his efforts rather to economic and scientific ends than to religion." "He was a man of the common people," concludes a fourth, "who fought a hard fight for their moral and economic welfare." In short, it has come to pass, as the author of the "Kernel and the Husk" anticipated, that the hand-workers are saying, "We used to think that Christ was a fiction of the priests; . . . but now we find that he was a man, after all, like us, — a poor working-man, who had a heart for the poor, — and now that we understand this we say . . . he is the man for us."[2]

Here, then, is a perplexing situation. To a vast

[1] See the exceedingly interesting series of opinions collected by Pastor Rade, in his paper before the Ninth Evangelical Social Congress, 1898, "Die Gedankenwelt unserer Industriearbeiter." Compare also Pflüger, "Kirche und Proletariat," 1899, s. 4: "The first proclaimers of the gospel, especially Jesus himself, belonged to the proletariat; . . . the preachers of the gospel to-day belong to 'good society.'"

[2] "The Kernel and the Husk" (Am. ed. 1887), p. 334 (quoted also, Contemporary Review, March, 1896, p. 429).

F

majority of those who are most concerned with the social question, the Christ of the churches is an object of complete indifference, if not of positive scorn; while to a Christ far removed from the traditions and creeds of Christian worship, — an unmysterious, human leader of the poor, — there is given an honor which as a supernatural being he no longer receives. On the other hand, to the vast majority of Christian worshippers this conception of Jesus as a labor-leader and social revolutionist appears a most inadequate and unhistorical picture of the Christ of the gospels. What have we here but a clean break between the tradition of the past and the need of the present? On the one hand is the ancient and precious story of the relation of Jesus to the individual soul, his revelation of the Father to the child, and his revelation of the child to himself, his message to the religious life in its experiences of sin, repentance, and spiritual peace; and on the other hand is this new and unprecedented appreciation of the external ills of environment and misfortune, of social wrong and injustice, and the discovery that here also Jesus Christ has a message of stern rebuke and pitying love. Is there, then, a permanent chasm set between the work of the Christian Church and the need of the modern world? Is there no unity to be discovered beneath these diverse conceptions of the teaching of Jesus? Must it happen that the force of the Christian religion shall be limited to spiritual and personal renewal,

and shall have no part in directing the social movement of the time ; or if, on the other hand, the
person of Jesus finds a place in the social question, must it be at the cost of his spiritual leadership and religious significance?   Must we choose
between Christ the Saviour and Jesus the Demagogue ; or is there in the religion of Jesus a quality and character which of themselves create a
social message such as the modern world needs to
hear?   These are the questions which confront
one as he observes the alienation between Christian teaching and social needs, and which invite
to fresh inquiry concerning the social teaching of
the gospel. [1]

[1] The literature which is of importance in its new appreciation
of the social teaching of Jesus may be said to begin with the " Ecce
Homo " of Professor Seeley, 1867.   The main thesis of this remarkable book — that Jesus was the founder of an external and
legislative commonwealth — may be regarded as an inadequate or
even a misleading statement of the purpose of Christ ("Christ
announced himself as the Founder, the Legislator, of a new State,"
p. 80; "To reorganize a society and to bind the members of it
together by the closest ties were the business of his life," p. 103;
"The first propelling power . . . is the personal relation of loyal
vassalage of the citizens to the Prince of the Theocracy," p. 95).
Yet the extraordinary insight of this book into the spirit of the
gospels and its beauty and vigor of expression make its publication
an epoch in the interpretation of the teaching of Jesus.

A second contribution of much originality and power was the
Bampton Lectures of Canon Fremantle, "The World the Subject
of Redemption," 1885 (2d ed. 1895, with an introduction by Professor R. T. Ely, and with important appendices of illustrative literature).   Less academic, but of the highest spiritual insight, and
of an importance not generally recognized by his readers, are the
Bohlen Lectures of Phillips Brooks, "The Influence of Jesus," 1879.

Two considerations give to such an inquiry a peculiar interest and encouragement. In the first place, as is evident from what has been already

Closer to the modern social spirit, more exegetical in character, and for the general student a sufficient guide, is the thorough and discriminating book of Shailer Mathews, "The Social Teaching of Jesus," 1897. (Compare also his article in the *American Journal of Sociology*, January, 1900, "The Christian Church and Social Unity.")

Of German literature, specifically devoted to this subject, the only comprehensive work lately produced is the learned but conservative book of M. von Nathusius, "Die Mitarbeit der Kirche an der Lösung der sozialen Frage," 2. Aufl., 1897; see also his "Christlich-soziale Ideen der Reformationszeit," 1897. Of less systematic German studies may be named : Schmidt-Warneck, "Die sozialen Verhältnisse und die ethischen Grundgedanken des Evangeliums," 1891 ; Uhlhorn, "Vermischte Vorträge über kirchliches Leben," 1875 (s. 353 ff., "Zur sozialen Frage"); Böhmer, "Brennende Zeit- und Streitfragen der Kirche," 1898 ; Sabatier, "Die Religion und die moderne Kultur" (übersetzt aus dem Französischen), 1898 ; Russland, "Die Wirtschaftspolitik des Vaterunsers," 1895.

Further should be noticed the increasing emphasis on the social aspects of the gospel in the general works of New Testament interpretation: *e.g.* Wendt, "The Teaching of Jesus " (tr. 1897); Beyschlag, "New Testament Theology" (tr. 1895); Weiss, "Biblical Theology of New Testament" (tr. 1882), I, 62 ff.; Bruce, "The Kingdom of God," 1891; and Gilbert, "The Revelation of Jesus," 1899.

Here also may be named less formal studies of the influences of Christianity on modern life : *e.g.* Fairbairn, "The Place of Christ in Modern Theology," p. 515 ff. ; and his "Religion in History and in Modern Life," 1894, Lect. III ; Gore, "The Social Doctrine of the Sermon on the Mount" (*Economic Review*, April, 1892); Rade, "Die Religion im modernen Geistesleben," 1898, and his "Religion und Moral," 1898 ; Söderblom, "Die Religion und die soziale Entwickelung," 1898 ; Church, "Christ's Words and Christian Society," in his "Gifts of Civilization," 1880, p. 39 ; G. Hodges, said, we here approach the one subject in Christian teaching where, on both sides of the present social issue, there is sincere appreciation and reverence. The theology of Christianity, as the slightest glance at its present tendency will indicate, is laying aside its confidence in metaphysical definitions and elaborate formulas, and with a new humility of mind is turning to the simpler task of interpreting and perpetuating the teaching of Jesus Christ. "The Church hears none but Christ," said the earlier and broader statement of this return to the gospels; the modern spirit, with more simplicity, inquires, "What would Jesus say?" To follow Christ, even though one cannot adequately define him; to be, not of those who name his name alone, but of those who desire to do his will; to direct the life of one's own soul and the life of the world in ways of which Jesus might say, "Well done, good and faithful servant,"—these principles, to the modern Christian, are not incidental to the Christian life, but are the essence of

"Faith and Social Service," 1896 ; E. W. Donald, "The Expansion of Religion," 1898 ; R. T. Ely, "Social Aspects of Christianity," 1889 ; J. Ll. Davies, "The Gospel of Modern Life," 1875, and his "Social Questions," 1885 ; "The Message of Christ to Manhood," Noble Lectures, 1895 ; Flint, "Socialism," 1895 (supplementary note, "The Church's Call to study Social Questions," p. 493 ff.); Washington Gladden, "Applied Christianity," 1886, and his "Tools and the Man," 1893 ; Westcott, "Social Aspects of Christianity," 1887 ; Harris, "Moral Evolution," 1896, Ch. IX and X ; Drummond, "Via, Veritas, Vita," The Hibbert Lectures for 1894, Lect. VI, p. 209 ff.; Lyman Abbott, "Christianity and Social Problems," 1897.

it; and this discernment and obedience, even when accompanied by a high degree of ignorance as to the interior nature of the Godhead and the purposes of the Infinite, may still, it is now widely believed, receive the great word of acceptance, "Thy faith hath saved thee; go in peace." [1]

And if it is thus true that the imitation of Christ has supplanted opinion about Christ as the test of Christian discipleship, it is equally true, on the other hand, that the social movement also has reached a point of peculiar reverence for the person of Jesus. Inadequate and superficial as may be the estimate on which this reverence is based, it gives a point of contact between the Church and the world. The ecclesiastics may argue their claim to authority, and the theologians may devise their systems of orthodoxy; yet all these assumptions and deliberations will wholly fail to impress the people of the trades-unions, or the social democracy of the city slums. Let the social teaching of the gospels, however, be told — ever so simply — with its tender summons, "Come unto me, all ye that labour and are heavy laden," [2] with its test of discipleship, "Inasmuch as ye did it unto one of these my brethren, even these least, ye did it unto me," [3] and the heavy laden and those who are least in the modern world become responsive to the teaching, and touched with reverence for the person whom they thus dimly discern. Hopeless, therefore, as one may

[1] Luke vii. 50.   [2] Matt. xi. 28.   [3] Matt. xxv. 40, 41.

be of coming to any understanding with the social movement through the prevailing methods of Christianity, there is still ground for hope that the teaching of Jesus may have new adaptations to the need of the new time. The talk of the churches is for the most part in a language as unintelligible as Hebrew to the modern hand-worker; but in the teaching of Jesus he seems to hear the welcome accents of a familiar tongue. A common reverence may beget a mutual understanding. The Christian believer and the social reformer may perhaps meet each other as they both approach the simplicity which is in Christ.[1]

To this characteristic of the present inquiry must be added a further encouraging consideration. The problem to which we are invited, of determining the relation of the teaching of Jesus to the special needs of the real world, is in its nature not, as may be supposed, a new problem, but a continually recurring one. Each period in civilization has had, in turn, its own peculiar interest and its own spiritual demands, and each, in turn, following its own path back to the teaching of Jesus, has found there what seemed an extraordinary adaptation of that teaching to immediate issues and needs. This is one of the most surprising traits of the

[1] Göhre, "Drei Monate Fabrikarbeiter," 1891, s. 190. "Only one quality (of religion) remains — respect and reverence for Jesus Christ. It is, indeed, a new picture of Jesus of Nazareth. He lacks the supernatural light in his eyes, the divinity assigned to him by the theologians is a subject for smiles ; . . . but they all stand reverently and quiet before his great personality."

gospel. It seems to each age to have been written for the sake of the special problems which at the moment appear most pressing. As each new transition in human interest occurs, the teaching of Jesus seems to possess new value. In one age the focus of human interest was at that point where the Greek mind met the Hebrew tradition, and developed the beginning of Christian theology; and to that age there spoke the great sayings of Jesus concerning his relation to the Father, as though the determination of the place of Jesus in theology were the essence of the gospel. To another age, absorbed in ecclesiastical development, the teaching of Jesus seemed specially directed to establishing the organization of the Church. This illumination of each view and tendency is felt in turn by each modern student of the gospels as he considers from some fresh point of view the teaching of Jesus. One scholar, on the watch — as was Renan — for the picturesque and Oriental traits of a Galilean peasant, finds in the visionary hopes of such a youth a key to the teaching of Jesus; another scholar, with the habit of mind of a constitutional historian, sees in the teaching of Jesus primarily the work of the framer of a constitution, and defines his mission as "the rise of a monarchy, the purest and most ideal that has ever existed among men";[1] still another scholar, profoundly impressed by the note of melancholy and despair which is heard in modern literature, turns again to

[1] "Ecce Homo," Ch. X, "Christ's Legislation."

this same teaching of Jesus, and finds its central quality to be " A Gospel for an Age of Doubt." [1] Does this divergence of impression mean that each age and each scholar creates a new Christ, and that what seems to be a historical figure is in reality only the reflection of the inquirer's mind thrown upon the screen of the past? Is it only the pious imaginations of successive students which make of Jesus now the source of a theology and now the founder of a church, now peasant, now king, now the deliverer from doubt? On the contrary, the life of Jesus has, in fact, all these aspects, and indeed many more; and it is not as false interpreters, but as partial witnesses, that men stand in their own place and report that view of the gospel which presents itself to their minds. This extraordinary capacity for new adaptations, this quality of comprehensiveness in the teaching of Jesus, which so many evidences of the past illustrate, prepares us in our turn for its fresh applicability to the question which most concerns the present age. As it has happened a thousand times before, so it is likely to happen again, that the gospel, examined afresh with a new problem in mind, will seem again to have been written in large part to meet the needs of the new age. Words and deeds which other generations have found perplexing or obscure may be illuminated with meaning, as one now sees them in the light of the new social agitation and hope. It will seem, perhaps, as it has

[1] Henry Van Dyke. "The Gospel for an Age of Doubt," 1896.

seemed so often before, that no other age could have adequately appreciated the teaching of Jesus; as if his prophetic mind must have looked across the centuries and discerned the distant coming of social conflicts and aspirations which in his own time were insignificant, but which are now universal and profound.

Such is the comprehensiveness of the teaching of Jesus. A great modern preacher has described this power of adaptation in the parable of the fairy tent.[1] Set in the king's palace, this magic enclosure was not too large for the smallest room; placed in the court-yard, it was large enough to shelter all the nobles; brought out upon the plain, it grew to cover the whole army of the king; there was "infinite flexibility, infinite expansiveness." Jesus himself, according to the fourth gospel, with still greater suggestiveness, repeatedly describes his mission through the parable of the light. "I am," he says, "the light of the world";[2] "I am come a light into the world";[3] "Yet a little while is the light among you; walk while ye have the light."[4] Light is by its very nature comprehensive, transmissible, ubiquitous. There is not too much for each man's need, and yet there is enough for all. Each separate chamber seems to have all the sunshine, while the unexhausted light radiates into a million other homes. It is the same with the in-

[1] Stopford Brooke, "Religion in Modern Life," first sermon.
[2] John viii. 12.   [3] John xii. 46.   [4] John xii. 35.

fluence of Jesus Christ. Each new age or movement or personal desire seems to itself to receive
with a peculiar fulness its special teaching, and it
is quite true that a direct ray of communication
and illumination enters that chamber of the mind
which reaches no other point. It is as if one stood
at night watching the moon rise from the sea,
and saw the glittering band of light which leads
straight to him, as though the moon were shining
for one life alone ; while in fact he knows that its
comprehensive radiation is for him, and for the
joy and guidance of a world besides. So the unexhausted gospel of Jesus touches each new problem
and new need with its illuminating power, while
there yet remain myriads of other ways of radiation toward other souls and other ages, for that
Life which is the light of men.

CHAPTER II

𝔉𝔬𝔯 𝔱𝔥𝔢𝔦𝔯 𝔰𝔞𝔨𝔢𝔰 𝔍 𝔰𝔞𝔫𝔠𝔱𝔦𝔣𝔶 𝔪𝔶𝔰𝔢𝔩𝔣.

WE turn to the story of the gospels, inquiring for the relation of the teaching of Jesus to various social questions of the present age. Before entering, however, into the details of such an inquiry, it may be of advantage to survey the story as a whole, and to consider whether there are any general characteristics or principles which lie plainly on the face of the gospels, and which indicate the habitual attitude of the mind of Jesus toward such problems of social reform.

On opening the gospels with this general purpose in mind, one is immediately impressed by the abundance of material presented. Jesus was no recluse or ascetic. He lived in a world of social intimacies, problems and companionships. The first act of his ministry was to gather about him an intimate group of friends through whose associated activity his teaching was to be perpetuated. He entered with unaffected and equal sympathy into the joys and the sorrows of social life.[1] He was familiar with the most various social types,

---

[1] John ii. 1–11 ; xi. 1–44.

fishermen [1] and Pharisees,[2] tax-gatherers [3] and beggars,[4] Jews [5] and Romans,[6] saints [7] and sinners.[8] Almost every social question known to his age was in some form brought before him, either to receive his judgment or to make a snare for his teaching. The integrity of the family, the relations of rich and poor, the responsibilities of the prosperous, — all these, which seem to be modern questions, receive from Jesus reiterated and often stern consideration, so that it would seem to be a matter of slight difficulty to determine from such ample material the character of his social teaching.

There are, however, several aspects of his ministry which must be clearly recognized before this teaching can be interpreted in its full significance or scope. In the first place, as one sums up his general impression of the gospels, it becomes obvious that, whatever social teaching there may be in them, and however weighty it may be, the mind of the Teacher was primarily turned another way. The supreme concern of Jesus throughout his ministry was, — it may be unhesitatingly asserted, — not the reorganization of human society, but the disclosure to the human soul of its relation to God. Jesus was, first of all, not a reformer but a revealer; he was not primarily an agitator

---

[1] Matt. iv. 18.   [5] John iii. 1.
[2] Acts xxiii. 6.   [6] Matt. viii. 5.
[3] Matt. ix. 9; Luke v. 27.   [7] Luke x. 42.
[4] Mark x. 46; John ix. 1.   [8] Luke xix. 7; vii. 37.

with a plan, but an idealist with a vision. His mission was religious. His central desire was to make plain to human souls the relation in which they stand to their heavenly Father. "Lord, shew us the Father," say the disciples, "and it sufficeth us."[1] "The gospel," as a great German scholar remarks, "is not one of social improvement, but one of spiritual redemption."[2]

Still further, there was at times in the spiritual attitude of Jesus a certain quality of remoteness and detachment from the social problems which were presented to his mind. He refused to be entangled in them. Distribution of property was not within his province: "Man," he says, "who made me a judge or a divider over you?"[3] Forms of government were not for him to change: "Render therefore unto Cæsar the things that are Cæsar's."[4] There was political oppression about him to be remedied, there were social unrighteousness and iniquity to be condemned; but Jesus does not fling himself into these social issues of his time. He moves through them with a strange tranquillity, not as one who is indifferent to them, but as one whose eye is fixed on an end in which these social problems will find their own solution. The social questions met him, as it were, on his way, and his dealing with them is occasional and unsystematic. Sometimes, when confronted with

[1] John xiv. 8.
[2] A. Harnack, 5ter Evang.-soz. Kongress, s. 120.
[3] Luke xii. 14.   [4] Matt. xxii. 21.

such a question, he turns from it to the question of spiritual motive which lies beneath the social demand. He is asked to deal with the special problem of inheritance, and his answer opens the larger question of the love of money: "Take heed, and keep yourselves from all covetousness."[1] In short, Jesus will not be diverted by the demand for a social teaching from the special message of spiritual renewal which he is called to bring. In many of the processes of applied science, there are certain results known as by-products, which are thrown off or precipitated on the way to the special result desired. It may happen that these by-products are of the utmost value; but none the less they are obtained by the way. Such a by-product is the social teaching of Jesus. It was not the end toward which his mission was directed; it came about as he fulfilled that mission. To reconstruct the gospels so as to make them primarily a programme of social reform is to mistake the by-product for the end specifically sought, and, in the desire to find a place for Jesus within the modern age, to forfeit that which gives him his place in all ages.[2]

To this characteristic of the teaching of Jesus must be added another which has equal significance in its bearing on the social question. It is

[1] Luke xii. 15.

[2] See also "The Message of Christ to Manhood," Noble Lectures, 1898, II, F. G. Peabody, "The Message of Christ to Human Society," p. 66.

the occasionalism of his teaching. Jesus was not the maker of a system. He considers each case by itself. He is not posing at every turn as though the future were listening to him. He gives himself, with complete disinterestedness, to the single person or special group or specific case before him. "Jesus," says Wendt, "was not a scientific teacher, but a popular preacher. He did not present his practical demands in abstract form and systematic development. He applied them to those persons with whom he had directly to do, and to their concrete relations and needs; . . . without qualifying them by limitations and conditions which might come into notice from other points of view." [1] In short, Jesus is primarily thinking of individuals. The initial impulse of his word and work is this thought of the preciousness of personality. The shepherd leaves the ninety and nine sheep and seeks the one that is lost; [2] the woman sweeps the house to find the one piece of money. [3] General principles issue indeed from the discourse of Jesus, as an aroma rises from a rose; but the source of this pervasive fragrance is in that special and individual flower which blooms in his conversation or his deeds.

The teaching of Jesus, being thus fragmentary, is often, in its details, inconsistent. One who proposes to follow literally the specific commands

---

[1] 8ter Evang.-soz. Kongress, 1897, "Das Eigentum nach christlicher Beurteilung," s. 23.

[2] Matt. xviii. 12. [3] Luke xv. 8.

of Jesus finds himself immediately plunged into contradictions or absurdities. He accepts the teaching of Jesus concerning non-resistance: " To him that smiteth thee on the one cheek offer also the other;" [1] but soon he hears this same counsellor of peace bid his friends sell their garments " and buy a sword." [2] He joins with the modern agitator in repeating the passionate rebuke of Jesus, "Woe unto you that are rich;" and then he looks again and sees the same Jesus meeting the young man who had great possessions, and loving him. He proposes to abandon all luxury and domestic peace in order to follow him who " hath not where to lay his head;" [3] and then he looks again and finds this same Jesus serenely sharing the gayety of a wedding feast [4] and the peace of a comfortable home. [5]   To interpret, therefore, the teaching of Jesus there is needed more than willingness of heart. The study of the gospels calls for common sense. In fact, the devotion to the letter of the New Testament is one of the chief impediments to the perception of its spirit. The very essence of its interpretation lies in the discernment, through the medium of detached utterances, of the general habit of mind of the Teacher. Jesus himself repeatedly intimated that he required this thoughtfulness in his disciples. Those who had ears to hear, [6] he said, could receive his teaching, but to others it

[1] Luke vi. 29.   [3] Matt. viii. 20.   [5] John xi. 6.
[2] Luke xxii. 36.   [4] John ii. 2.   [6] Mark iv. 9.

G

was not given to understand. His teaching was
like that of the artist, who does not argue concerning beauty, but utters it, in color or in form, and
leaves the problem of appreciation for those who
can hear or see. He throws his truth into the
world for those who can receive it. "Go, . . ."
he says to those who ask for his doctrine, "and
tell John what things ye have seen and heard."[1]
By his teaching concerning specific cases the disciples are trained in a certain habit of mind, which
in its turn interprets other cases as they arise. It
is as Jesus promised that it should be to those who
followed him: "When he, the Spirit of truth, is
come, he shall guide you into all the truth."[2]

Thus the problem presented to a hearer of Jesus
in his own time, or to a reader of his words in the
present time, is to receive the teaching of Jesus in
the light of the special circumstances and suggestions which prompted it, and to deduce therefrom
the general principle which this teaching represents.
"If," as Wendt again remarks, "we examine the
recorded words of Jesus in an isolated way, we find
more than one meaning apparently possible, and
are able to decide with certainty for one of those
meanings by virtue of our knowledge of the mode
of teaching acquired by extensive observation in
other cases."[3] The study of the law has been of

[1] Luke vii. 22.   [2] John xvi. 13.

[3] "Teaching of Jesus" (tr. 1897), I, p. 106. Compare also
Paulsen, "Ethik," s. 72, "The universal applicability of the gospel
proceeds from the fact that it is not a philosophical or theological

late in a great degree transformed by the introduction of what is known as the case-system. Instead of lectures on the fundamental principles of jurisprudence, the learner is now confronted with detached and genuine cases, from scrutinizing which, in their likeness and variations, he is encouraged to deduce the principles which they combine to illustrate. Something like this is the method in which are communicated the principles of the teaching of Jesus. They are not unfolded in a philosophical system, but are involved in the treatment of specific cases; and to the observant student this occasionalism of the teaching of Jesus is precisely what gives it a perennial freshness, vitality and force.[1]

Here, then, are two characteristics of the gospel which would seem in some degree to obscure its social teaching, — an evident subordination of social problems, and an equally evident limitation of instruction to specific instances and occasions. Jesus speaks chiefly of God, and speaks chiefly to the individual. It would seem, then, as if we must have been misled in anticipating from him a clear and impressive teaching concerning the social world. If Jesus was not primarily devoted to the social question, and if again his teach-

system. Systems pass away, . . . but great poems are as eternal as their subject — human life itself."

[1] Compare also the interesting proposition to apply the same method to the study of medicine: W. B. Cannon, "The Case-method of teaching Systematic Medicine," *Boston Medical and Surgical Journal*, January 11, 1900.

ing was chiefly personal and occasional instead of
systematic and universal, is it not difficult to derive
from it any general principles which shall be applicable to the problems of modern social life? On
the contrary, one must answer, it is precisely these
two characteristics, his relation to God and his relation to the individual, the loftiness of his Theism
and the precision of his occasionalism, which open,
as we consider them, into the social principles of
the teaching of Jesus.

On the one hand, this tranquil elevation of mind
above the social issues of his day is what gives to
Jesus his wisdom and insight concerning them.
He only truly sees things who sees round them
and beyond them. Breadth of wisdom requires a
large horizon of the mind. The man of details is
shut in by them, so that they obstruct rather than
enlarge his view. The wise physician deals best
with the sick man, not by being a participator in
the emotion and distress involved in the single
case, but by detaching himself from them and
examining the single case with the tranquillity and
self-control of a broader view. The wise general
does not throw himself into the smoke of battle,
but stands apart from it and above it, where he
can survey and direct the whole. The wise counsellor is he who stands above the issue which calls
for judgment and sees it in the perspective of a
wide experience. Sometimes it happens that the
highest wisdom in affairs of the practical world is
an endowment of the most unworldly men. They

see into life by seeing over it, and men of business turn to such advisers for counsel because of the horizon which their judgments survey.[1]

This quality of wisdom is not the trait most commonly associated with the life of Jesus. His tenderness of heart has obscured from observation his sagacity of mind. Yet one cannot approach his dealings with the questions which were brought to him without being impressed by this quality of insight, foresight, comprehensiveness, wisdom. The traditions of the Church ascribe to Jesus almost every other virtue rather than that of sagacity. He is the type of submission and resignation. His features, as portrayed by Christian art, represent, almost invariably, a feminine, spiritual, patient personality, not one that is virile, commanding and strong. He has become the ideal of the monastic and ascetic character, and in many minds would have no consideration as a wise guide in practical affairs. A more careful study of the teaching of Jesus leads to quite an opposite impression. He was indeed a man of sorrows and acquainted with grief, but he was none the less truly a man of wisdom and acquainted with human nature. His sanity of judgment is as extraordinary as his depth of sym-

[1] Compare also Seneca, "De Clementia," II, 6, "He will dry another's tears, but will not weep with him. . . . This he will do with calmness of mind, and with an unchanged countenance." (Succuret alienis lacrimis, non accedet. . . . Faciet ista tranquillâ mente, voltu suo.) And the saying of Neander (Preface to Vinet's "Socialisme"), "Um sich hinzugeben, muss man sich angehören."

pathy. The first impression made by the boy Jesus on those who met him was of his budding wisdom; he "advanced in wisdom and stature."[1] The first comment of many hearers upon his teaching concerned its sagacity: "Whence hath this man this wisdom?"[2] Christian art and reverence, in remembering the prophecy fulfilled in him, "In all their affliction he was afflicted,"[3] has forgotten that other hope of a just and discriminating guide, which was equally fulfilled in him: "The government shall be upon his shoulder: and his name shall be called Wonderful, Counsellor;"[4] "and the spirit of the Lord shall rest upon him, the spirit of wisdom and understanding."[5] The picture of Jesus which Christian art has yet to paint is that of the masculine Christ, a personality who teaches with authority, and whose large horizon gives him comprehensiveness of view.

Jesus himself testified whence this wisdom came. It was, he said, his detachment from the world which gave him insight concerning the things of the world. "And I, if I be lifted up from the earth, will draw all men unto myself."[6] His leadership in the affairs of earth comes of his being lifted up from it; his religious mission created his social authority. At the end of his ministry he promises to his disciples that their power for social service shall be enriched by the continuity of relationship which he was to bear to the life of

[1] Luke ii. 52.   [3] Is. lxiii. 9.   [5] Is. xi. 2.
[2] Matt. xiii. 54.   [4] Is. ix. 6.   [6] John xii. 32.

God : "Greater works than these shall he do, because I go unto the Father."[1] It is said of Count Zinzendorf, the pious nobleman who welcomed the exiled Moravians to his home, that as a young man he could ride the wildest horse in his father's stables; and on being asked how it could happen that one could be at the same time a pietist and an athlete, he answered, "Only he to whom earthly things are indifferent becomes their master."[2] There was this masterly quality in the social teaching of Jesus. Instead of being entangled by social questions, he moved through them with a quiet authority and even a delicate irony. His conversation was in heaven; therefore the world was at his feet.

Here is one of the most striking contrasts between the teaching of Jesus and that of the prophets of the Old Testament. They threw themselves into the midst of the struggle for national righteousness, exhorting, rebuking, upbraiding their people as they wavered or retreated into wrong ; Jesus surveys this struggle, as it were, from above, as an incident of the great campaign of God. The prophets wrestled with the waves of social agitation ; Jesus walked upon them. The difference was not so much one of social intention as of social horizon. The work of a reformer is for his own age ; that of a revealer for all ages. The social teaching of Jesus is universal, precisely because it was a by-product, issuing from his universal teaching of the

[1] John xiv. 12.   [2] Nathusius (op. cit.), s. 317, note.

life of God in the soul of man. Jesus looks at the social world from above, and that point of view gives him courage, optimism, comprehensiveness, vision, hope.

The second characteristic of the gospels which we have noticed is not less fruitful in social consequences. Jesus, as we have seen, primarily addressed himself in his teaching to individual cases and immediate ends. Once only, and that at the beginning of his ministry, and to his selected group of personal disciples, does he approach anything like a formal announcement of what may be called general principles.[1] For the most part he uses a "case-system"; he discourses with a few; he heals people one at a time; he lavishes his richest instruction on individuals; and finally, having attached to his teaching only a handful of plain people, he gives back his work to the Father with a strange sense of completeness in it. "It is finished,"[2] he says; "Having accomplished the work which thou hast given me to do."[3] He is not only indifferent to numbers, but often seems disinclined to deal with numbers. He sends the multitudes away; he goes apart into a mountain with his chosen disciples;[4] he withdraws himself from the throng in Jerusalem to the quiet home at Bethany;[5] he discourses of the profoundest purpose of his mission with the twelve in an upper room;[6] he opens the treasures of his

---

[1] Matt. v–vii.
[2] John xix. 30.
[3] John xvii. 4.
[4] Matt. xvii. 1.
[5] John xii, 1.
[6] Luke xxii. 12–38.

wisdom before one Pharisee at night,[1] and one unresponsive woman by the well.[2] What does this extraordinary individualization of teaching indicate as to the attitude of Jesus toward social reform? It indicates the instrument to which he was willing to trust his hope for the world. What he had to give he gave to individuals, to be given again through individuals. "As the Father has sent me," he says, "even so send I you."[3] His way of approach to the life of his age was not by external organization or mass-movements or force of numbers, or in any way from without; but by interior inspiration, by the quickening of individuals, by the force of personality, or, so to speak, from within.

When one considers the traditions and hopes of his people, and the sense of capacity in himself of which he must have been aware, it is simply amazing that Jesus did not put himself at the head of a movement, or establish an organization, or direct his teaching to the whole-sale conversion of the multitude. Yet hardly any problem of exegesis is more difficult than to discover in the gospels an administrative or organizing or ecclesiastical Christ. On the contrary, there is, in his teaching, a remarkable quality of reserve and privacy. Sometimes he charges his hearers not to tell what he has said or done.[4] He interprets privately to his friends the teaching

---

[1] John iii. 1–21.   [2] John iv. 7–29.   [3] John xx. 21.
[4] Matt. viii. 4 ; Mark viii. 26 ; Luke v. 14 ; Matt. xvii. 9.

which others have not understood.[1] Never did
a popular leader leave his work so little systema-
tized. The sense of incompleteness in it gave his
friends in his last days a sense of bewildered helplessness. The only light they had was in his life,
and when he told them that it was expedient for
them that he should go away, the light seemed to
them to go out.[2] " But we hoped," they said, " that
it was he which should redeem Israel." [3] He had
given them no indication of the external form
which should issue from his teaching. He trusted
to the capacity of individuals, if only their hearts
should have received the spirit of truth, to deal
with problems of form and organization as they
arrived. In short, instead of regeneration by
organization, Jesus offers regeneration by inspiration. He was not primarily the deviser of a social
system, but the quickener of single lives. His
gift is not that of form, but that of life. " I came,"
he says, " that they may have life " ; [4] " The words
that I have spoken unto you are spirit, and are
life " ; [5] " Because I live, ye shall live also." [6] The
communication of vitality, the contagion of personality, the transmission of character, — these
are the ends he seeks, and these are possible only
through that individualization of teaching which
marks his ministry. As Phillips Brooks once said,
" Jesus was not primarily the Deed-Doer, or the

[1] Mark iv. 34.
[2] John xvi. 7.
[3] Luke xxiv. 21.
[4] John x. 10.
[5] John vi. 63.
[6] John xiv. 19.

Word-Sayer, he was the Life-Giver." [1] Even of himself and of his own mission, he announces that it begins with the individual. "For their sakes," he says, I do not, first of all, organize an associated life or announce a scheme of salvation; but, first of all, " I sanctify myself." [2] Jesus, in short, not only surveys human life from above, but he approaches it from within.

These two qualities, however, of social wisdom and social power, are not the only principles which govern the social teaching of Jesus. Indeed, they are but introductory to the most conspicuous and central of his social principles. Beyond the point of view from which he looks at the world, and the instrument to which he intrusts his work for the world, lies his ideal for the world, — a social ideal whose significance and scope are to be interpreted only when one has first recognized that Jesus surveys life from above and approaches it from within. This social ideal, which presents itself continuously and vividly to the mind of Jesus, is summed up in that phrase which occurs more than a hundred times in the first three gospels, — the "kingdom of heaven," or the "kingdom of God." [3] From

[1] Noble Lectures, 1898, I. A. V. G. Allen, "The Message of Christ to the Individual Man," p. 18. Compare also the sermon of J. H. Newman, "Personal Influence the Means of propagating the Truth."

[2] John xvii. 19.

[3] The two titles appear to be practically identical in signification. Beyschlag, "New Testament Theology," I, 42, "That both expressions mean the same thing is manifest from the parallels of Matthew

the beginning of the ministry of Jesus to its close, this is the subject of his prophecy, parable and prayer. "Jesus," begins the gospel of Mark, "came into Galilee, preaching the gospel of God and saying, The time is fulfilled and the kingdom of God is at hand."[1] The kingdom was the one end to be desired; it was the pearl of great price for which all else might be sold;[2] it was the piece of money to find which the house was diligently swept;[3] it was to be the theme of daily prayer for the followers of Jesus: "Thy kingdom come."[4] It is a phrase which, on the face of the record, is often obscure, and which in different passages appears to have inconsistent meanings. The kingdom is described as both a present and a future state, as both an inward and an outward condition. Now it seems to be a remote and glorious consummation of the Messiah's reign in the day of the last things: "Then shall appear the sign of the Son of man in heaven: and then shall all the tribes of the earth . . . see the Son of man coming on the clouds of heaven with power and great glory."[5] Again, it is obviously not remote and supramundane, but near and of this world: "There be some here of them that stand by, which shall in

on the one hand and of Mark and Luke on the other." For possible grounds of the variation in use see the interesting note in Wendt, "Teaching of Jesus," I, 370 ff.

[1] Mark i. 14, 15.　　[2] Matt. xiii. 46.　　[3] Luke xv. 8.
[4] Matt. vi. 10.　　　　[5] Matt. xxiv. 30.

no wise taste of death, till they see the kingdom of God come with power." [1]   Yet again, it is a silent, spiritual, immanent presence: "The kingdom of God cometh not with observation: neither shall they say, Lo, here! or, There! for lo, the kingdom of God is within you." [2]

What unity of teaching is it possible to discover within these apparently conflicting and incompatible aspects of the kingdom? [3]   In the first place, certain difficulties of interpretation may be removed by recalling the circumstances under which the teaching of Jesus was given. The phrase was familiar to his hearers. It summed up to their minds the fulfilment of their national hopes and of their Messianic dreams. [4]   Yet to the Hebrews themselves it had become a confused and waver-

[1] Mark ix. 1.

[2] Luke xvii. 20, 21.

[3] The history of modern interpretations of the doctrine of the kingdom is told in detail by Schnedermann, "Jesu Verkündigung und Lehre vom Reiche Gottes," I, 86 ff. The conclusion of the author which, he remarks (s. 173), "has been recognized by no other inquirer," and which subordinates the idea of the kingdom in the teaching of Jesus, seems unlikely to obtain acceptance; *e.g.* s. 173, "The assumption that Jesus laid great weight on the idea of the kingdom for its own sake is wholly unfounded" (aus der Luft gegriffen); and s. 195, "The conception of the kingdom lies, in the teaching of Jesus, in the Israelitic background."

[4] Ex. xix. 6 ; Dan. ii. 44. See: Wendt, "Teaching of Jesus," I, 174, and note ; Holtzmann, "New Testament Theology," I, 225 ff. ; Stevens, "Theology of New Testament," p. 28 ff. ; Beyschlag, "New Testament Theology," I, 43 ; and the detailed and learned survey of four "stadia" in Jewish thought in Toy, "Judaism and Christianity," 1896, 303-371.

ing conception. Sometimes it had taken the form
of a political scheme of national emancipation;
sometimes it was the expression of a religious
dream of Messianic glory. Thus, even to those
who were looking and longing for the kingdom
of God, it was not a clearly defined and specific
hope. On this flexible phrase, then, with its
capacity for spiritualization, Jesus fastens when
he desires to describe his mission. He knows
that his conception of it is not that which is
popularly current among his people, but he utilizes the only phrase which is in the least adequate
for his teaching, believing that the kingdom of
which he speaks is not only in no way contrary to
the national hope, but in reality represents the
interior truth of that national ideal.

One misinterpretation of his message he distinctly
meets. The kingdom, as he announces it, is certainly not to take that form of a political restoration
to which many of his contemporaries had degraded
their social ideal. The blessings of that kingdom
are not for the great or powerful, but for the
humble ministers of others' needs. "Whosoever
therefore shall humble himself as this little child,
the same is the greatest in the kingdom of heaven."[1]
"Whosoever would become great among you, shall
be your minister."[2] "My kingdom," he explicitly
says, "is not of this world;"[3] and again, "Take
heed, beware of the leaven of the Pharisees and

---

[1] Matt. xviii. 4.   [2] Mark x. 43.   [3] John xviii. 36.

the leaven of Herod," [1] — the desire, that is to say, of political supremacy or of party rule. [2]

A second conception of the kingdom of heaven current in the time of Jesus cannot be so lightly dismissed. It is that of an apocalyptic consummation of the Messiah's rule, — a view which obviously prevailed in much Jewish literature of the time, and which is deeply imbedded in the gospel story. It has been held, therefore, with ingenuity and learning,[3] that Jesus shared, with his people and his age, these eschatological ideals, and that the key of his teaching concerning the kingdom is to be sought, not in his more spiritualized sayings, but in the apocalyptic utterances and prophecies of the gos-

---

[1] Mark viii. 15.

[2] Wendt, I, 364 ff. ; Beyschlag, I, 47 ; Shailer Mathews, " Social Teaching of Jesus," 45.

[3] This view has been elaborated, with variations in detail, in two prize essays of the Hague Society for the defence of the Christian Religion, by Issel, " Die Lehre vom Reiche Gottes im N. T.," 1891 ; and Schmoller, " Die Lehre vom Reiche Gottes in den Schriften des N. T.," 1891 (s. 102 ff.); and in the more famous treatise, confessedly suggested by Schmoller, of Joh. Weiss, " Die Predigt Jesu vom Reiche Gottes," 1892. See the summary of his conclusions, ss. 61, 62 ; and his intention, announced at the outset, " to exhibit the thoroughly apocalyptic and eschatological character of the idea of Jesus." See also, of the same tendency, Bousset, " Jesu Predigt in ihrem Gegensatz zum Judentum," 1892 (s. 100 ff.); Schnedermann (op. cit.), s. 190, " This kingdom of God is in no sense a result to be achieved (Aufgabe). The refutation of the utterances of Ritschl to this effect by Haupt, Köstlin, Schmoller, J. Weiss, and others, is to be recognized and commended as an important achievement of the latest inquiry. Rather it is a free gift (Gabe) as Schmoller and J. Weiss have made plain."

pels. There are, beyond doubt, many passages which lend themselves to this view; and the method of those New Testament critics who interpret the teaching of Jesus in its relation to the antecedent traditions and ideals of Hebrew faith, has been most illuminating and fruitful. It is difficult, however, to subordinate in the teaching of Jesus the spiritual sayings to these Hebraic hopes. In disposing of one difficulty of interpretation another difficulty is introduced. If the mind of Jesus was thus supremely concerned with an apocalyptic kingdom, how can he have referred to it as "within"? To believe that the spiritual and ethical teaching concerning the kingdom should have been superimposed by the followers of Jesus on the view really held by their Master, is contrary to every indication in the gospels of the true relation between Jesus and his disciples. The well-known phrase of Matthew Arnold, "Jesus above the heads of his reporters," is one of the safest canons of the New Testament interpretation. The more spiritual and ethical a teaching is, the more likely it is to have come from the Teacher's lips. Thus, if the apocalyptic passages are to be accepted at all, it must at least be in connection with that other form of proclamation which describes the kingdom as a spiritual and already present reality. "Blessed are the eyes which see the things that ye see;"[1] "the kingdom of God is come upon you."[2]

[1] Luke x. 23.
[2] Matt. xii. 28. So with much force, Erich Haupt, "Die escha-

What interpretation, then, shall be offered of this relationship between a kingdom which is at hand and a kingdom which is to come to pass in the world of heaven? Three possibilities have had serious consideration. It may be, in the first place, suggested, in opposition to the view just presented, that it is the apocalyptic passages which are super-added, and that they represent the thought of the disciples, derived from the Hebrew tradition, rather than the mind of the Master.[1] Such a conclusion, however, would seem to be the last resort of criticism. It may be, indeed, believed that to many a saying of Jesus there was given a heightened color through the report of evangelists steeped in apocalyptic literature; but to eliminate from the record all anticipation on the part of Jesus of a future consummation is to reject without other cause large portions of the narrative.

tologischen Aussagen Jesu," 1895, s. 77 ff., "The solution of the problem appears to me attained only when our inquiry begins at the opposite point from that now usually occupied, with those passages in which the kingdom of God is described as present. . . . These passages form the interior climax of the message of Jesus. Here he shows that it is no new and noble Judaism that he brings. The chief element in the kingdom of God — communion with God, the relation of children to a Father — is a present possession."

[1] See the restrained yet candid judgments of Toy, " Judaism and Christianity," p. 260 ff., " That they [the eschatological discussions] were not delivered by Jesus in the form in which we now have them may probably be inferred from the consideration already mentioned — that the disciples for some time after his death show no knowledge of their contents. . . . The power of the founder of Christianity was in his moral personality and in his conception of a thoroughly spiritual society."

H

A second possibility which deserves consideration is that the thought of Jesus himself had a
gradual development during his ministry, and
passed by degrees from the external to the spiritual view of the kingdom, so that, while at the
beginning of his teaching he shared the popular
Messianic ideal and preached a kingdom which
was to appear in the clouds of heaven, he became
by degrees aware that this consummation was not
to happen, and that the real kingdom was, even
while he taught, being spiritually realized in the
hearts that accepted him.[1] This view, however, is
also not without grave difficulties. There are,
indeed, indications that, as the ministry of Jesus
proceeded, the meaning and end of it grew clearer
and more commanding to his mind. The hopes
with which no doubt he began, of finding acceptance among his people, turned out to be vain; the
cross disclosed itself to him as an inevitable end;
and at last he "set his face," as we read, "to go
to Jerusalem."[2] Yet, on the other hand, the brief
limits of his ministry give scanty room for any
radical reconstruction of his thoughts concerning
the kingdom. Indeed, his first teachings recognized as fully as his later utterances its spiritual
nature. What is called his temptation was the

---

[1] Beyschlag, "Leben Jesu," I, 229 ff., "The probability is that he
came gradually to think of himself as the deliverer promised by the
prophets"; and the criticism of Wendt, I, 380 ff. For the con-
verse of this view, see Toy, p. 352.

[2] Luke ix. 51.

deliberate putting away by him of material tests and rewards. If any deepening spirituality can be traced in his language as it proceeds, it is much more probably to be traced to his gradual instruction of the disciples in the profounder view than to a gradual illumination of his own mind. There are, in fact, many indications which suggest a deepening and spiritualizing of the idea of the kingdom, not so much in the mind of Jesus as in the minds of his hearers and followers. It may well have been to them, at the first hearing, difficult to realize that Jesus was enriching an old phrase with a new signification, and his bold use of traditional language may have been accepted by them, as it has been accepted by many modern scholars. By degrees, however, it may have come to pass that one after another, in recalling their impressions of the teaching of Jesus, became aware of the deeper meaning which at first they had missed, until at last the very phrase, " The kingdom of God," is in the fourth gospel lost in the larger conception of "life" and "eternal life." This gradually dawning consciousness of the interior meaning of the teaching of Jesus seems to find its fulfilment in the mind of Paul. To him the spiritual view has become the only conceivable one: "The kingdom of God is . . . ," he says without qualification, "righteousness and peace and joy in the Holy Ghost."[1]

We are brought, then, to the apparently para-

[1] Rom. xiv. 17.

doxical conclusion that the kingdom of God had to Jesus both significations, that of a future and that of a present state, that of a heavenly and that of an earthly society. This apparent paradox, however, disappears when we consider the conception of the kingdom in the light of the two principles which we have already laid down. Jesus, as we have seen, views the world from above. He sees in it the movement of the life of God on the souls of men. Wherever, then, this spirit of God finds welcome in a human life, there, immediately, unostentatiously, yet certainly, the kingdom of God has already come; and when at last that same spirit shall penetrate the whole world, then there will result a social future which language itself is hardly rich enough to describe. This is no inconsistency or confusion of thought. The thought of Jesus considers both what is and what is to be; the present potentiality of the kingdom and its future realization. Here is the significance of the parables of the leaven [1] and of the mustard seed. [2] The kingdom has as its very essence the capacity for expansion. It has as real an existence in the seed as in the tree, but not less real in the future glory than in the present seed. It is hidden in the leaven, but it is not less demonstrably to be revealed in the mass. The social ideal, then, of Jesus Christ, is to be interpreted only through his religious consciousness. He looks

[1] Matt. xiii. 33 ; Luke xiii. 21.
[2] Matt. xiii. 31, 32 ; Mark iv. 31, 32 ; Luke xiii. 19.

on human life from above, and, seeing it slowly shaped and purified by the life of God, regards the future of human society with a transcendent and unfaltering hope. In the purposes of God the kingdom is already existent, and when his will is done on earth, then his kingdom, which is now spiritual and interior, will be as visible and as controlling as it is in heaven.[1]

On the other hand, Jesus approaches life from within, through the inspiration of the individual. Here is his answer to that question which the disciples themselves asked, "When shall these things be? and what shall be the sign of thy coming?"[2] The kingdom is to come, answers Jesus, not by outward force or social organization or apocalyptic dream, but by the progressive sanctification of individual human souls.[3] And does one

[1] Holtzmann, "New Testament Theology," I, 200, "The kingdom of God is both a gift to be received and a result to be achieved" (ebensosehr Gabe wie Aufgabe). So Harnack, "History of Dogma," I, 62, "Jesus announced the kingdom of God . . . as a future kingdom, and yet it is presented in his preaching as present; as invisible, and yet it was visible — for one actually saw it." B. Weiss, "Biblical Theology of New Testament" (tr. 1882), I, 72, "It is this interpretation of present and future, it is this certainty of its completion at every stage of the empirical realization of the kingdom of God, which has become an inalienable moment of the Christian consciousness, in consequence of the teaching of Jesus." See also Stevens, "Theology of the New Testament," 1899, 37 ff. Holtzmann, s. 208, collects in a note a long series of definitions of the kingdom.

[2] Matt. xxiv. 3.

[3] On the kingdom as spiritual, see Bruce, "The Kingdom of God," 4th ed., 1891, Ch. I; "Christ's Idea of the Kingdom," p. 58,

ask again what is to be the motive of this personal
sanctification? It is to be found, according to
Jesus, in the thought of the kingdom. On the
one hand the kingdom is an unfolding process of
social righteousness, to be worked out through
individuals; on the other hand, the individual is
prompted to his better life by the thought of
bringing in the kingdom. Thus the individual
and the kingdom grow together. The individual
discovers himself in the social order, and the social
order, like that "whole creation" of which Saint
Paul wrote, "waiteth for the revealing of the sons
of God."[1]

In other and more modern language, the social
teaching of Jesus Christ is this, — that the social
order is not a product of mechanism but of personality, and that personality fulfils itself only in
the social order. Thus the social philosophy of
Jesus is but another statement of his philosophy
of religion. Speaking as a religious teacher, Jesus
says that the life of man is discovered to itself
in the service of God. The son comes to himself
when he says, "I will arise and go to my father."[2]
His sense of dependence, in the language of Schleiermacher, is the beginning of his religious life.
Religion is freedom from the world through de-

"In all probability the title was used alternatively [kingdom of
God, or of heaven] by Jesus, for the express purpose of lifting the
minds of the Jewish people into a brighter region of thought"; and
on the kingdom as social, see Mathews, "Social Teaching of Jesus,"
Ch. III, and his "History of New Testament Times," 1899, p. 171 ff

[1] Rom. viii. 19.   [2] Luke xv. 18.

pendence upon him, "Whose service," in the beautiful words of the English Prayer-book, "is perfect freedom." [1] The same spiritual process is to be traced in the social teaching of Jesus. Again, the individual is the point of departure, but he finds his own self-realization only in the service of the social world. As has been lately said, " The true individuality is to be found in a fully organized society, and a worthy society in a fully developed individual." [2] The world of social ethics, then, lies in the mind of Jesus like an island in the larger sea of the religious life; but the same principle of service controls one, whether he tills the field of his island or puts forth to the larger adventure of the sea. Shall we, then, say that Jesus was an individualist, or shall we say that in

[1] Schleiermacher, "Christlicher Glaube," 1801, I, 19, "The common element in all the varied expressions of piety which distinguish religion from all other feelings — that is to say, the essence of religion — is this, that we are conscious of ourselves as absolutely dependent, or in other words, in relation to God." In the reconciliation of the sense of freedom with the sense of dependence, the two German tendencies in the philosophy of religion, proceeding from Hegel and Schleiermacher, meet; Pfleiderer, "Die Religion," 1869, I, 78, and more distinctly in his " Religionsphilosophie," 1878, s. 298, "In Gott eins mit der Weltordnung und durch Gott frei von der Weltschranke . . . das ist das Wesen der Religion "; Biedermann, " Dogmatik," 1869, s. 30, "The content of the religious process in the spiritual life of man is the freedom of the finite spirit from finite conditions in an infinite dependence "; Lipsius, " Dogmatik," 1876, s. 28, "Religion is the reconciliation of the longing for freedom with the sense of dependence."

[2] *New World*, September, 1898, Henry Jones, " Social and Individual Evolution."

any sense of the word he was a socialist? Was his mind directed toward personal education or toward social reform? His method, we must answer, admits of no such antagonism between spiritual life and the social good. The one is his means, the other is his end. The first word of his teaching is character, the second is love. Love has its watchword, "for their sakes"; and character its command, "sanctify thyself"; and the Christian social law is fulfilled in the whole saying of Jesus, "for their sakes I sanctify myself." [1]

Here

Such, in their most general statement, seem to be the social principles of the teaching of Jesus, — the view from above, the approach from within, and the movement toward a spiritual end; wisdom, personality, idealism; a social horizon, a social power, a social aim. The supreme truth that this is God's world gave to Jesus his spirit of social optimism; the assurance that man is God's instrument gave to him his method of social opportunism; the faith that in God's world God's people are to establish God's kingdom gave him his social idealism. He looks upon the struggling, chaotic, sinning world with the eye of an unclouded religious faith, and discerns in it the principle of personality fulfilling the will of God in social service. It is for later chapters to indicate how these social principles may be applied in detail to specific social problems of the modern world. For the

[1] John xvii. 19.

present, let us note in advance the general effect which they may have on one's total view of social life.

There has probably never been an age in human history which could compare with the present time in its capacity for appreciating these principles which we seem to discover beneath the words and conduct of Jesus Christ. The social question, as we saw at the outset, is an all-environing and all-engrossing interest. Even those who are not consciously concerned with it are none the less involved in it. Indeed, this indifferent and neutral element in modern social life makes one of the most threatening elements of the modern social question. Those, on the other hand, who recognize the present situation are often much burdened and perplexed by it. Some of them are shut in by the multitude of details involved in social duty. Their special work is at best but a fragment, and they often wonder how it can have a place in the whole movement of social progress. At times it seems to them that they are doing more harm than good, and that perhaps it would be better to do nothing. They are like detachments of an army, fighting in the skirmish line, without knowing how their service counts in the general's plan. They are oppressed with a sense of incapacity. They observe that the philosophy of society which is most current at the present time is a philosophy of materialism. To it the fundamental problems are economic ; in its teaching the reconstruction of society proceeds from below, and the ideals of an age are the corollaries of its industrial order. To such observers, then, the social question brings with it a new wave of social pessimism, as if the problems of modern society were too bewildering and portentous to give any ground for courage or hope.

To this frame of mind, hemmed in, disheartened, vainly attempting the interpretation of life from below, there offer themselves the social principles of the teaching of Jesus. In the first place, he contributes a new point of view, — the view from above, the sense of horizon, the capacity for comprehensiveness and wisdom. Passionate activity, beautiful self-sacrifice, indignant emotions, — all these are abundantly offered in our day for social service; but what a lack there is of breadth of view, of social courage, of a justified and stable optimism! How are these qualities to supplant the narrowness and irritation and despair which make social hope appear a Utopian dream? They are to come, answers Jesus, through an application to the social question of the spirit of rational religion. What the modern reformer needs is the capacity to look beyond the bounds of his own special work, and to perceive its relations, its causes, and its effects, as a part of the movement of a Divine plan. Nothing could be more contrary to the teaching of Jesus than the vulgar notion that he diverts attention from this world and fixes 't on another. His ministry is for this life, quite

is much as for any world. " Thy kingdom come,"
he prays, " on earth."   It is, however, the point of
view which transforms the scene.   The landscape
is more truly studied from the hilltop than from
the underbrush below. The general, standing apart
from the battle, surveys it more completely than
the rank and file in the midst of the smoke.   Precisely thus the spiritual companionship of Jesus
with the life of God gives him perspective and
hope in his view of the world below. He looks
at life from above, and its confusion and conflict
fall into order and reveal their purpose as parts of
the large intention of the Father.   He looks over
the partitions of social provincialism, and sees the
dimensions and unity of the world.

When one asks, then, as many reformers are
tempted to ask, "What part has religion in these
practical affairs?   What right have I to pause
in my generous activity and contemplate life
in the spirit of Jesus?" the first — though not
the complete — answer to such self-inquiry is
this, — that the capacity for detachment and the
contemplation of practical affairs from the religious point of view are precisely what make practical activity most patient, comprehensive, and
wise.   The special weakness of modern social
activity is its impulsiveness, its fickleness, its
fragmentary interest, its specialized enthusiasm.
What the work of philanthropy and the reform
of industry need is the larger horizon of the view
from above. Jesus heals the demoniac boy the

more gladly and firmly because he has just been on the mount of transfiguration.[1] It is the same with many a devoted and overburdened modern life as it turns to heal the social distresses of the time. The patience and courage which administer wise relief come of the antecedent transfiguration of life through communion with God. Many a modern life, if asked to define the significance and usefulness of its religious experience, would have little more to say than this : " My faith in God makes me able to do my work. It rescues me from narrowness and hopelessness, and gives me persistence and courage from day to day. It preserves for me the large view of my duty, and sustains me when my immediate results are bitterly meagre and small. In short, it is what stands between me and overwhelming weariness or social despair." The just still live by their faith. The view of life from above gives a rational courage for the service of life below.

The second aspect of the teaching of Jesus is equally applicable to modern life. Next to narrowness of view, what is the special peril of the present social movement ? It is, beyond doubt, its externalism. Wherever one looks, he sees progress defined in terms of organizations, schemes, majorities, social machinery. Industrial life has reached a degree of complexity in which the individual worker is little more than one cog in a vast machine. Political methods have magnified

[1] Matt. xvii. 15–18.

enormously the function of government. Officialism supplants more and more the demand
for individual initiative; until, as has been said
of German militarism, every effort seems now
devoted to the making of a man into a machine.
The creed of scientific socialism is frankly and
aggressively external. Its programme has rarely a
word to say of any change of character; it makes
no appeal to the working-man to cultivate prudence,
self-restraint or patience. On the contrary, these
qualities, which have been generally recognized as
virtues, often seem to stand in the way of the working-man's aim. Let him demand more pay, it is
urged; more comfort, better external conditions;
and then these changes in the outward industrial
order will of themselves develop the inward capacity to use it. Even religion itself runs grave risk
of being institutionalized and externalized out of
all self-recognition. Organization and ritual, ecclesiastical machinery, leagues and associations, —
all these external methods have attained such
terrific dimensions and importance that it has come
to appear an elementary Christian duty for persons to become, as Stevenson remarked, "joiners";
and it is even announced as one conspicuous mark
of Christian progress that on a certain day, under
one organized arrangement, some millions of associated believers will, in sixteen different languages,
beseech the throne of grace.

What has Jesus Christ to say to this marvellous
development of social machinery? He has no

direction to give and no criticism to offer. It may well be an admirable, as it is certainly an inevitable, phase in the evolution of society. The methods of the "great industry" are transforming the habits of the Church, as they have already transformed the habits of the business world. All these subjects lie outside of the sphere of the teaching of Jesus. He is not a social mechanic or a social organizer. The complexity of the modern world presents a problem of external arrangement which was never before his mind, and with which, even if it had been set before his mind, he would probably not have felt himself deeply concerned. Jesus, however, turns to the other factor of social life, whose significance the tendency to externalism gravely obscures. It is quite true, as modern teachers are urging upon us, that environment modifies personality, that social and economic conditions now exist which make a healthy human life very hard to live, that the reorganization of society is a pressing task, and that such improvement in organization may fortify the individual life, as a single soldier's courage is stronger when he is conscious of an organized army at his back. The teaching of Jesus, however, is of the person who can modify his environment, of the man who transforms conditions, of the courage which is nurtured in solitude and is not alone, because the Father is with it. In short, Jesus approaches the social question from within; he deals with individuals; he makes men. It is for others to serve the world by organization; he serves it through inspiration. It is for others to offer what the theologians once called a scheme of salvation; the only salvation Jesus offers is through saviours, and saviours are those who have sanctified themselves for others' sakes.

Does this mean that the teaching of Jesus is indifferent to external methods of reform, and is absorbed, as many of his followers have been, in mystical communion with God, and in the saving of one's own soul? Was Jesus unaware that there may be circumstances in life in which it is almost impossible to save one's soul? Would he, if he could survey the life of the modern world, take no interest in such bettering of external conditions? Would he expect to communicate spiritual inspiration where people are living, male and female, ten in a room, or where a family of four are subsisting on the casual earnings of one? Is he so feeble a sentimentalist as to think that good will come from within if the way is not prepared for it from without? We shall soon see how far from such indifference to external conditions is the teaching of Jesus, and how radical are his instructions concerning the environment of life. If the primary aim of Jesus is to set forth the principle of personality, to awaken the higher life of persons, to make a man "come to himself," then no social conditions have, under his teaching, any right to exist which can obstruct or which even fail to encourage this end of individual growth, oppor-

tunity, initiative and character.   All this we shall
observe as each successive aspect of the social
order claims our attention.   Yet within this problem of the better social order lies always the
problem of the better man.   " There is no political alchemy," said Mr. Spencer, "by which you
can get golden conduct out of leaden instincts." [1]
It is vain to imagine that a change of external
conditions will of itself bring about a change of the
human heart.   The fact is that conditions which
seem extraordinarily favorable may become the
very cause of the wreck of character and of the
weakening of the will, and that conditions which
seem severe and meagre have in them often the
making of men.   Many a phase of civilization in
which prosperity has been most freely lavished on
a people has turned out to be an epoch of political
or moral decline ; and many of the fairest blooms
of strenuous and fragrant living have sprung from
a bare rock like that of Athens, or from an obscure
province like that of Galilee.   The method of externalism, in short, deals at most with but one half.
of the social question.   It is a great and honorable
task which seems offered to the present generation, — the task of perfecting social organization,
the levelling and broadening of the way by which
the better life of the future may have its entrance
into the world ; but if there is no better life to
enter ; if after crying, " Prepare ye, prepare ye

[1] Essay on "The Coming Slavery," *Popular Scientific Monthly,*
April, 1884.

the way of the Lord!" we wait in vain to see the Son of man approach, — with what a sense of futility and purposelessness are we left, with our organizations and schemes and committees, all prepared for a day of triumph which does not come!

Indeed, complexity of organization brings with it a new and threatening peril. What shall it accomplish if the organization becomes the tool of designing men; what gain shall there be in the municipalization of industry if the municipality is the instrument of a "boss"; wherein is the mechanical perfection of charity effective if it is in the hands of stupid officials? The more perfected the social machinery becomes, the better trained must be its engineers. The external order calls for the inward control. The teaching of Jesus, then, does not pretend to cover the whole range of the social question. It recognizes that the problem of adjusting social environment must be a new problem with each new age; it concerns itself, therefore, with the making of persons who shall be fit to deal with the environment which each new age in its turn presents. "Cleanse first," says Jesus, "the inside of the cup and of the platter."[1] "For what doth it profit a man, to gain the whole world, and forfeit his life?"[2]

In Mrs. Browning's dramatic contrast between the mission of the reformer and the vocation of the poet, she sets forth this Christian doctrine : —

[1] Matt. xxiii. 26.   [2] Mark viii. 36.

I

"I too," she says,

> "have my vocation, — work to do, . . .
> Most serious work, most necessary work,
> As any of the economists. Reform,
> Make trade a Christian possibility,
> And individual right no general wrong.
> . . . What then, indeed,
> If mortals are not greater by the head
> Than any of their prosperities ? . . . It takes a soul
> To move a body : it takes a high-souled man
> To move the masses, even to a cleaner sty.
> . . . Ah! your Fouriers failed
> Because not poets enough to understand
> That life develops from within." [1]

Still more dramatically, Jesus himself, in that profound experience which we call the temptation, was directly approached by the spirit of externalism. "If thou art the Son of God," said the tempter, "command that these stones become bread." [2] How modern the proposal sounds! It is precisely the use of power which the modern agitator would call most beneficent — the utilization of spiritual forces for economic production. It might seem, indeed, to such an agitator nothing short of cruel, in a world where there was hunger, to use power for anything else than to make more bread. Jesus, however, approaches the social question from within. He has nothing to say against bread-making ; in another place he feeds a great multitude. When, however, it is a question of the

[1] "Aurora Leigh," Book II.   [2] Matt. iv. 3.

supreme need of life, he knows that there are necessities more profound than hunger. " Man," he says, " shall not live by bread alone, but by every word that proceedeth out of the mouth of God." [1] The fundamental craving of human life, he well knows, — and many a human being, though oppressed by poverty and hunger, still feels the deeper need, — is for capacity, inspiration, regeneration, personality, power.

There is another aspect of the social question to which this second principle of the teaching of Jesus recalls our attention. The fact that he approaches, first of all, the individual indicates how large a part of social ills proceeds, in his opinion, not from social maladjustments, but from the fault of human beings themselves, in their own interior, misdirected and redeemable lives. One need not here strike a balance between the external and internal causes of social wrongs. When the bacteria of disease fasten on a human body, it is not possible to determine whether the poison from without or the susceptibility from within is chiefly responsible ; it is enough to say that much of the external change and decay comes from internal predisposition, and that the constitution may be in many instances fortified against such disease. In the same way it may be affirmed of a vast amount of social suffering, that its cause and prevention are to be in large degree determined by an inquiry into one's own heart, and that the beginning of a great part

[1] Matt. iv. 4.

of social amelioration is in the recognition of that personal responsibility which the Bible does not hesitate to call sin. We have become so accustomed to the language of externalism, that there may seem something antiquated and theological in this reference of social wrongs to so personal a cause as sin. We are much more apt to trace the evils of society to unfavorable environment, to imperfect legislation, or to the competitions of industry; and it is quite true that these causes, and many more, contribute to the social question. No tendency in modern life, however, is more destructive to social progress than the tendency to weaken the sense of personal responsibility for social imperfection, and to fix the blame on unpropitious circumstances. The obvious fact is, that for a very large part of social disorder, the chief responsibility lies in the passions and ambitions of individual men, and that no social arrangement can guarantee social welfare, unless there is brought home to vast numbers of individuals a profounder sense of personal sin. A social curse, for instance, like that of the drink habit is legitimately attacked by legislation and organization; but these external remedies will be applied in vain if there is any slackening of the conviction that, with most persons, drunkenness is not a misfortune for which society is responsible, but a sin for which individuals are responsible. Or, again, the problem of charity will remain an ever increasing problem of relief and alms unless there is included, within the problem of relief, the stirring of individual capacity to do without relief, and to enlarge the range of initiative and self-respect. Or, once more, the problem of industry will open into no permanent adjustment between capital and labor, so long as capitalists are rapacious and merciless, and laborers are passionate and disloyal. To whatever phase of the social question we turn, we observe, within the sphere of social arrangements, the interior problem of the redemption of character. Much social suffering is due to the social order; but much, and probably more, is due to human sin.

To this point, then, of personal responsibility Jesus addresses much of his teaching. He will have no part in the limp fatalism which regards character as the creature of circumstances. He makes a masculine appeal to a man's own will. He allows no shirking of the truth. The publican whom he commends throws no blame on his vocation or his circumstances: "God," he says, "be merciful to me a sinner!" [1] The prodigal does not return to his father with an indictment against the social conditions which have prevailed in the far country of riotous living; he returns with the manly and frank confession, "Father, I have sinned." [2] There are, perhaps, profounder aspects than this of the Christian doctrine of sin, as there have been many technical and unreal ways of expressing that doctrine; but this bearing

[1] Luke xviii. 13.   [2] Luke xv. 18.

of the doctrine of sin on social life has been reserved for the present age to appreciate, and a time
when the social question is the centre of human
interest is a time when we need more than ever
to recall the personal causes of social progress
and decay. The chief difficulty with modern
social life, as we shall repeatedly see, is not a
mechanical difficulty, but a moral fault. It is quite
true, that one legitimate prayer of the Christian
reformer in the present age may be: "Create a
better social order, O God, and renew a right relation between various classes of men;" but a much
deeper and worthier petition of one who desires
to shape the social order of the time would be, as
it was of old: "Create in me a clean heart, O
God; and renew a right spirit within me."[1] The
teaching of Jesus meets the need of the time
when he thus approaches the social question from
within.

Persons, then, with horizon of view and with
interior initiative, — these are the instruments on
which Jesus depends to correct the narrowness and
the outwardness of the social movement. What is
it, one finally asks, which shall create in persons
this scope of social purpose and this capacity for
social service? To answer this question we must
recall the third and the most characteristic social
principle of Jesus, the principle of the kingdom.
What delivers one from small views of social duty
and from externalism of social method is, accord-

[1] Ps. li. 10.

ing to the teaching of Jesus, the devotion of the individual to a spiritual ideal of social life. The thought of the kingdom makes the man, as the service of the man in its turn makes the kingdom. Among the harassing incidents of routine, incompleteness, and misdirected effort which abound in modern tasks of social service, the secret of effectiveness and courage, according to Jesus Christ, lies with the idealist. Such a man, as Matthew Arnold says of Sophocles, "sees life steadily and sees it whole." He finds himself because he has found an end to which he can commit himself. He is obedient to the heavenly vision ; he sanctifies himself for others' sake; and wisdom, sanity, and power are given to him as he thus gives himself to the kingdom.

How far such language seems to carry us from the prevailing temper of the modern social question ! What room is there, it may be asked, for the idealist among scenes of destitution and overcrowding, of starvation wages and industrial slavery, where the masses of men are fighting, not for ideals, but for daily bread ? Remote, however, as a spiritual ideal appears to be from the intensely practical world of social service, it is none the less certain that the lack of such an ideal is the chief curse of modern social life, and that the unspiritual character of the ends proposed as substitutes for such idealism constitute their chief social peril. What is it which we must admit to be the most depressing and heart-breaking quality of the ordinary work of average modern life? It is, beyond doubt, its deadening, downward-looking, dehumanizing dulness, its mechanical round of unilluminated and uninspired routine. It is this which brings with it the sense of limitation, insignificance, and purposelessness, which converts men into machines and robs them of vitality, imagination, faith, and hope. The high walls of their vocation shut in the narrow road of their lives and shut out all vistas beyond, until they trudge like beasts of burden rather than walk like children of God. And what is it that can restore color and meaning to such a life? Much, no doubt, can be accomplished by improving conditions, by the levelling of the walls of vocation, by escape from mechanism. Yet this sense of imprisonment in one's life is by no means a consciousness of those alone whose conditions are most deplorable. The prosperous quite as much as the poor are thus ensnared. Despondency and *ennui* are social diseases which afflict the luxurious quite as much as they do the hand-working class. Behind the problem, then, of improving social conditions lies the problem, for all sorts and conditions of men, of interpreting life as it is, and as it must be, under all conditions, and of illuminating that routine which is inevitable with a sense of significance, unity, intention, and worth.

This transfiguration of common life is what Jesus offers to men in his vision of the kingdom of God. He looks upon the striving, struggling world of social movement as contributing to that social intention.   He sees the

> " One far-off, divine event
>   Toward which the whole creation moves."

Neither the turbulence of the stream, nor its reactionary eddies, make him forget the ocean to which it flows. The pettiness, the toil, the routine, the insignificance of life, — even its pain and bitterness, — are swept into the movement of his mighty hope, and become a part of its greatness instead of an obstacle to its course.   Thus the teaching of Jesus gives meaning to many an obscure life, caught in the perplexity of the modern world. It offers to such a life, not first of all a new set of circumstances, but a new insight into and through its circumstances. A man cries out for the interpretation of his experience, and finds it as he prays, "Thy kingdom come." It is his social ideal which makes a place for his personal service. His insignificant task gets a meaning because it is taken up into the Divine plan. What he regards as his successes and what he calls his failures may be of equal importance in the vast campaign of God. He regains composure, self-respect, and courage, because he has enlisted in that service. It is not his universe. He is set, as a man under authority, to do his duty in the ranks. Not for him, indeed, the glory of a triumphant commander, but for him perhaps at last the commander's summons : "Well done, good and faithful servant : thou hast been faithful over a few things, . . . enter thou into the joy of thy lord !" [1]

The significance of such a social ideal may be indicated from quite another point of view. We turn to the substitute now most confidently proposed for these spiritual interpretations of social life, and at once observe that here also the spirit of idealism is the effective motive power. Nothing is more pathetic than to see an ideal created out of ends which are essentially unspiritual and material, and to observe this fictitious idealism exciting a passionate and self-sacrificing loyalty. The social end proposed by the philosophy of socialism may be in one sense described as an ideal ; for it is, at least, a visionary, remote, and Utopian end. In the more accurate sense, however, it is as far as possible from a spiritual ideal ; it is a sheer material, external rearrangement of possessions and facilities. Yet how devoted and profound an attachment is felt by millions of plain people for this economic creed ! It is an emotional loyalty which, we may be sure, has been awakened, not by a programme of industry, but by the ideal elements which have become associated with it ; by such maxims as " Liberty, equality, fraternity " ; by the sense of justice, and the hope of a golden age of righteousness ; in short, by those aspects of the socialist gospel which it has in common with the Christian gospel of the kingdom of God.

[1] Matt. xxv. 21.

It is by no means true, then, that the modern world has outgrown the idealist. On the contrary, it is his habit of mind which makes persuasive the doctrines of industrial revolution. Indeed, it may not improbably come to pass, as we shall later in more detail point out, that the modern world may have to take its choice of idealisms — on the one hand, the materialized hope which inspires the socialist propaganda; or, on the other hand, the spiritual vision which inspired the teaching of Jesus. One thing only, among the many uncertainties of the social future, may be regarded as reasonably sure, — that no social teaching will be likely to win the hearts of men which is not in some way colored by an idealist's faith. The things that are unseen are, after all, the things for which human hearts most care. "Where there is no vision, the people perish." The permanent influence of the teaching of Jesus on the minds of the human race was assured when he made it his first duty and highest joy to proclaim the coming of an ideal order of Divine righteousness and truth, and "came into Galilee preaching the good news of the kingdom of God."

Such appears to be the relation of the social principles of Jesus to the social questions of the present day. His contribution is not one of social organization or method, but of a point of view, a way of approach, and an end to attain. His social gospel is not one of fact or doctrine, but one of spirit and aim. If it is true that the

social movement is obstructed by narrowness of
view and lacks wisdom and horizon, if it is
gravely tempted by externalism and needs to be
recalled to the problem of the individual, if its
ideals are unspiritual and fictitious, then the teaching of Jesus has something still to offer to social
life even among conditions which he could not
have foreseen, and for which, therefore, he could
have made no regulative law. We are to consider
in detail the bearing of this teaching on various
forms of social organization presented by the
modern world. There are, in particular, three
such groups of relationship which lie, like concentric circles, round the individual life. Closest
to him is the circle of the family, the interior and
elementary social group; beyond this circle is the
larger group of a community of families, compre-
hending diverse conditions of prosperity and poverty, and presenting to the individual the problems
of the rich and of the poor; and still again, round
both these circles sweeps with a larger radius the
industrial order of the present age. Each of these
circles of social life holds a social question which
is in one aspect wholly unprecedented and purely
contemporaneous. The institution of the family,
the distribution of property, and the organization of
industry are all at the present time subjects of
fresh consideration, and conceivably open to radical change. Of such problems, therefore, considered as temporary social arrangements, the
teaching of Jesus, given as it was to a wholly

different age, can have little to say. The teaching of Jesus, however, concerns itself with the principles which these social phenomena illustrate. He views them from above, in the light of his religious vocation ; he approaches them from within, through the development of personality ; he judges them in their end, as contributory to the kingdom of God. Into each circle of social life he enters with these social principles, and it is as one who from within fits his key into door after door and passes out into the open air.

In short, we are brought to the point social organization and social inspiration — the mass and the person — meet as factors in social progress. The teaching of Jesus, being chiefly concerned with the latter factor, may perhaps seem to be of decreased significance under the conditions of the present age. Never was a time which appeared more wholly given over to the principle of organization. It is an age of mass-meetings, majorities, democracies, combinations, machinery. What scope is there left, it may be asked, for the free growth and creative service of the individual ? The fact is, however, that the growth of organization, instead of displacing the principle of inspiration, only provides a larger opportunity for its effectiveness. The two factors of social movement are not substitutes for each other ; they are mutually dependent on each other, as wings which on opposite sides sustain a bird's strong flight. Personality finds in organization the multiplication of power; organization, the more complex it grows, makes greater demands on personality. Modern machinery calls for better training in its engineers; modern industry requires more skill in its mechanics; modern politics, statesmanship, administration, have become more and more dependent upon competent men who shall control and direct the mighty power which modern organization has devised. All things, said the apostle, wait for the entrance into organization of the power of personality: "The earnest expectation of the creation waiteth for the revealing of the sons of God."[1]

When, therefore, we admit that the chief social contribution of Jesus is the production of spiritual personality, we do not dismiss his teaching as unimportant for the modern world. On the contrary, we turn to him with fresh attention, as perhaps providing that element of social progress of which the modern world stands most in need. If it is true that in every form of social activity the cry of the time is for personality; if we are in danger of being overwhelmed by social mechanism and robbed of social power; if in the tendencies of the time

"The individual withers and the age is more and more";

if the Church of Jesus Christ itself, with its vast development of organization, is in danger of being deserted by the active and thoughtful because it

[1] Rom. viii. 19.

does not seem to be the instrument of wisdom and of power, — then, even if Jesus makes no important contribution to the external factors of social progress, it may be a fitting time to recall the teacher who said, "I am come that they may have life, and may have it more abundantly."

Among many evidences that the modern world is recognizing afresh the significance of personality, the most notable is the renewal of general interest in the personality of Jesus himself. Here was a person who, in the modern sense, accomplished little, was but in the slightest degree an administrator or organizer, and contented himself with the general statement of his mission, "I am the Way and the Truth and the Life." Yet through all the uncertainties of Christian theology and all the conflicts of Christian ecclesiasticism, there has disclosed itself to the world an influence proceeding from him which turns out to be that which the world most desires, — the influence of a person viewing life from above, judging it from within, and directing it to its spiritual end. It is one of the most extraordinary signs of the times that, while the doctrines which centre about Christ have to great multitudes almost lost their meaning, his personality has acquired fresh loyalty and homage. People who are absorbed in the ways of modern life feel a fresh accession of spiritual loyalty to one who, in the midst of these tangled interests, proves to be a wise and trustworthy guide. In a great orchestra, with all its varied ways of musical expression, there is one person who performs on no instrument whatever, but in whom, none the less, the whole control of harmony and rhythm resides. Until the leader comes, the discordant sounds go their various ways; but at his sign the tuning of the instruments ceases and the symphony begins. So it is with the spiritual leadership of Jesus Christ. Among the conflicting activities of the present time his power is not that of one more activity among the rest, but that of wisdom, personality, idealism. Into the midst of the discordant efforts of men he comes as one having ████ ; the self-assertion of each instrument ████ service is hushed as he gives his sign; and in the surrender of each life to him it finds its place in the symphony of all.

CHAPTER III

There was a marriage in Cana of Galilee; . . . and Jesus also was bidden, and his disciples, to the marriage.

THE social problem of the family, it need hardly be said, is not comprehended by practical considerations of domestic duty. It is not a question of behavior within the domestic group, but a question of the continued existence of this form of social relation. Even thus defined, the problem of the family usually confronts one at such close range that its real dimensions and significance are not easily appreciated. Before approaching, then, the teaching of Jesus on the subject, it will be necessary to indicate briefly some aspects of the question which may seem to be remote from the immediate issues of the present age.

The problem first presents itself when we become aware that the coherence and permanence of family life are, under existing social conditions, seriously threatened. Domestic instability, it is observed, tends in a most startling manner to become an epidemic social disease. The number of divorces annually granted in the United States of America is, it appears, increasing, both at a rate unequalled in any other civilized country, and at a constantly accelerating rate.[1] In all Europe, Canada, and Australia in 1889 the total number of divorces granted was 20,111; in the United States in this same year it was 23,472. In 1867 there were granted in the United States 9937 divorces; in 1886 there were granted 29,535. The increase of population in those twenty years was 60 per cent; the increase of divorces was 156 per cent. The total of married couples living in the United States to one couple divorced was in 1870, 664, and in 1880, 481. The ratio of marriages celebrated to one couple divorced was : in Massachusetts in 1867 forty-five to one, and in 1886 thirty-one to one; in Illinois in 1867 twenty to one, and in 1886 thirteen to one. It may even be computed[2] that if the present ratio of increase in population and in separation be maintained, the number of separations of marriage by death would be at the end of the twentieth century less than the number of separations by divorce.

Many causes contribute to this result. Looseness in the law of divorce and in its administration, diversity of law in the different States, and an almost equal looseness in the law of marriage, —all have their part in creating a situation in which, as has been remarked, less care is observed

[1] United States Commissioner of Labor, " Report on Marriage and Divorce," 1889; "Columbia College Studies," I, 1; Willcox, "The Divorce Problem ; a Study in Statistics," 1891 ; Mayo-Smith, "Statistics and Sociology"; A. P. Lloyd, "A Treatise on the Law of Divorce," 1889.

[2] Willcox (op. cit.), p. 12.

in arranging a contract of marriage than is involved in a contract concerning a horse or a piece of land.[1] This situation, which has become so familiar as to make the instability of the marriage tie a matter even of current jest, is in itself sufficient to constitute a problem of extreme gravity, and it is most natural that many communions of the Christian Church are urging upon the consciences of their adherents the insidious nature of the social peril involved, and are procuring more stringent legislation, both of State and Church, concerning marriage and divorce.

In these practical efforts for domestic integrity, however, there is in reality involved a much larger issue than at first appears. It is, in fact, nothing less than an issue between two theories of the marriage tie, — the conception of it as a temporary contract, involving the interests of those who are known as "the parties concerned"; and the conception of it as a social institution, involving the fabric of the social order. Indeed, the family is but one element in a general struggle for existence of two types of civilization, one dominated by an interest in the development of the individual, the other characterized by a concern for the social order. The first of these conceptions of society

[1] *Atlantic Monthly*, April, 1888, F. G. Cook, "The Marriage Celebration in the United States"; S. W. Dike, "Reports of National Divorce Reform League"; *Political Science Quarterly*, December, 1889, "Statistics of Marriage and Divorce"; C. F. Thwing, "The Family : an Historical and Social Study"; C. D. Wright, "Practical Sociology," 1899, p. 151 ff.

has for a long period controlled English thought. "The movement of progressive societies," said Sir Henry Maine, "has been uniform in one respect. Through all its course it has been distinguished by the gradual dissolution of family dependency and the growth of individual obligation in its place. The individual is steadily substituted for the family as the unit of which civil law takes account."[1] This substitution has been for several generations the key of English jurisprudence, philosophy, and economics, as well as of the religious life and thought of Protestantism.[2] The second conception of society, on the other hand, has come to its full expression within the present generation. It takes fresh account of the stability and progress of the social order. It is illustrated by the mass of new legislation which deals with questions of social welfare; by the new expansion of philosophy into problems of social structure, evolution, and obligation; by the transition of economic science from issues of individual competition and harmonies of self-interest to the adjustments

---

[1] Maine, "Ancient Law," 3d Amer. ed., 1878, p. 163; so also Horace Bushnell, "Christian Nurture," 1871, p. 91, "All our modern notions and speculations have taken on a bent toward individualism." Compare, "The Message of Christ to Manhood," Noble Lectures, 1899; H. C. Potter, "The Message of Christ to the Family," p. 193.

[2] So of the Catholic judgment of Protestantism, "Life of Father Hecker," N. Y., 1894, "Protestantism is mainly unsocial, being an extravagant form of individualism. Its Christ deals with men apart from each other and furnishing no cohesive element to humanity."

of associated industry; and, finally, by the new emphasis of Christian theology upon the organic life of the Church or of the world.

In the midst of this conflict of tendencies in civilization stands the problem of the family. If the individual is the end for which social life exists, if it is the "parties concerned" alone who are to be considered in a case of marriage, then the legislation of self-interest, which takes account of nothing more than the happiness or even the whims of individuals, will be set to make and break this contract. If, on the other hand, marriage is an elementary expression of organic social life, a witness of that social continuity which is coming to be recognized in the Church, the industrial order, and the State; or, to say the same thing in the language of Christian philosophy, — if the individual comes to his self-realization only in and through his service of the social order, — then the integrity of the family, as the most elementary group of social life, will be reverently guarded and stringently secured. In the issue, then, between a reversion of social type to the individualism which is elsewhere outgrown, and the safe-guarding of the social organism in its most elementary form, lies the first aspect of the problem of the family.

Even this conflict of contemporary types, serious as it is, does not present to us the problem of the family in its full significance. Behind this direct attack of sheer self-interest on the integrity of the domestic group, there lie more subtle perils which can be appreciated only when one recalls the history and evolution of the institution of the family. Here is a social group which, in its present form, is by no means an original and outright gift to the human race, but is the product of a vast world-process of social evolution, through which various types of domestic unity have been in turn selected and, as it were, tested, until at last the fittest has survived. From this point of view, the problem of the family is not merely a contemporary issue between expediency and ideal- ism, but is one element in the vastly larger prob- lem of human progress and destiny; and one's judgment concerning the place and future of the family is determined by observing the gradual processes of social selection through which, in the history of the human race, the modern form of the family has been by slow degrees evolved. Here, at last, we meet in its full scope and social impor- tance the problem with which the divorce courts and the ecclesiastical councils are trying to deal; and here also we meet one of the most curious chapters of modern research, which has come to play a most unexpected part in practical discus- sions.[1]

[1] Westermarck, "The History of Human Marriage," 2d ed. 1894; Lubbock, "Origin of Civilization," etc., 3d ed., 1879; McLennan, "Studies in Ancient History," 1886; Starcke, "The Primitive Family," 1889; Schurman, "The Ethical Import of Darwinism," 1887, Ch. VI; Coulanges, "The Ancient City," 1874, Book II.

The first aspect of this historical evidence to win attention was formulated in the so-called " Patriarchal Theory." In the social life of ancient Rome, and in many indications of social conditions in ancient Israel, it was observed that the family was the unit from which national coherence was derived, and that this unit was perpetuated through the supremacy of the oldest male. Thus the patriarchal theory seemed the key of the primitive history of the family. Through the expansion of the family group there appeared to be evolved the clan, the tribe, the nation, and the authority of the father became in turn that of the chief, the ruler, the king. It is not easy to overestimate the importance of the emphasis thus laid on the place of the family in human history. " The unit of an ancient society," in the familiar words of Sir Henry Maine, " was the Family, of a modern society the Individual."[1] Social progress proceeds, not through relations of isolated atoms, but through the multiplication of organized cells ; not through association of individuals, but through the perpetuation of families. " A cohesive family," says Mr. Bagehot, " is the best germ for a campaigning nation. . . . Nothing of this is possible in loosely bound family groups."[2] Yet the patriarchal theory, illustrated as it was by the more familiar types of ancient civilization, has not only had enormous expansion, but has been in important respects supple-

[1] Maine, " Ancient Law," 3d Amer. ed., 1878, p. 121.
[2] Bagehot, " Physics and Politics," Ch. III, p. 517.

mented and corrected by the more extended study of primitive society. It remains true that the family is the unit of civilization, but it is also true that this unit has had its own evolution, so that the family is not only a cause of modern society, but is in its turn an effect of ancient society. Human relationships, it is in the first place pointed out, were probably, even under the rudest conditions, not the promiscuous relations of a herd, but, — as in the case of most of the higher mammals, — a relation of pairing animals, so that even in the most primitive society, either through force, or jealousy, or common possessions, or the care of children, or necessities of self-defence, a more or less permanently associated group-life was maintained. "We may indeed conclude," said Mr. Darwin, "from what we know of the jealousy of all male quadrupeds, that promiscuous intercourse in a state of nature is extremely improbable." [1]

What was it, then, that gave to this pairing group its original coherence and continuity? The most striking suggestion which has been made in answer to this question is that of Mr. John Fiske, in his discussion of the physiological conditions of human infancy.[2] The young of most higher animals, Mr. Fiske reminds us, are at birth able to

[1] "Descent of Man," pp. 590, 591.
[2] This epoch-making doctrine was first expounded in "Cosmic Philosophy," 1875, II, 363; reappears in "The Destiny of Man," 1889, p. 57; and is finally described in autobiographical form in "A Century of Science," 1899, p. 100 ff.

care for themselves ; while the human infant must be cared for through months of helplessness. This prolongation of infancy brings with it the genesis of sociality. It bridges the gulf which seems to divide the human from the brute world. It gives a profound meaning to the phenomenon of helpless babyhood. "From of old we have heard the monition, 'except ye be as babes, ye cannot enter the kingdom of heaven.' The latest science now shows us — though in a very different sense of the words — that, unless we had been as babes, the ethical phenomena which give all its significance to the phrase 'kingdom of heaven' would have been non-existent for us."

Still more significant for the philosophy of the family have been the later researches of the ethnologists. Turning from the comparatively advanced social conditions indicated by the Roman or Hebrew literature to more primitive social types, these students of Aryan tribes and of North American aborigines discover in the beginnings of human society a far more varied and more curious series of domestic relationships than the patriarchal theory covers. The family, it appears, which is to be the unit of further civilization, has emerged into its present form through various experimental types, assuming all possible variations of grouping, until the fittest to survive had been attained. First, out of the original relation of pairing animals there comes into view a domestic unity and continuity represented by the woman, who with her children creates a more or less coherent social group among wandering and predatory males. The matriarchal domestic type precedes, as a rule, the patriarchal ; children belong, first of all, to the mother's stock ; polyandry appears to be more primitive than polygamy. It is a type which still survives in many an Oriental tribe and many an Indian tradition, and it may even be suggested that this primitive institution of the practical supremacy of the wife is not without its survivals in the administration of many a modern home. Again, in this dim chapter of social evolution, as possessions multiply and the competition for wives becomes keen, the unity of the family is determined, in many tribes, not by reference to the woman, but by the supremacy of the man. Perhaps the series of incidents suggested by McLennan occurs : first, in a state of constant warfare, the neglect of female infants ; then a consequent lack of women within the tribe ; then the necessity for exogamy, or the procuring of wives from outside the tribe, and, as a consequence, the custom of marriage by capture, or the recruiting of domestic life from other tribes. Finally, out of this unity in the male, emerges, under more advanced social conditions, the patriarchal family, with its profound effect, through Roman law and ecclesiastical custom, on modern views of marriage and divorce.

Out of such a struggle for existence among social types, the modern family is born. The

relation of individuals which it represents, with
personal rights and obligations, is a relation
unattained in primitive social groups. Prophesied though monogamy may be by the evolution
of the domestic group,[1] the family as we understand it, with its mutual sacrifices, its personal
self-surrender, its discovery of the higher self in
the social group, appears to be an end toward
which the movement of social evolution has been
for ages tending. The social order, in St. Paul's
language, has groaned and travailed in pain, waiting for the revelation of the higher type. Here,
then, at last the problem of the family begins to
be seen in its true dimensions. It is not merely
a problem of contemporary or local expediency,
or even one of social philosophy alone, but one
which has the entire history of the race for its
background and the entire future of the social
order for its consequence. The immediate questions of marriage and divorce which agitate the
modern world should be considered in the light
of this long story of social evolution or reversion.
With the integrity or instability of the unit of
civilization is likely to stand or fall the structure
of that civilization. The most fundamental question which can be asked of any phase of social
condition is this : What are the character, form,
and habits of its family life?

It is at precisely this point, however, that we
now meet the most uncompromising and undis-

[1] Spencer, " Principles of Sociology," I, 673 ff.

guised attack upon the modern family, — the attack of the scientific socialist. It would be by no means just to say that the encouragement of domestic instability is an essential part of the socialist programme. Many strenuous advocates of common industrial ownership shrink from the thought of a coöperative commonwealth of wives and children.[1] Yet it must be admitted that, with great ingenuity and candor, the leaders of the German school, by utilizing the researches of the evolutionists to which we have just alluded, and applying them to the problem of social revolution, have obtained a philosophy of history which has had profound effect upon the practical beliefs of millions of plain people.[2] To those who would substitute common ownership for individual liberty, the institution of the family presents one of the most persistent obstacles. Domestic unity is inconsistent with an absolute social unity vested in the State. The thrift, economies, and centralized interest of the isolated home tend to detach those who are devoted to such homes from complete devotion to the socialist ideal. "Family suprem-

[1] L. Stein, "Die soziale Frage im Lichte der Philosophie," s. 77, "In a socialist state of any civilized character, the institution of monogamy must remain undisturbed."

[2] Bebel, "Die Frau und der Sozialismus," 10. Aufl., 1891, ss. 7–72; F. Engel, "Der Ursprung der Familie, des Privateigentums und des Staates," 4. Aufl., 1892; Dritter Evang.-soz. Kongress, 1892, s. 8; F. Naumann, "Christentum und Familie"; Neunter Evang.-soz. Kongress, 1898; Rade, "Die sittlich-religiöse Gedankenwelt unsrer Industriearbeiter," s. 117 ff. ("Ehe und Familienleben",

acy will be absolutely incompatible with an inter-dependent solidaric commonwealth." [1]

To these practical considerations, moreover, there is added a new application of the doctrine of social evolution. The family, as we have seen, has had its primitive origin, its changeful phases, its gradual growth ; it is now, according to many socialist philosophers, to have its further period of transition and final decline. It is "a historical phenomenon which has been developed in course of time, and in time will vanish." What originally consolidated the domestic group was the desire to transmit private property. The family was "an economic unit, and such it still remains." [2] It is an instrument of the capitalist class. Indeed, without such private property the unity of the family can hardly exist. How can we speak of the sanctity of the home, it is asked, when the man

[1] Gronlund, "The Coöperative Commonwealth in its Outlines," 1884, p. 224. Bebel (op. cit.) s. 199, "The final result is this : Marriage, as at present understood, is an arrangement most closely associated with the existing social status and stands or falls with it;" s. 5, "The complete solution of the woman question . . . is, like the solution of the labor question, impossible under our present social and political conditions." E. and E. M. Aveling, "The Woman Question" (a tract), 1897, p. 16, "The contract between man and woman will be of a purely private nature. . . . For divorce there will be no need." K. P., "Socialism and Sex" (undated), London, Reeves, "Economic independence is essential to all humans. . . . The current type of sex relationship . . . is inconsistent with economic independence, and therefore is a type destined to extinction. The socialistic movement with its new morality . . . must surely and rapidly undermine our current marriage customs and marital laws."

[2] Naumann, "Christentum und Familie," s. 12.

and his wife have no home or private possessions, and both work all day in the mill or the street? "For a large part of the working population of our great industrial cities," remarks a German student, "the traditional form of the family no longer exists."[1]

It is still further pointed out that even as regards its contribution to industrial life the importance of the family is already enormously lessened. Once every form of industry went on within the family circle; but, as the methods of the great industry are substituted for work done in the home, the economic usefulness of the family is practically outgrown. Women are no longer the slaves of domestic service. They can lead their own lives and earn their own bread. "Machinery has become their saviour."[2] Thus, with the coming of the socialist State, family unity will be merged in a higher end. The wife, being no longer doomed to household drudgery, will have the

[1] Göhre, "Drei Monate Fabrikarbeiter," 1891, s. 37, "Dass infolge dieser Zustände in weiten Kreisen unsrer grossstädtischen Industriebevölkerung die überlieferte Form der Familie heute schon nicht mehr vorhanden ist." So Morris and Bax, "Socialism," p. 299 ff., "The present marriage system is based on the general supposition of economic dependence of the woman on the man. . . . The basis would disappear with the advent of social economic freedom. . . . A new development of the family would take place on the basis of . . . mutual inclination and affection, an association terminable at the will of either party. It is easy to see how great the gain would be to morality and sentiment."

[2] Naumann, s. 14; see also his "Der Christ im Zeitalter der Maschine," in his "Was heisst Christlich-Sozial?" 1894.

greater blessing of economic equality. Children will be cared for by the community under healthful and uniform conditions, and we shall arrive at what has been called "the happy time when the continuity of society no longer depends upon the private nursery."[1] Childbearing and non-childbearing women will have separate consideration, so that both production and liberty shall be insured.[2] The evolution of the family will have proceeded from simplicity to simplicity. Its history will have been a spiral progress, beginning in the promiscuous freedom of savagery, and ending in the equally incidental and loose relations of individual and temporary desire.

It is difficult for one who is unfamiliar with the socialist propaganda to believe that these speculations concerning social evolution can have had serious influence upon the lives of the working-people to whom socialism has become a practical creed; but the fact is that in popularized, and often in grosser, form, this protest against family exclusiveness has become a positive part of the German gospel of discontent. The German hand-worker is constantly reminded that his economic welfare is to be found in a complete break with that social order of which capitalism, religion, and family unity are the bulwarks; and his eager mind is con-

---

[1] Bernard Shaw, quoted *Pall Mall Magazine*, April, 1898.

[2] The practical arrangement of this stock-farm scheme is described by Karl Pearson, "The Ethics of Free Thought," 1888, p. 379 ff.

stantly fed by the literature of domestic revolt. Still more insidious is this same doctrine as it is expounded in English as well as German literature, addressed not to working-people, but to light-minded and self-indulgent readers of the prosperous classes. The modern novel appears to find no theme more lucrative than that of the failure of marriage, and discusses in more or less undisguised language the next steps which may be proposed in domestic evolution. In short, it has become clear, not only that a transformation of economic conditions is likely to bring with it a radical change in domestic relations, but that, on the other hand, until a new set of ideas about family life are made thoroughly familiar, the greatest obstruction to radical economic change will remain unremoved. Nothing is stranger in the modern social agitation than this transfer of its storm-centre from the issue with capitalism, in which it began, to the apparently remote and tranquil region of the family; and it is not inconceivable that the judgment of history on the programme of economic socialism may be determined, not so much by the main issue for which the programme appears to stand, as by the effect of the changes proposed upon the integrity of the family.

Such, then, is the place in modern thought of the problem which, in its obvious and temporary form, presented itself as a mere question of the regulation of marriage and divorce. Two forces appear to threaten the stability of the present social order, — the reactionary force of self-interested individualism, and the revolutionary force of scientific socialism; and at the point where these forces meet stands the institution of the family. On the one hand it is in danger of being shattered into its atoms, on the other hand it is in danger of being lost in a larger unity. On the one hand is a possible social reversion, and on the other hand a possible social revolution. The problem of the family is not only theoretically fundamental in social philosophy, but it is also the practical issue whose decision is most likely to determine the future of human society, government, and religion. With this problem, therefore, brought to its larger statement and seen in its far-reaching effects, we turn to the teaching of Jesus, and proceed to inquire whether the social principles of his gospel which we have already considered appear to open into any definite instructions concerning this special case.

As one sets himself to such an inquiry he is struck at once by the extraordinary emphasis repeatedly laid by Jesus on the institution of the family. There were many other problems concerning which his judgment was sought, where it must be inferred either from slight allusions or from complete silence or from some single illuminating phrase. Toward the politics, the larger social institutions, and even the theological issues of his time, his attitude was, as a rule, one of

L

extraordinary reserve, which is as disappointing
to many a modern reformer as it was perplexing
to many a hearer of his message.[1] On the other
hand, with quite unparalleled fulness of detail,
the teaching of Jesus deals with the nature and
obligations of the family. With unusual identity
of language the first three gospels record his
sayings on this subject, and their reiteration of
the teaching indicate how profound an impression
it originally made.[2] Still further, this is the only
aspect of social life concerning which Jesus de-
scends from the announcing of general principles
to the further duty of prescribing specific legislation. When, for instance, the Pharisees are in-
formed that the new teaching concerning marriage
and divorce is not what "was said to them of
old time,"[3] and come to Jesus, "tempting him,"[4]
Jesus does not, as in so many other cases, refuse
to be ensnared by their questions, but proceeds to
expound with candor and thoroughness the Christian law of the family in its relation to the Mosaic
law. When, again, the Sadducees bring him the
problem of marriage ingeniously converted into a
theological puzzle, Jesus again, instead of answer-
ing, "Why tempt ye me, ye hypocrites?"[5] seems
glad to use this ill-intended occasion as an opportunity for defining the place of marriage in the

---

[1] "Ecce Homo," p. 336, "It was Christ's fixed resolution to enter
into no contest with the civil power."

[2] Matt. v. 31 ; Matt. xix. 9 ; Mark x. 11 ; Luke xvi. 18.

[3] Matt. v. 21.   [4] Matt. xix. 3.   [5] Matt. xxii. 18.

spiritual world, and his doctrine is set forth with such force and clearness that "when the multitudes heard it, they were astonished at his teaching."[1]

More significant still of the sentiment of Jesus concerning the family is his general use of this relationship as the type which expresses all that was most sacred to his mind. His entire theology may be described as a transfiguration of the family. God is a Father, man is his child; and from the father to the child there is conveyed the precious and patient message of paternal love. When the prodigal boy, in that parable which most perfectly tells the story of the sinning and repentant life, "came to himself," his first words were, "I will arise and go to my father";[2] and while he is yet afar off the waiting father sees him coming and is moved with compassion. Repentance, that is to say, is but the homesickness of the soul, and the uninterrupted and watching care of the parent is the fairest earthly type of the unfailing forgiveness of God. The family is, to the mind of Jesus, the nearest of human analogies to that Divine order which it was his mission to reveal.

To all these aspects of his teaching, which indicate the thought of Jesus concerning the family, may be further added his habitual sympathy for domestic life itself and his habitual reverence for women. Jesus, though having "not where to lay his head,"[3] was as far as possible from the habits of celibate asceticism. He shared the gayety of

[1] Matt. xxii. 33.　　[2] Luke xv. 18.　　[3] Luke ix. 58.

the wedding feast;[1] he lived until manhood in the tranquil simplicity of a village home; he was subject unto his parents;[2] he found respite from the strain of his last days in the family circle at Bethany.[3] His attitude toward women was marked both by insight and by courage. Nothing could be more contrary to the spirit of Jesus than to say with Bebel that "Christian doctrine exhibits the same contempt for women which all Oriental religions manifest." On the contrary, without entering into discussion of the rights of women to special consideration, Jesus honors them in conversation and in deed. He speaks to one unresponsive woman his momentous words, "God is a Spirit: . . . I that speak unto thee am he";[4] he interprets and welcomes the affection which prompts another woman to lavish on him her costly offering;[5] he reads the heart of the woman who is a sinner;[6] he lifts the thoughts of Martha above her household cares[7]; in his doctrine of marriage he explicitly guards the rights and enforces the duties of the woman; and finally, his last thought upon the cross is for his mother in her solitary home.[8] His teaching moves in an atmosphere of domestic interests, and his profoundest thoughts are colored by respect for the family.[9]

[1] John ii. 1–11. [3] Matt. xxvi. 6. [5] John xii. 7, 8.
[2] Luke ii. 51. [4] John iv. 24, 26. [6] John viii. 7–11.
[7] John xi. 21–27. [8] John xix. 26, 27.
[9] Compare Shailer Mathews, "Social Teaching of Jesus," p. 98 ff. So "Ecce Homo," p. 233, "Family affection in some form is the almost indispensable root of Christianity."

No sooner, however, does one observe these characteristics of the teaching of Jesus, than he perceives a striking analogy between that teaching and the discussions which we have already described as characteristic of the present age. The considerations which made the problem of the family conspicuous in the thought of Jesus were, of course, infinitely removed from the speculations and apprehensions of the modern world ; but the identity of conclusion concerning the place of the family in the social order is impressive. The social teaching of Jesus, proceeding from a wholly different point of view, lays its hand on the same key of social progress which is now indicated by the social philosopher ; and the character of the teaching of Jesus on this subject is one whose importance could not be adequately appreciated until the researches of the present generation had recalled attention to the problem of the family. In the teaching of Jesus, as in these last inquiries concerning the evolution of society, the crucial problem is that of the nature and stability of the domestic group. Modern research observes the coherent family system working its way through the history of tribes and nations, and moulding whole races into firmer stuff ; Jesus, on the other hand, with a wholly different horizon before his mind, sees this same relationship of the family set in the still wider sphere of the Divine order, and finds in the unity of the family that social force which moulds all mankind into one great family under the Fatherhood of a loving God. Modern learning, using the language of research, says, "The family is the unit of civilization"; Jesus, using the language of Hebrew scripture, says, "The twain shall become one flesh. . . . What therefore God hath joined together, let not man put asunder."[1]

Approaching, then, the teaching of Jesus concerning the family with this recognition of its central position in his thought, we observe still another likeness to the modern situation. There are, as we have seen, two distinct aspects of the present issue, — its contemporary, immediate, legislative form, involving the practical treatment of marriage and divorce; and, on the other hand, its more comprehensive, philosophical, prophetic form, in which the problem of the family becomes one element in the process of social evolution. The same distinction may be observed in the teaching of Jesus. Far as he is removed from any academic division of his discourse, none the less, in dealing with the family, he speaks at times in terms of social legislation concerning the family, and at times in terms of moral education through the family. On the one hand, he offers a specific doctrine concerning marriage and divorce, and, on the other hand, he announces principles of social life which immediately and profoundly affect the constitution of the family. The first aspect of his teaching, being the more obvious and explicit, has

[1] Matt. xix. 5, 6.

attracted the greater attention from students of
the Christian law of social life, as though Jesus
were primarily a social reformer; the second way
of teaching, being in his more accustomed manner
of general instruction, is less defined and external,
but lies in reality much deeper in the purpose of
Jesus and is of greater significance for the modern
question of the family.

As to the explicit doctrine of Jesus concerning
marriage and divorce, there would seem to be
little difficulty of interpretation. Indeed, it is
not easy to see how this subject has come to provide such inexhaustible material for ecclesiastical
discussion. Unwelcome the teaching of Jesus may
be to many modern minds; impracticable or injudicious it may appear under modern conditions;
"overstrained morality," it may be, as Renan called
it; but in its main features this teaching certainly cannot be called complicated or equivocal
or obscure.

In the passage which presents its most formal
statement, the teaching of Jesus begins, as it so
often does, with a text from the Hebrew scrip-
tures, which Scripture, as he had solemnly told his
people, he had come not to destroy, but to fulfil.
"He which made them, . . ." says Jesus, quoting
from the book of Genesis, "made them male and
female, . . . and the twain shall become one flesh."[1]
The unity thus formed, Jesus goes on to say, in
answer to those who were "tempting" him, is

[1] Matt. xix. 4, 5.

absolute. "They are no more twain, but one flesh."[1] To put away one's wife, therefore, and marry another is, Jesus does not hesitate to say, for the man to commit adultery; and to put away one's husband and marry another is for the wife to commit adultery.

In one important detail, it is true, a difference is to be observed between this legislation as recorded by Matthew and the parallel passages in Mark and Luke.[2] The first gospel, in both the passages which occur in it concerning divorce and remarriage, inserts the clause, "saving for the cause of fornication"; while in the other two gospels not even this single exception is noted. Various interpretations have been given to this divergence in the tradition.[3] It may be urged, on the one hand, that, as adultery practically ruptures the unity of the flesh, it is *a priori* more probable that Jesus should have

---

[1] Matt. xix. 6.   [2] Mark x. 1–12 ; Luke xvi. 18.

[3] On the one hand, Keim, " Jesus of Nazareth," III, 310, "This addition is interpolated"; V, 32, " Jesus softened his vigorous statement by no exception, not even by the most conciliating exception of the wife's adultery, which the later Church, and first of all our Matthew, introduced." Weiss, "Life of Christ," II, 150 (note), "The form of Jesus' remarks against remarriage Luke has preserved in the originals," II, 295 (note). On the other hand, Meyer's " Handbook " (tr. 1884), on Matt. xix. 9, "The words are not to be regarded as an addition of the evangelist. . . . The exception which they contain to the law against divorce is the *unica et adæquata exceptio.*" Reconciliation of the two views is urged by Wendt, " Teaching of Jesus," I, 354, "The exception noted by the first evangelist is no real exception to the rule which Jesus so emphatically laid down, that the obligation of marriage is absolute."

recognized it as putting an end to the marriage relation. It may even be suggested that the two gospels which omit to mention this ground for remarriage have omitted it because they regarded it as a matter of course. It must be, in any event, admitted that the first gospel gives its support to those who would permit remarriage for the innocent party in a divorce for adultery, though not even here is there any substantial support for those who would extend the definition of adultery to undefined causes like desertion or alienation, or still more trivial offences now often held to be sufficient. On the other hand, it may be reasonably argued that in a matter so closely concerning practical life it is more probable that Matthew should have been led to add an exceptive clause than that the two other evangelists should have omitted to mention so important a qualification. It may be still further urged that it is precisely the admission of this single cause which has brought with it, in all manner of disguises, that very laxity which Jesus was bent upon excluding, as though the one devil should return bringing seven other devils more wicked than himself.[1]

[1] An interesting analogy to the variation concerning an exceptive clause is provided by the variation of the text of Matthew in the passages concerning self-control (Matt. v. 22). The Authorized English Version, following some manuscripts, reads: " Whosoever is angry with his brother without a cause " ; while the Revised Version, on better authority (see the critical note of Meyer on Matt. v. 22, 1864, s. 136: "Es ist ein unpassender, aus Befangenheit geflossener, obwohl sehr alter . . . Zusatz.") omits the qualifying clause altogether.

Important, however, as this question of interpretation is, and prolonged as have been the discussions based upon it in the councils of the Christian Church, the really significant element of the teaching is not that in which the various records differ, but that in which they agree. The main intention of the teaching has been greatly overshadowed by this discussion of a single detail. The emphasis of Jesus is, in reality, laid — not upon the terms of a possible separation — but upon the question of remarriage after such separation. "Whosoever putteth away his wife and marrieth another," say all the passages. It is against the provoking of alienation by this anticipation of remarriage that Jesus makes his special protest; and the modern world, with its voluntary desertions often suggested by antecedent and illegitimate affection, knows well how grave a social peril it is with which Jesus deals. He teaches no prohibition of voluntary separation in case of conjugal failure; he makes no cruel demand upon the innocent to sacrifice children or love or life for one terrible mistake; but, except at the utmost for one cause, — and perhaps not even for that cause, — the mistake is one which, in the judgment of Jesus, involves a permanent burden. Marriage when undertaken must be regarded, not as a temporary agreement, but as a practically indissoluble union.

It is not surprising to observe that both the Pharisees, to whom Jesus offered this teaching, and the disciples, who listened to it, were united in their protests against it. On the one hand, the Pharisees said, "This is a harder doctrine than that of Moses," and Jesus admits that this is so. You, he says, live by the law of Deuteronomy, but even in your own tradition there is the older law of Genesis. "Moses . . . suffered you to put away your wives : but from the beginning it hath not been so." [1] Behind the conception of a sacrament, that is to say, even when that sacrament was ordained by Moses himself, there is the still more primitive law of nature, the essential adaptation described in Genesis of monogamy to human life ; or, as Jesus said, that which has been "from the beginning." On the other hand, the disciples say, "If the case of the man is so with his wife, it is not expedient to marry," [2] and this is precisely the criticism frequently offered in modern times to any strict construction of the marriage tie. The common habit of the political or the legal mind inclines it to inquire, not for ideal social relations, but for temporary security against immediate perils. Stringent regulation of marriage, it is urged, tends to increase the probability of promiscuous relations, and in some cases to throw doubt on the legality of well-intentioned marriages or on the legitimacy of children. In the interest, therefore, of good order, the marriage contract should be simplified and relief from its bonds should be within easy reach. This is the defence

[1] Matt. xix. 8.   [2] Matt. xix. 10.

of laws concerning marriage which authorize it without preliminary license, or solemnizing magistrate, or witness ; and of laws concerning divorce which permit it for a hasty temper or a passing whim. If the case of the man with his wife, it is said, is more strictly regulated, "it is not expedient to marry."

To all such suggestions that the way to sanctify marriage is to make it less binding, the teaching of Jesus is absolutely opposed. The alternative he presents to permanent acceptance of the marriage bond is not that of a contract which may be hastily made and hastily broken ; still less is it the probability of living in vice if one is not living in matrimony. The proposition of Jesus, which would seem to be not unreasonable, but which, in the light of much modern legislation and social custom, appears in an extreme degree ascetic and unattainable, is simply this, — that the alternative to permanent union in marriage is permanent purity out of marriage. There are, he admits, cases in which "it is not expedient to marry," [1] though they are by no means cases of mere insufficient self-control, such as seek relief in the modern courts. Physical reasons of temperament or of heredity may sometimes fitly prohibit matrimony. Such persons, in the language of Jesus, "are born eunuchs from the mother's womb." Again, a profound spiritual demand is sometimes inconsistent with the married state, as it was indeed with Jesus himself.

[1] Matt. xix. 10–12.

Such persons, as he says, "make themselves eunuchs for the kingdom of heaven's sake." The alternative in all such cases is not of more sexual liberty, but of less. They sacrifice family life for a duty which in their case is higher. It is, as he had said just before, like plucking out the right eye or cutting off the right hand if they cause to stumble.[1]

Concerning the general rule of marriage and its logical consequences, his teaching is explicit and undisguised. Marriage, being ordained of God for the union of two in one flesh, is in its intention for two and for two only, so long as they both shall live. Even to look upon another woman to lust after her is to commit adultery with her already in the heart. Jesus recognizes neither contemporaneous, nor, as it has been called, consecutive, polygamy.[2] Precisely as the other relations of family life, of parent with child, of brother with brother, have never been regarded as to be "put away"; precisely as there may be in these relations alienation and even separation, but cannot be divorce, permitting new alliance with new sons or brothers, — so, according to the teaching of Jesus, is the relation of husband and wife. Persons on entering Christian marriage, as in becoming parents after marriage, are undertaking a responsibility from which they may not look to escape. The son,

---

[1] Matt. xviii. 8, 9. So Mathews, "Social Teaching of Jesus," p. 93.
[2] *Princeton Review*, July, 1882, Leonard Bacon, "Polygamy in New England."

however prodigal, still belongs to the father; and the husband, though in a far country of permanent separation, still belongs to the wife. The Christian law is not primarily designed to make allowance for social failures, but to establish the principles of the kingdom of God.

This severity, which it is impossible to eliminate from the teaching of Jesus, was precisely what made it unwelcome when first delivered. It was a time when in Rome the domestic integrity, which had been the foundation of the State, was corrupted by ostentation and extravagance; a time when in Judea the teachings of Scripture were being learnedly interpreted so as to permit the very license which they were written to forbid. Thus the teaching of Jesus, while true to the better tradition of both countries, was too uncompromising for the self-indulgent aristocracy of Rome, and too unmistakable for the subtle theologians of Jerusalem. Indeed, it was the more an offence to both because both were forced to recognize that it was the ideal from which they had fallen away. With something of the same searching of hearts, the teaching of Jesus still meets both self-indulgent desire and theological ingenuity. Every kind of argument about unhappy homes and uncongenial tempers and newly discovered affinities is answered by the simple words of Jesus, "What therefore God hath joined together, let not man put asunder." [1]   Every soft-hearted evasion of his legislation by those who

[1] Matt. xix. 6.

profess to be his ministers is confronted by his undisguised language, "Whosoever shall put away his wife, . . . and shall marry another, committeth adultery."[1] The family is, to Jesus, not a temporary arrangement at the mercy of uncontrolled temper or shifting desire; it is ordained for that very discipline in forbearance and self-restraint which are precisely what many persons would avoid, and the easy rupture of its union blights these virtues in their bud. Why should one concern himself in marriage to be considerate and forgiving if it is easier to be divorced than it is to be good?

Finally, it is most interesting to notice that this high strain of exalted idealism in Jesus concerning marriage is not inconsistent with an equally remarkable quality of sanity and common sense. Being asked one day by the Sadducees what would happen under his strict doctrine of the marriage tie if "in the resurrection"[2] a woman found herself among many legitimate claimants, Jesus does not hesitate to say that the relation of marriage is based on physical conditions, and is not to be a characteristic of the heavenly life. "In the resurrection they neither marry, nor are given in marriage, but are as angels in heaven."[3] It might have been anticipated of a mystic and visionary, as Jesus no doubt appeared to those who were tempting him, that he would use no discrimination in his teaching, and could be easily lured into discourse

[1] Matt. xix. 9. [2] Matt. xxii. 28. [3] Matt. xxii. 30.

about spiritual marriages and affinities, like many a feeble mystic of the modern world. Jesus, however, is in this matter no mystic or ascetic. He recognizes that in marriage physical affection is an element in spiritual unity. He looks at the things of the flesh, not as things that are wrong, but as things that are real. The very fact that, as Jesus says, "He which made them made them male and female," limits the marriage relation to the physical life; while it is also true that this physical relationship makes marriage a permanent relationship while physical life lasts.

Such seems to be the nature of that one form of social legislation which Jesus ever concerned himself to give. To great numbers of persons who have desired to harmonize domestic inconsistency with Christian loyalty, it is a teaching which has seemed hard to receive; to many innocent persons it is a teaching which, no doubt, has brought grave suffering; to many persons who have "lightly or unadvisedly" become married, the penalty for their mistake has often appeared intolerable. Jesus, however, views the problem of marriage, like other social problems, from above, — in the large horizon of the purposes of God. Like a wise physician, he detaches himself from entire absorption in specific cases of social disease, and considers them in relation to the general principles of social reform. His teaching may, as he says, bring, not peace, but a sword. It may happen that a daughter-in-law will be set against her mother-in-law, and a man's foes shall be those of his own household. None the less, in the teaching of Jesus, the stable mono-gamic family remains the type of the unity of the kingdom of God; and his hope for the world is to be fulfilled through the expansion of those affections which are naturally born in the uncorrupted and uninterrupted unity of the home. To this mainte-nance of the home in the interest of the kingdom his legislation is directed. Those who, by fault or misfortune, are involved in domestic instability are permitted by the teaching of Jesus to admit their failure and to part ; but they may not, except possibly for a single cause, — and by no means certainly even for that cause, — forthwith begin a new alliance. Among those marriages which have been deliberately wrecked on some well-known rock of neglected duty, that one or the other party might, with full insurance, embark in another ven-ture, the teaching of Jesus stands like a lighthouse to mark the channel and to make such disasters criminally inexcusable. Special cases of social dis-ease must not, according to the teaching of Jesus, be permitted to menace the general social health. Social wreckage must not obstruct social navigation. The view from above gives significance and justi-fication to much in the teaching of Jesus which, when seen from below, may seem unreasonably severe.

Such considerations as these, however, growing out of the legislation of Jesus, carry us, it will be

M

seen, far beyond the actual sphere of legislation itself, and into the region of the general conse-quences of his teaching; and here, as has been remarked, we come upon that which is more charac-teristic in the teaching of Jesus than legislation in any form can be. If it is true, alike according to the con-clusions of modern scholarship and the gospel of Christ, that the maintenance of family integrity is the basis of the present social order, then it must be true that those tendencies and enterprises in modern society which make for domestic stability are most directly in line with the purpose of Jesus; and it must be still further true that many tendencies and enterprises of modern society which may seem in themselves of slight social disadvantage must be regarded as grave social perils if they are seen to threaten the integrity of the family. Indeed, we must go further, and admit that the chief defences of the family are not to be sought in any form of legislation, either political or Christian, but in much more remote sources of social wisdom and strength. Much of the energy which is devoted to establishing rules about marriage and divorce is like energy devoted to maintaining a dike, after the ocean has begun to trickle through. Outside such remedial legislation presses the force of a great flood of restless desire, against which amendments of legislation are of but slight avail; and the in-creasing stream of divorces which now penetrates the barrier of the family is in reality the indication of a storm which is produced by causes lying often very far away. There are social conditions in modern life in which promiscuity and homelessness are almost inevitable, and where it is a mockery to talk of the sanctity of the home; and there are other social conditions, far removed from the first, where an almost equal peril to the family is to be found in social ambition and publicity. To apply, then, the teaching of Jesus to the world as it now is, one must take account of things which lie apparently quite beyond the specific problem of the family, and must observe some of the tendencies in modern life which make on the one hand for social integrity, or on the other hand for social disintegration.

These remoter causes which at the present time work for or against the stability of the family are in the main of two kinds. In the first place, there are causes which proceed from the economic movements of the age; and, in the second place, there are those which proceed from the prevailing standards of social life. The economic influences have their effect chiefly on our social customs; the moral causes have a still graver effect upon what we may call our social creed.

Of economic changes which tend to modify domestic life, the most conspicuous is the unprecedented concentration of population in urban and industrial life. In 1791 but three per cent of the population of the United States lived in towns having more than five thousand inhabitants each. As late as 1840 but eight per cent so lived. Then began the drift to the cities, until in 1880 twenty-two per cent, and in 1890 twenty-nine per cent, or nearly a third of the population, were housed in cities and large towns.[1] The growth of the "great industry" is but another aspect of the same migration ; it masses population, and draws together producer, seller, buyer, and trader, until rural life, even far away, feels what Mr. Charles Booth has called the indraught of the city. To affirm that this migration, and the congestion of population which ensues, necessarily lessen domestic unity would be, of course, quite unjustifiable ; but it is certainly true that these conditions are unfavorable for family life. The number of divorces annually granted to residents in cities in the United States is from one-third to one-half greater than the number granted to residents in the country.[2] Rural life, on the other hand, does not insure affection and forbearance ; indeed, it is often the monotony and solitude of the country which drives restless spirits, for good or evil, to the vivacity and companionship of the great industry and the great town ; yet, in general, the life of the city is pervaded by a sense of temporariness and homelessness, while the life of the country encourages domestic integrity. It is but a small minority of

[1] *Quarterly Journal of Economics*, January, 1890, A. B. Hart, "The Rise of American Cities" ; C. D. Wright, "Practical Sociology," 1899, Ch. VIII (with references).

[2] "Report of Commissioner of Labor," 1889, p. 162.

the population of a great city which is able to maintain privacy of domestic arrangement and to train those sentiments and traditions which gather about a home. The great proportion of the city's population are industrial nomads, likely any day to fold their tents like Arabs and migrate to some better market for their labor or their wares; and, of these, a pitifully large proportion have not even tents to detain them, and herd together in the accidental companionship of the lodging-house, the tenement, and the street. Indeed, the migratory habit, which is forced upon the poor, begins to be a matter of choice among the prosperous, and, instead of any place which can be permanently regarded as a home, we now observe, even among the luxurious, a preference for the publicity and changefulness of the "flat" or the hotel. Whatever advantages of economy or convenience there may be about this congregated and shifting life, it certainly tends to discourage, either among rich or poor, that sentiment which maintains the unit of civilization. The Roman family had its symbol of continuity in the sacred fire, burning on the ancestral hearth; but it is not without difficulty that this sense of a sacred and permanent unity can be maintained round the cooking-stove of the tenement, the hot-air register of the boarding house, or even the steam radiator of the apart-ment hotel.

The problem of the city, which is thus involved in the problem of the family, is however by no means so formidable and overwhelming a social peril as it at first appears to be. Within this congestion of social life there are many signs which point to a restoration of social health and a renewal of domestic integrity. First, may be mentioned the now widely extended provision of better lodgings for the poor. One of the greatest achievements of modern philanthropy has been the discovery that under proper conditions model dwellings are a remunerative investment. To be charitable without being unbusinesslike has long been the unfulfilled ambition of the well-disposed ; and the lodging-house business has come to offer at least one form of benevolence which justly commends itself to generous but prudent philanthropists.[1] In these practical undertakings, however, one rule of construction is essential for permanent success, and the neglect of this rule has brought to many a well-meant plan unanticipated disaster. It is the rule which guarantees to each family its domestic independence and seclusion. However much the prosperous may be inclined to undomestic pleasures, the healthier instincts of the self-respecting poor demand something that can be

[1] Of the abundant and rapidly multiplying literature on the housing of the poor may be named : United States Commissioner of Labor, 8th special report, "The Housing of the Working People," by E. R. L. Gould ; "Report of New York Tenement House Committee," 1895 ; American Economic Association, XIII, Reynolds, "Housing of Poor in American Cities" ; Post, "Musterstätten persönlicher Fürsorge von Arbeitgebern," 1893, II, s. 215 ff.; H. H. Estabrook, "Some Slums in Boston," 1898.

called a home. For this reason blocks of model dwellings must be so constructed that each family shall have its own front door, within which are all the necessities of life. For this reason also, when feasible, it is wiser to build detached cottages than solid blocks. This also is the reason why great industrial settlements, absolutely controlled by an employer or a corporation, though equipped with every comfort, are often unwelcome to hand-workers, even on the most economical terms. What the good workman wants is not benevolent patronage, but fair pay and independence. He wants a sense of proprietorship and an object for his thrift; and many a bewildered employer has fancied his plans thwarted by sheer ingratitude and stupidity when in reality they were confronted by the healthy instinct of the home. The industrial problem of dwellings for the poor, that is to say, indicates in a most unexpected manner the fundamental significance of the problem of the family.

A second hopeful characteristic of the present congestion of population is the rapidly increasing tendency to suburban life. The provision of rapid transit from the centre of a city now sweeps each day a great multitude of plain and unambitious people into more natural conditions of rural life; so that the time may not be remote when a city shall be little more than a vast warehouse and shopping-place, in which, as in the case of that part of London specifically called "the City," the population may even tend to decrease. In this tide of population, flowing into the city each morning and ebbing again at night, we observe a social movement which, beyond doubt, makes for the cleansing of social life and the establishment of domestic unity. A suburban home is not a guarantee of domestic happiness, but it certainly makes a centre of mutual attachment, thrift, and simplicity; and the endless rows of unpretentious and often tasteless homes which now surround each great city are to be reckoned by the thoughtful observer as a significant contribution to the problem of the family.

Still another corrective tendency in city life which makes for the integrity of the family is to be found in the principles now commonly accepted for the judicious care of children. The modern science of child-saving rests on faith in the restorative quality of a good home. It regards city institutions as not only the most extravagant, but as also the least hopeful, way of caring for dependent children, and its hope is in the deportation of such children from the influences of the city to rural and domestic surroundings.[1] All countries in which any alertness of mind is applied to official relief have come to accept the placing-out system as the way of charity appropriate to children, and the first principle of that system is not only

[1] J. A. Riis, "The Children of the Poor," 1892, p. 277, "He is saved from becoming a tough to become an automaton." See also *Forum*, January, 1895, p. 52 ff., F. G. Peabody, "Colonization as a Remedy for City Poverty."

that of "out-door relief," but that of out-of-town relief, and the farther out the better. The instinct of family life, that is to say, which is threatened by the growth of the city, indicates in its turn the most wholesome and fruitful way for the city's salvation.

The same restorative tendency is to be observed in the habits of the prosperous. The demands of business and the passion for social herding force many prosperous persons into a form of city life which bears hardly any semblance to the life of a family, and which strains and frets the marriage tie with divided interests and undomestic obligations. As soon, however, as these preposterous demands of the city appear to be satisfied, the healthier domestic instinct reasserts itself, and the prosperous — often, indeed, to escape the city's tax-bill, but often also to escape from its publicity and promiscuity — join the efflux to the country, until in many cities, for at least half the year, the streets of the more luxurious city-dwellers are like streets of tombs. Still more significant is the procedure of many such persons in the education of their children. Being instinctively aware that a child needs, first of all, a home, and being conscious that their own domestic establishment cannot be fairly called by that name, they transfer the care of their children, and especially of their boys, to schoolmasters in the country. It is but another application of the placing-out system, which has for a long time been applied with success to the children of the homeless poor, and which is now having great extension among the children of the homeless rich. In such instances the utmost credit should be given to the teachers who by consecrated devotion convert a school into a family; but what, on the other hand, is to be said of the family which is confessedly not as wholesome for one's children as a school? Occasionally, no doubt, there may be an occurrence of domestic disaster or necessary rupture or unavoidable circumstances, in which the deporting of a child to the custody of a stranger is advisable in the case of the rich as in that of the poor. In general, however, the growth of the boarding-school system is an indictment of the home. A school may be a better training-place of child-life than a home; but that is because the home, for sufficient or insufficient reasons, is not what a home ought to be. On the other hand, the placing-out system is a most striking witness of the significance of the home in education. Parents thus colonizing their children are indicating in the most emphatic manner that, even if domestic unity and seclusion are impossible to themselves, some substitute for these blessings must be secured to insure the moral and physical health of those whom they most love. The same evils of the city streets and of the undomestic home threaten rich and poor alike, and beneath the problem of the city, as in a palimpsest, one reads the underlying signs of the significance of the family.

There are many other economic changes which are, in the same way, vastly enlarging the scope of the problem of the family, and contributing to the solution of a question with which they have nothing designedly to do. Each judicious investment in well-constructed dwellings for the poor, each extension of suburban railways and reduction of their rates, each encouragement on the part of a corporation or employer of permanence and thrift among employees, each amelioration of the city's own life by checking the evil of drink, or by multiplying popular resources of popular recreation, instruction, and health, — is a contribution to domestic integrity and peace. We observed at the outset that the unfolding history of human civilization is at each step epitomized in the evolution of the family ; we now observe that the maintenance of the family provides a test of the wisdom both of economic movements and of philanthropic endeavor.

Yet these economic rearrangements and philanthropic enterprises, however beneficent they may be, do not disclose to us the most fundamental causes of the problem of the family. The main sources of domestic instability are not economic, but moral. The problem of the family is not chiefly a result of defective social arrangements, but chiefly the result of a defective social creed. The truth of this statement is at once verified when one recalls the fact that divorce, like nervous prostration, is a disease which afflicts the prosperous more than it does the poor. Temptation enough, indeed, to promiscuous living is forced upon the poor by the crowded conditions of their life, yet one of the most distinctive and most touching characteristics of the poor is a clinging conjugal attachment, unbroken by the strain of destitution or even of vice. Many a well-intentioned philanthropist has tried to lift a family out of want by separating the wife from her degraded husband, and has been dismayed and possibly offended by the unreasonable loyalty of the innocent to the unworthy partner. Domestic instability, that is to say, is not chiefly the result of unpropitious circumstances, but of unspiritual and undomestic views of happiness and success. It is the consequence, not of a hard life, but of a soft creed ; its chief provocations are not external, but internal ; and its cure must begin with a finer social morality and a more worthy conception of the ends of human life. The problem of the family is but one aspect of the whole drift of social standards and ideals in modern life ; and the loosening of the marriage tie is, from this point of view, the premonition of a general landslide of social morality, as in the Alps the occasional fall of icy fragments indicates a general softening of the crust which may culminate in a mighty avalanche.

Of such a threatening thaw of ethical standards there are two conspicuous indications in modern social life. One is the interpretation of life in terms of egoism, and the other is the estimation of life in terms of commercialism. One is the love of self and the other is the love of money. On the one hand is the ancient heresy which makes one's self the centre round which the social world revolves, — the Ptolemaic philosophy of the selfish life; on the other hand is the special temptation which confronts social life at the present time, as a consequence of the prodigal productiveness and abundance of the modern industrial world.

Of the effect on domestic stability of mere selfishness, whether in the form of fleshly brutality or of ungenerous self-consideration, little need be said. The family, in its very nature, represents a transition from the self-considering to the self-subordinating life. The individual yields his isolated self in entering the social unity. A marriage, therefore, in which one member assumes all the rights and the other performs all the duties is not a domestic relation, but a relation of supremacy and servitude; a reversion of type to one of those primitive groups, patriarchal it may be, or matriarchal, from which the race by the slow processes of evolution has emerged. Marriage in its modern form is the most elementary expression of the life in common.

Elementary as such a proposition would seem to be, the discovery that it is true brings to many persons a shock of surprise. Such persons have imagined that domestic unity would endure the brutality of passion or the domineering temper

or the self-indulgent complaint in which selfishness expresses itself ; and when they discover that
marriage involves mutual rights and mutual sacrifices, they chafe under these unanticipated and
irksome restraints. They have thought of marriage as little more than the satisfaction of lust
or of ambition or of whatever other form self-
love may assume, and they suddenly find themselves involved in a moral situation, demanding of
them the continual exercise of those generous
instincts of which, perhaps, their first love was
full. Here, then, are indicated both the chief peril
and the chief social function of the institution of
the family. The chief peril which besets the family is not to be found in imperfect legislation or
inadequate social arrangements, but in the undis-
ciplined will, in the unsocialized desire, in the
survival in human life of the instincts of the beast
of prey, the viper, or the hog. On the other
hand, the chief social function of the family con-
sists in the contribution which it makes to the
socialization of the will. The family sets the individual at birth in a relation of altruistic interest ; it
renews and matures this joy as discovered in self-
sacrifice, when the individual creates a new family
of his own ; it continues only as such self-discov-
ery through self-surrender becomes the law of life.
The family, that is to say, is not designed to make
life easier, but to make life better. It rests upon
the generous instincts of natural and self-forget-
ting love. To contemplate a marriage from any

other point of view is simply to court disaster. Domestic stability comes, not through the domination of one will and the suppression of another, but through the discipline of each in mutual service, the giving and receiving of mutual correction, the sharing of mutual burdens and mutual joys. Such conditions necessarily involve friction, adjustment, self-discipline, and self-sacrifice; but it is precisely these ethical demands which make the chief contribution of the family to the moral education of the human race.

To the attack on the integrity of the family made by sheer selfishness, must be added the equally familiar peril created by the spirit of commercialism. Money-making is in itself no sin. Few desires in life are more honorable or more contributory to character than the ambition to win by honest work enough money to free one's self and those one loves from harassing and sordid cares. Commercialism, however, estimates life in terms of money, and expects to get from money blessings which money cannot buy. It proposes, among other uses of money, to buy an insurance on domestic happiness, as on other commodities. It talks of a "good" marriage as it talks of other lucrative ventures, though goodness may be sheer badness except to the trader's mind. Yet no one can read the signs of the times without observing that money and happiness are quite as often found apart as together. In fact, commercialism supplies the soil in which the malaria of domestic infelicity most easily spreads. The competitions of trade are duplicated in the competitions of social life; the advertising habit reappears in the habit of social ostentation; the value of money for making money is mistaken for a value in making friends; and finally, precisely as in the fluctuations of trade, a time of strain arrives, and the home, like the business firm, becomes bankrupt and is dissolved. It is a tragic Nemesis which thus follows the enshrining of Mammon as one's household god! Luxury, long desired, brings with it restlessness; freedom from real cares is succeeded by a more exhausting slavery to imaginary cares; "good" as the marriage may have seemed to be, it is difficult for those joined in it to be good, and still more difficult for children born of it to remain virile and unspoiled; finally, the natural end of a misplaced ideal comes in one overwhelming shock, and the idol set above the family hearth falls from its niche and crushes the home.

Nor is the effect of commercialism on the family to be observed in the commercially successful alone. There is a much larger and much more pathetic group of cases in which domestic instability proceeds, not from prosperity ill endured, but from the unsatisfied thirst for unattained prosperity. Such cases are affected by the contagion of commercialism, but have not the experience which fortifies against it. They imagine that ostentation and notoriety bring with them a happiness which simplicity and seclusion miss, and that a substitute for the home may be found in imitation of the foolish rich. One of the most startling evidences which the pitiful records of the divorce courts disclose is the fact that domestic instability in the United States prevails chiefly, not among the poor, or among the foreign born, or the hand working class, but among the ambitious, commercialized, migratory middle class of native-born Americans. It is, in short, one incident of that general restlessness of modern American life, in which the prizes of commercialism are the only visible rewards of social competition. The perverted standards and ideals of the commercialized rich filter down, like the water of an infected spring, through the social strata, poisoning many a life which has no direct contact with the temptations of prosperity, but is thirsty for satisfactions which the prosperous appear to enjoy.

If, then, the self-centred mind and the commercialized life are sources of such widespread contamination, then the restoration of social health must begin in nothing less than the purifying of the prevailing social creed. Family integrity can no more be insured by enactment or legislation than the health of a city can be secured by city ordinances while the water supply is tainted at its spring. The problem of the family is but one aspect of the much larger problem of socializing and spiritualizing the habits and aims of social life. At this point, however, and perhaps with a

N

certain surprise, we find ourselves once more confronted by the social principles of Jesus Christ. Precisely this issue, between a selfish and materialized aim and a socialized and spiritual ideal, was what lay before his mind, as it now lies before the mind of the modern world; and then as now the *crux* of the situation was seen to lie in the problem of the family. Jesus pictured to himself a perfect spiritual unity of social life, which he called the kingdom of God; and of that final fulfilment of his desire the germ and type were in the unity of the family group, where the self-realization of each individual was found in loving self-surrender. Jesus, therefore, with an explicitness used in no other case, announced definite legislation concerning the family. If that initial group, he seems to say, can be established in integrity, then within its familiar circle can be easily verified the principles of the kingdom, which on a larger scale might be obscure. Yet Jesus did not trust to such legislation to bring in the kingdom. He surveyed social life from above, with the detachment of the idealist; and he approached social life from within, by changing, not social circumstances, but human hearts. No amount of social regulation, he knew, can assure social stability, unless the interior ideals of individual lives are cleansed and refined at their source. Jesus seeks therefore, first of all, the springs of personal life, which if left unclean are sure to infect the whole social stream into which they flow.

"Cleanse first the inside of the cup and of the platter,"[1] he says; "and even now is the axe laid unto the root of the trees."[2] In short, as we have been led to trace the remoter causes of the problem of the family, so finally we are led to that solution of the problem which is most characteristic of the teaching of Jesus. It is nothing less than the redemption of personal life from the spirit of selfishness and from that curse of commercialism which the New Testament calls the love of the world. Selfishness dries up the springs from which the stream of the kingdom flows; commercialism poisons that stream in its course. Where the institution of the family is converted into an instrument of self-interest or into a commercial transaction, it is vain to hope for its transformation by regulation from without; where, on the other hand, an unselfish temper and a spiritual desire express themselves in domestic life, there no problem of the family is left to solve.

Must one, then, conclude that this comprehensive and spiritual solution of the problem of the family has met with no success? Has the teaching of Jesus concerning the unselfish and unworldly life given to the institution of the family no assurance of stability? Is it true that the very existence of the family is at present seriously threatened, and that we are likely soon to pass from a period of "family exclusiveness" into an age of domestic looseness or of communistic control? On the con-

[1] Matt. xxiii. 26.　　　[2] Matt. iii. 10.

trary, we must answer, grave as are the facts which we have traced in this chapter, they have no such significance as this. It is startling enough to be told that out of every thousand marriages in the United States upward of sixty are likely to end in divorce; but it must not be forgotten that, out of the same thousand, nine hundred and forty are to continue in some degree of unity and love. An epidemic of disease such as we have traced, though it be serious, still leaves the vast majority of the population uninfected; an Alpine avalanche, though it be destructive, still leaves the mountains strong. No self-deception could be greater than that of the socialist who fancies that we are really on the brink of a general break-up of the family system. No literature could be more untrue to the main movement of modern thought than the books and dramas which take for granted that licentious imaginings and adulterous joys have displaced in modern society pure romance and wholesome love. The eddies of dirty froth which float on the surface of the stream of social life and mar its clearness are not the signs which indicate its current. Beneath these signs of domestic restlessness the main body of social life is yet untainted, and the teaching of Jesus concerning unselfishness and unworldliness is practically verified in multitudes of unobserved and unpolluted homes.

What is a Christian family? It is not an extraordinarily angelic or ascetic group. It is simply a domestic group in which the spiritual ends of marriage are not obscured either by uncontrolled selfishness or by contaminating commercialism. Such a marriage has been created by the natural leadings of a pure love, and this single-minded affection becomes a permanent instinct of life. A Christian marriage expects to have its friction of interests and its moments of turbulence, like a stream that has its rapids and its falls; but these incidents do not block the movement of life, and the stream of love grows deeper and more tranquil as it flows. A Christian family does not forfeit its simplicity, genuineness, and interior resources when it becomes prosperous, or find itself stripped of the essentials of happiness when it becomes poor. In a Christian home the discipline of children is not so much a work of exhortation as of contagion. The prevailing climate of unaffected idealism strengthens the moral constitution of the child. Thus the Christian family gets its unity and stability, not by outward regulation, but by the natural processes of its inward life. It has its troubles, and they draw hearts together. It has its joys, and they are multiplied by being shared. When, finally, the children of that family grow up to hear of larger truths, — truths of the kingdom and of the Father in heaven, and of the son for whose return the Father is waiting, — then they interpret these great mysteries of the eternal world, as Jesus prompted them to do, in the language of their own loving and united home. Are there many such Christian families? Millions, we confidently answer. This is the normal type of the civilized home. The teaching of Jesus, so slightly accepted in many ways of life, has actually taken firm root in the soil of the family. If Jesus should come again, and consider the obvious effects of his teaching on the habits of social life, he would perhaps find no change so dramatic as that which is to be observed in the coherence and mutual devotion of the modern home. To the vast majority of any modern community, the problem of the family is but a remote and uninteresting sign of the time, heard by them as the roar of the ocean is heard by dwellers inland, reporting to them a storm far out at sea. Homes enough there are, as we have seen, wrecked in such storms, and lives enough which are tossed on rough waters with nothing that can be called a home to hold them up, but the continent of our civilization is not seriously threatened by the encroaching sea. The pure love which creates a stable family still sanctifies multitudes of such homes, set far back from the stormy agitations of the time; and among such homes the spirit of Jesus enters from day to day, as one day he came to the newly married pair at Cana, and changes the water of commonplace and prose into the wine of romance and joy.

CHAPTER IV

THE TEACHING OF JESUS CONCERNING THE RICH

How hardly shall they that have riches enter into the kingdom of God!

Who, then, is the faithful and wise steward whom his lord shall set over his household? . . . Blessed is that servant, . . . of a truth, he will set him over all that he hath!

WE pass from the innermost circle of social relationship—the family—and find ourselves in a larger but concentric circle. At the centre the individual is inquiring concerning his place and function in the social order, but round him now sweeps the life of a community, made up of many families associated in the complexity of the modern world. No sooner does the individual contemplate this larger circle environing his life, than a new social problem confronts him. He observes the extreme diversity of social conditions which each such community represents. Some of these families are hungry, for food or for work, and some, on the other hand, seem overburdened by superfluous possessions. Some of these homes are tempted by their poverty, and some by their prosperity. The individual looks about him at the scene presented by the modern distribution of wealth, and it is not a peaceful or sunny

183

prospect. About him lie, it is true, great tracts of general prosperity, a rolling country with gentle undulations of greater or less possessions; but in the midst of this smiling landscape rise a few abrupt and overshadowing peaks, making more sombre and sunless the deep cañons of incompetency and want which lie between. It is a spectacle abounding in suggestions of pathos, not unmingled with an element of irony. Each extreme of this diversity involves its own special peril; each social type — the dwellers on the heights and those who never see the sun — has its own temptations; each type tends to become isolated and fixed in its conditions; yet within each type there are groups which have a curious kinship in habit and needs. On the one hand is the group of the unemployed and laboriously idle rich, and on the other hand is the group of the unemployed and professionally idle poor. The two groups have much in common. Each is a detachment of what is known as the army of the unemployed. Each is characterized by loss of respect for work. Each, therefore, has its share of responsibility for the revolutionary agitation of the time. The instruments of this revolt are likely to be found among the exasperated poor; but the provocation to revolt is likely to proceed from the unemployed and self-indulgent rich, the spenders of that which others have gained, the persons of whom Mr. Ruskin said that their wealth should be called their "ill-th," because it is not well, but ill, with their souls. Thus, while the main current of social life is healthy and free, its motion has thrown up upon the surface a kind of life which may be described as social froth, and has deposited at its bottom another kind of life which may be described as social sediment; and who shall say which is the more threatening social peril, — the submerged poor or the light-minded rich; the restlessness of the social sediment, or the thoughtlessness of the social froth?

It should be noticed that this diversity of social condition, which appears to create a new social question, is not itself a new situation or one of unprecedented gravity. On the contrary, one of the most obvious facts of modern civilization is the enormous advance in general prosperity and in purchasing power of every social class. It is by no means true that as the rich grow richer the poor are growing poorer. The concentration of great wealth in a few hands is accompanied by an extraordinary distribution of comfort among many millions, so that conveniences and resources, which two generations ago were the luxuries of the few, have come to be within easy reach of the humblest. This progress in general prosperity has not, however, been a uniform progress. While the rich have been growing richer, the poor have been growing less poor, but they have not maintained the same pace of progress. Thus, while general progress may be admitted to be real, it may be still indicted as inequitable, and it is this sense of inequity which gives to the present social situation its specific character. It is not true that the hand-working class have less, but it is true that they know and feel and desire more. Thus, the modern social question is one fruit of the education of the masses. It is not a sign of social decadence, but a sign of social progress. "The people had been made blind, like Samson," remarks Mr. Graham, "the better to toil without being dangerous. . . . In 1870 it was felt . . . that a measure of education was necessary and politic, and Lord Sherbrooke (then Mr. Robert Lowe) expressed a very general feeling in his well-known aphorism, 'We must educate our masters.'"[1]

In such a situation, however, the social question presents itself in a much more radical form than it has, under other conditions, assumed. It is not a question of economic reforms or philanthropic schemes. It considers the very existence of these extremes of condition. Ought there to be any such types in social life as the rich and the poor? Is the possession of wealth on any terms justifiable? Is poverty by any means eradicable? Is a social order just and rational which permits great accumulation of wealth in single hands? If not, shall not a new social order be established, where the valleys of social life shall be exalted and its mountains and hills brought low? We speak of a rich man as being "worth" a certain sum. How much, asks the modern spirit, is a rich man in fact

[1] Graham, "The Social Problem," 1886, pp. 23, 25.

worth? Is he worth what he costs? In a time when the majority have the power, but have not the wealth, is it not possible, either by legislation or by revolution, greatly to restrict or hamper the accumulation and perpetuation of wealth? May not the way of the rich, like that of the transgressor, be made very hard? If the private ownership of wealth brings with it no public utility, or if, still worse, it turns out to be a source of demoralization, are there not ways of dealing with it as one deals with any common nuisance, so that it may be in large degree abated?

Thus the modern social question tests the institution of private property by its contribution to the public good. Does it foster a quality of social life which is worth perpetuating? Does money-getting fulfil a moral purpose? Is it, on the whole, best that the way to wealth shall be left open toward the top, so that a man who has the gift for getting rich may have all the benefits of that gift; or, on the other hand, ought rich people to be abolished, because it is impossible to be both rich and good? What is this fact of diversity of condition in modern social life, but a challenge to the poor to use their power, like a Samson who is no longer blind, to drag down the pillars of a perverted civilization?

Such are the questions which, often with bitterness, often with apprehension, are being asked by the present age. Wealth is brought to the test of utility. If it cannot be proved to fulfil some public service, then it is very probably digging its

own grave. With such questions, then, we turn
to the teaching of Jesus Christ; and at once we
are confronted by those principles of his teaching
which in their general form we have already recalled. Jesus views the social order from above,
in the horizon of the purposes of God; he approaches the social order from within, through the
awakening of individual capacity; he judges the
social order in its end, as a means to the kingdom
of the Father. What has Jesus, then, to say of
the contrast which was conspicuous in his time,
as it is in ours, between wealth and poverty?
Does the possession of wealth appear to Jesus
likely to make that kind of man who in his turn
may help the kingdom? May a rich man be an
accepted follower of Jesus Christ? Or is poverty,
on the other hand, of the essence of Christian
discipleship, and is a rich man necessarily shut out
of the kingdom? What is the teaching of Jesus
concerning the rich?[1]

No sooner does one ask these questions than he
recalls the reiterated and unmitigated language of
warning and rebuke with which Jesus addressed
the prosperous. "How hardly shall they that have
riches enter into the kingdom of God!"[2] "Woe
unto you that are rich;" "Blessed are ye poor;"[3]
"Lay not up for yourselves treasures upon the
earth;"[4] "For a man's life consisteth not in the

---

[1] See also *Christian Register*, January 5, 1893, F. G. Peabody,
"The Problem of Rich Men."

[2] Mark x. 23.   [3] Luke vi. 20, 24.   [4] Matt. vi. 19.

abundance of the things which he possesseth;"[1] "Ye cannot serve God and mammon;"[2] "It is easier for a camel to go through a needle's eye, than for a rich man to enter into the kingdom of God."[3] Few modern agitators, urging the dispossessed poor to resist their oppressors, have ever ventured upon stronger language than this; few, indeed, have gone so far as to say to their followers: "Sell all that thou hast, . . . and come, follow me."[4] It is not surprising that such sayings have been greeted as conclusive testimony concerning the teaching of Jesus, and as establishing his place in history as the great forerunner of modern protests against the industrial system which is based on private capital. "When Jesus," it is confidently asserted, "says, 'Lay not up for yourselves treasures upon earth,' he shows himself on ethical grounds a radical opponent of all accumulation of wealth."[5] "The democracy of property, which is the larger revelation of Christ, . . . is the condemnation of the wage-system."[6] "If the man who best represents the ideas of early Christians were to enter a respectable society to-day, would it not be likely to send for the police?"[7] "The practice of the preacher-carpenter who had not where to lay his head, who is not re-

[1] Luke xii. 15. [3] Matt. xix. 24.
[2] Matt. vi. 24. [4] Luke xviii. 22.
[5] Naumann, "Was heisst Christlich-Sozial?" s. 9.
[6] Herron, "The New Redemption," p. 63.
[7] Leslie Stephen, "Social Rights and Duties," I, 21 (quoted by Mathews, "Social Teaching of Jesus," 149 [note]).

corded as having possessed a single coin, who had nothing to leave his mother, and whose grave was borrowed from a friend, accords fully with the message he delivered."[1]

Estimates like these of the teaching of Jesus must not be lightly dismissed. There is no way of breaking the force of these solemn sayings of the gospels concerning the deceitfulness of riches, or of eliminating from the teaching of Jesus his stern warnings to the prosperous and his beautiful compassion for the poor. Is it possible, however, that so obvious and so limited a message as this, a teaching so slightly distinguishable from the curbstone rhetoric of a modern agitator, can be an adequate reproduction of the scope and power of the teaching of Jesus? Is it not, on the contrary, more probable that we have here a new illustration of that easy literalism which through all Christian history has distorted and limited the teaching of the gospel? No vagary or extravagance of opinion has been too extreme to claim for itself the authority of the teaching of Jesus, or to fortify that claim through a fragmentary and haphazard eclecticism. The gospels, however, are not a series of disconnected aphorisms; they are the record of a continuous life, whose complete intention is not disclosed in single incidents or detached sayings, but reveals itself in the general

[1] Article in *The Outlook*, December 10, 1898. Compare also O. Holtzmann, "Jesus Christus und das Gemeinschaftsleben der Menschen," 1893, s. 17 ff.

habit and movement of the Teacher's mind. If, then, one seriously desires to know what Jesus thought about the rich and the poor, he must scrutinize, compare, and weigh the scattered sayings of the gospel and derive from them a general impression of the life which gave authority to the teaching; and as he thus passes from the letter of the gospel to its spirit, there may perhaps disclose itself a scope and character of teaching which no isolated saying adequately represents, but which, the more one examines it, draws the learner to the Teacher with a profounder impression of reverent awe.[1]

As one thus approaches the teaching of Jesus concerning the rich, he is, first of all, confronted by an extraordinary difference of emphasis in the different evangelists.[2] The fourth gospel hardly

[1] 8ter Evang.-soz. Kongress, 1897, Wendt, "Das Eigentum nach christlicher Beurteilung," s. 10, "A trustworthy Christian judgment concerning property is to be derived, not from single Biblical utterances or parables, but from the fundamental principles and religious conceptions of Jesus."

[2] On these notable differences of social teaching see, on the one hand, Keim, "Jesus of Nazareth," III, 284, "We have [in Luke] gross, naked Ebionitism." . . . "The naked doctrine of poverty." IV. 81, "In the glorification . . . of poverty as such . . . we have the direct reverse of the teaching of Jesus." More moderately, H. Holtzmann, "Die ersten Christen und die soziale Frage," s. 44, "The view of Jesus is of the peril of riches; . . . the view of the third Gospel is that riches are in themselves disgraceful, and poverty in itself saving." On the other hand, Renan, "Life of Jesus" (tr. Allen), Ch. XI, "The Gospel in his [Jesus] thought of it, is for the poor." The Ebionitic note of the third gospel is emphasized, perhaps with exaggeration, by Colin Campbell, "Criti-

touches the question of material possessions at all. It moves in quite another world, — a world of lofty philosophy, spiritual biography, and Divine communion. With the exception of two unimportant passages [1] the very words "rich," "poor," "wealth," "poverty," "to be rich," "to be poor," do not occur either in the fourth gospel or in the Johannine epistles. The second gospel also, — though for opposite reasons — offers practically no material concerning poverty or wealth which does not also present itself either in Matthew or Luke, or in both. The fourth gospel loses sight of these human interests in its flight of spiritual meditation; the second gospel hastens by these general problems of social life in its absorbed and concise records of the words and acts of Jesus. Thus the teaching of Jesus concerning social conditions must be sought almost wholly in the gospels of Matthew and Luke; and here we come upon abundant material.

Yet here also we meet a still more striking

cal Studies in Luke's Gospel," 1891, Ch. II. Compare, Plummer, "Commentary on Luke," 1896, p. xxv. "Is there any Ebionism in St. Luke? That Luke is profoundly impressed by the contrast between wealth and poverty . . . is true enough. But this is not Ebionism. He nowhere teaches that wealth is sinful and that rich men must give away all their wealth, or that the wealthy may be spoiled by the poor." Observe also the discussions of B. Weiss, "Life of Christ," Book I, Ch. IV, V; J. Estlin Carpenter, "The First Three Gospels, their Origin and Relations," 1897, Ch.VIII–X; and especially the painstaking and convincing study of Rogge, "Der irdische Besitz im N. T.," 1897, s. 9 ff.

[1] John xii. 5; xiii. 29.

difference. In the first place, while the record of the two gospels is often obviously identical in origin, it happens in almost every instance that, where Matthew and Luke report the same incident or saying concerning the rich or the poor, the passage in Luke takes a severer or more universal form of condemnation of the one class, or of commendation of the other. Where Matthew says, "Give to him that asketh thee" ($\tau\hat{\varphi}$ $a\dot{i}\tau o\hat{v}\nu\tau\acute{i}$ $\sigma\epsilon$ $\delta\acute{o}\varsigma$),[1] Luke says : "Give to every one" ($\pi a\nu\tau\grave{i}$ $a\dot{i}\tau o\hat{v}\nu\tau\acute{i}$ $\sigma\epsilon$ $\delta\acute{i}\delta o\nu$);[2] where Matthew says, "Sell that thou hast" ($\pi\acute{\omega}\lambda\eta\sigma o\nu$ $\tau\grave{a}$ $\dot{v}\pi\acute{a}\rho\chi o\nu\tau a$),[3] (Mark, $\ddot{o}\sigma a$ $\ddot{\epsilon}\chi\epsilon\iota\varsigma$), Luke says, "Sell all that thou hast" ($\pi\acute{a}\nu\tau a$ $\ddot{o}\sigma a$ $\ddot{\epsilon}\chi\epsilon\iota\varsigma$ $\pi\acute{\omega}\lambda\eta\sigma o\nu$).[4] Where the beatitude in Matthew reads : "Blessed are the poor in spirit,"[5] Luke says, "Blessed are ye poor,"[6] and reënforces this modification with the added phrase, "But woe unto you that are rich!"[7] Where Matthew says, "But lay up for yourselves treasures in heaven,"[8] Luke says, "Sell that ye have, and give alms."[9] According to Matthew there are brought to the great supper both bad and good,[10] but in Luke the Lord of the supper says, "Bring in hither the poor and maimed and blind and lame."[11] To this marked difference of emphasis must be added the further fact that the most radical teachings and illustrations concerning the

[1] Matt. v. 42.
[2] Luke vi. 30.
[3] Matt. xix. 21.
[4] Luke xviii. 22.
[5] Matt. v. 3.
[6] Luke vi. 20.
[7] Luke vi. 24.
[8] Matt. vi. 20.
[9] Luke xii. 33.
[10] Matt. xxii. 10.
[11] Luke xiv. 21.

perils of wealth are to be found in the third gospel alone.   Here appear the story of Dives and
Lazarus,[1] of the foolish rich man,[2] of the unjust
steward,[3] and the conversation about inheritance.[4]
It is in Luke alone that the prophetic word is
utilized : " And the rich he hath sent empty
away." [5]   In short, between Matthew and Luke
there is as marked a difference of teaching as may
be found in modern literature between the teaching of an earnest philanthropist and the teaching
of a socialist agitator.   It is quite within the truth
to speak of Luke as the " socialist-evangelist." [6]

What is to be regarded as the probable cause of
this striking peculiarity of the third gospel ?   The
most obvious interpretation which suggests itself
is that the character of the gospel reflects the
character of its author.   Luke, it is said, like Paul,
with whom he lived and taught, had a larger social
experience and a keener human sympathy than
the other evangelists.   His mind, therefore, seized
on the radical sayings of Jesus in their original
sternness of tone, where Matthew softened and
spiritualized such words into conformity with provincial habits of mind.   Thus, the socialist-evangelist best understood his Master, and the teaching

---

[1] Luke xvi. 20.   [3] Luke xvi. 1–13.   [5] Luke i. 53.
[2] Luke xii. 16–21.   [4] Luke xii. 13.

[6] Rogge, p. 10 (citing H. Holtzmann in " Prot. Kirchenzeitung,"
1894).   But compare, also, as diminishing the significance of these
contrasts, the comment on the general habit of mind of Luke, in
Plummer, " Commentary on Luke," p. lxii.

of Jesus concerning the rich is to be found in Luke.

This view of the relation of the gospels, however, leaves out of account several of the most significant aspects of the New Testament. In the first place, it is inconsistent with the general principle of criticism, that of two readings of equal external authority the more spiritual reading is the more likely to reproduce the Master's words. Other things being equal, it is not probable that the more obvious meaning is original, and that the more spiritual signification is superimposed. Of the two readings, "Blessed are the poor in spirit," and "Blessed are ye poor," it is on the face of things not likely that the peculiar depth and beauty of the truth which the first passage expresses should be a gloss upon the superficial, not to say the questionable, teaching of the second passage. Further, without undertaking to enter elaborately into the much debated problem of the Paulinism of the third gospel, it is obvious that, in the attitude of that gospel toward poverty and wealth, we meet a characteristic which is very remote from the habitual teaching and example of Paul. To regard poverty as in any degree a test for admittance to the kingdom of God, or to discriminate against the prosperous simply because of their prosperity, is quite contrary to the spirit of the robust, sagacious, and independent apostle to the Gentiles. He perceives, it is true, that "Not many wise, . . . , not many mighty, not many noble, are called;"[1] but it is not a part of his purpose to reproach the rich or to identify holiness with poverty. For his own part he will be, he says, a charge to no man. " For ye remember, brethren, our labour and travail : working night and day, that we might not burden any of you."[2] It is true that Paul regards it a despising of the Church of God to " put them to shame that have not;"[3] and that he urges contentment with what one has ;[4] yet he has a place for the rich also in the world of Christian service. Within the churches which he organizes there are disciples prosperous enough to undertake missionary contributions. " So, then, as we have opportunity," Paul says to them, " let us work that which is good toward all men, and especially toward them that are of the household of the faith."[5] " God loveth a cheerful giver."[6] He welcomes missionary gifts from the church at Philippi as a sacrifice "acceptable, well-pleasing to God."[7] He bids Timothy to charge the rich "that they do good, that they be rich in good works."[8] Finally, in his most comprehensive statement of Christian character, he explicitly announces that the abandonment of possessions does not necessarily indicate holiness. "And if I bestow all my goods to feed the poor, . . . but have not love, it profiteth me nothing."[9] Here is a habit of mind so dif-

[1] 1 Cor. i. 26.
[2] 1 Thess. ii. 9.
[3] 1 Cor. xi. 22.
[4] Phil. iv. 11.
[5] Gal. vi. 10.
[6] 2 Cor. ix. 7.
[7] Phil. iv. 18.
[8] 1 Tim. vi. 18.
[9] 1 Cor. xiii. 3.

ferent from that which is illustrated in many pas
sages of the third gospel, that so far as this single
problem of the right to property has any bearing
on the general question of relationship between
Luke and Paul, it certainly seems to indicate no
close kinship of spirit or aim.

There is another and more general point of view
from which this contrast between Luke and Paul
may be considered. When we scrutinize the New
Testament as a whole we observe that the same
line of cleavage which is to be noticed between
the third gospel and the epistles of Paul appears
to run between other books also, and divides the
literature of the New Testament into two general
groups. With the third gospel seem to group
themselves the introductory chapters of the book
of Acts and the epistle of James; and with Paul's
epistles the gospels of Matthew and of Mark. A
situation thus presents itself which is in sharp contrast with the usual grouping of New Testament
books, and of which New Testament criticism has
thus far taken but small account. The first gospel,
for instance, is beyond question colored in many
respects by the Palestinian tradition, and the
third gospel is, in general, adapted to Gentile
readers; but when we examine the social teaching of the two there is exhibited a reversal of
these relationships, and the first gospel rather
than the third appears to free itself from the
pressing trials of Palestinian poverty and relief.
Into the interesting critical question thus opened

it is not possible here to enter, but the general line of cleavage is not easy to mistake.[1] The book of Acts begins in a tone of lofty ecstasy, prompted by that confident belief in an imminent cosmic catastrophe which made the first disciples indifferent to social conditions or social change. They testified to their freedom from the ordinary limitations of life by their gift of tongues,[2] and they expressed their indifference to social distinctions by having "all things common."[3] The epistle of James goes beyond indifference to possessions and positively indicts the prosperous as sinners. Its language is that of unsparing attack and bitter irony. "Go to now, ye rich," concludes this most radical of New Testament writers, "weep and howl for your miseries that are coming upon you."[4] On the other hand, the first two gospels move in a world of tranquil and unimpassioned narrative, less virile in teachings concerning worldly independence than the self-respecting judgments of Paul, but exhibiting no rigid discrimination between social classes.[5]

What does this general contrast among New Testament books indicate as to the prevailing conditions of primitive Christian life? It reminds us of that contrast of social condition and habit

[1] On this distinction of New Testament Books, see the interesting discussion of Rogge (*op. cit.*), s. 68 ff.

[2] Acts ii. 4.   [3] Acts ii. 44.   [4] James v. 1.

[5] See the essay of Th. Zahn, " Die soziale Frage und die innere Mission nach dem Briefe des Jakobus," in his " Skizze aus dem Leben der alten Kirche," 1898, s. 93.

of mind which, as has been frequently observed, existed between the Palestinian and the Gentile communities. The disciples at Jerusalem, in the lofty enthusiasm of their first fellowship, threw down the barriers of ownership as they did those of language, and had one speech and one purse. It was, as we have already seen, not a prearranged and institutional communism, but, as Peter expressly calls it,[1] a voluntary sharing of what was needed. While it remained, it remained one's own, and when it was sold it was still in one's power. Even this relation, however, was one which could not be realized in an enlarging Church. As we proceed in the book of Acts itself, the social types associating themselves with the new religion become more and more varied, until persons of every social condition, Pharisees[2] and fishermen,[3] the treasurer of Candace,[4] the proconsul Paulus,[5] Dionysius the Areopagite,[6] Crispus,[7] the head of a Jewish synagogue, together with many who must be cared for by alms from "the daily ministration,"[8] come into view as acceptable members of Christian congregations.

Nor must we forget the inevitable effect upon the congregations of Palestine of the social teaching represented by the epistle of James. The less honorable poor flocked, it would seem, with the devout to such communities, until at last the

[1] Acts v. 4.
[2] Acts xxiii. 6.
[3] Matt. iv. 18.
[4] Acts viii. 27.
[5] Acts xiii. 7.
[6] Acts xvii. 34.
[7] Acts xviii. 8.
[8] Acts vi. 1.

church in Jerusalem, in spite of its noble desire to have all things in common, was so impoverished as to lose the capacity for self-support, and became dependent on alms contributed by the Gentile churches. It was a curious nemesis which followed the identification of the religion of Jesus with a special economic condition. James might continue to fulminate against the iniquities of the rich, but the communities to which he wrote sank into a progressive pauperization from whose results they were relieved by the more virile and thrifty congregations bred in the spirit of the self-supporting Paul.

Such, it may not unreasonably be believed, were the circumstances in which two different ways of regarding wealth and poverty came to exist within the literature of the New Testament. In the Palestinian communities, where the faithful found themselves more and more impoverished and defenceless, every saying of Jesus was cherished which seemed to comfort the poor or to rebuke the prosperous; in the missionary churches, on the other hand, the distinctions and animosities of social classes were subordinated to the larger mission to which the Christian religion was called; and when the same sayings of Jesus were repeated, it was their spiritual significance which was recalled. " Blessed are ye poor," [1] says the church in Palestine, for the solace of its oppressed disciples; "Blessed are the poor in spirit," [2] repeats the spiritual tradition, for

[1] Luke vi. 20.   [2] Matt. v. 3.

the humbling of unchristian pride. "So also shall the rich man fade away in his goings," says James.[1] "For all things are yours; . . . and ye are Christ's,"[2] answers Paul.

These conjectures, however, carry us somewhat beyond our present purpose. It is enough to recognize, running through the New Testament, two radically divergent traditions concerning the relation of riches to the Christian life. According to the one tradition the only consistent Christian is a poor man; according to the other the true riches and the real poverty are of the soul. If then we are to inquire which of these two traditions represents the original teaching of Jesus, it is impossible to rest on the authority of any single passage in the gospels or even on the authority of any single gospel. Behind these partial expressions of the teaching, one must observe the more general aspects and relations of the Master's life. What, we must ask, was the habitual attitude of Jesus toward the rich and the poor as he walked and talked with both? With whom did he most naturally live? To whom did he most entirely give his heart? Whom did he welcome as his friends and followers? What is the relation of his teaching to the views which prevailed in his own time and nation concerning poverty and wealth? Summing up his scattered instructions, comparing his various parables, and observing the general direction of his mind and

[1] James i. 11. [2] 1 Cor. iii. 21, 23.

the habitual rule of his life, what was the burden of his message to the rich?

In order to reach an answer to these questions it is necessary, first, to recall the social environ- ment of the ministry of Jesus, the world of people and of ideas into which he entered and through which he moved. The people who were the first to welcome him were certainly not of the rich and ruling classes, but, as a rule, plain and unassum- ing folk. This, however, is by no means equiva- lent to saying that the immediate followers of Jesus were drawn exclusively from those who in the modern sense, could be called poor. On the contrary, the gospel story, with all its tender feeling for the poor, moves for the most part through a social environment quite above the range of poverty. Jesus himself was born in a home which cannot be classified either as rich or poor. He was educated, both in letters and in handicraft. When he entered upon his public life, there is no sign that the social peril of wealth was in any degree burdening his heart. When at the outset of his ministry he was tempted of the devil, the solicitations which were presented to him were not those of riches, but those of fame, power, and self-display.

When, further, we consider the social condition of the persons first won by his teaching, we are met by many different social types.[1] Among those who

[1] Rogge, p. 20 ff.; H. Holtzmann, "Die ersten Christen und die soziale Frage," s. 23; *New World*, June, 1899, p. 305.

flocked to a teacher who renewed their hope and
self-respect were indeed many penniless and bur-
den-bearing outcasts; yet within the circle of his
intimacy and confidence there were persons of all
degrees of prosperity. The fishermen who were
first called by him were by no means penniless
or homeless, but were people of reasonable
prosperity. They "left their father . . . with
the hired servants, and went after him."[1] One
of them "was known unto the high priest, and
entered in with Jesus into the court of the high
priest."[2] At the death of their Master they
returned to their boats and trade.[3] Peter was a
householder, to whose home Jesus came when
Peter's wife's mother lay sick.[4] In the house
of Matthew the tax-gatherer, Jesus sat at meat;[5]
"and many publicans and sinners sat down with
Jesus and his disciples."[6] Zacchæus was a chief
publican, "and he was rich." "The half of my
goods," he said to Jesus, "I give to the poor;"
and Jesus commends him and welcomes him, saying, "To-day is salvation come to this house."[7]
Nicodemus, "a ruler of the Jews,"[8] is addressed
by Jesus with astonishing candor; but there is
no rebuke of the Pharisee's prosperity. The
captain of the guard,[9] a person of social importance and authority, is not censured by Jesus,
but honored with special praise. "Joanna the

[1] Mark i. 20.
[2] John xviii. 15.
[3] John xxi. 3 ff.
[4] Matt. viii. 14.
[5] Matt. ix. 10.
[6] Mark ii. 15; Matt. ix. 10.
[7] Luke xix. 2, 8, 9.
[8] John iii. 1.
[9] Matt. viii. 10.

wife of Chuza Herod's steward, and Susanna, and many others," being — it must be in-ferred — women of means, "ministered unto them of their substance." [1] The home at Bethany, in which Jesus repeatedly found tranquil release from the pressure of his public life, was a home of comfort, if not of luxury, and there was in it "an ointment of spikenard, very precious." [2] Fi-nally, Joseph of Arimathea, "being a disciple of Jesus," provides a tomb for the crucified Master, and comes with Nicodemus, "bringing a mixture of myrrh and aloes, about a hundred pound weight." [3]

Here are sufficient indications that no single social type monopolized the sympathy or accept-ance of Jesus. Whatever may be gladly ad-mitted concerning the special tenderness of his teaching when he speaks of the poor, and how-ever true it is that "the common people heard him gladly," [4] there is certainly no ground for believing that Jesus proposed to array the poor against the rich or to set the one social class on his right hand and the other on his left. The fact is that his teaching moved in a world of thought and desire where such distinctions be-came unimportant, and a profounder principle of classification was applied. He gathered about himself all sorts and conditions of men and women ; he passed without any sign of conscious

1 Luke viii. 3.   3 John xix. 38, 39.
2 John xii. 3.   4 Mark xii. 37.

transition from the company of the rich to that of the poor and back to that of the rich again. He was equally at home at the table of the prosperous Zacchæus, in the quiet home at Bethany, and in the company of the blind beggar by the wayside.[1] He lavished his great utterances with equal freedom on the scholarly Nicodemus[2] and on the ignorant and foolish woman by the well.[3] In short, his categories of social judgment are not those of wealth and poverty. His thought is directed toward the fulfilment of the kingdom of God. Whatever type of character he discovers which seems contributory to that ideal he spontaneously and often abruptly accepts, and whatever circumstances, on the other hand, appear to hinder that great consummation must be, according to his teaching, at any sacrifice escaped or overcome. Here must have been one source of joy in listening to Jesus. Men found themselves no longer identified with a single social class, having special limitations of teachableness or capacity; they were brought into sight of the comprehensive unity of human ideals and needs, in which the distinctions of social groups were lost in a larger companionship. It was the joy of the narrow stream when it flows out at last into the comprehensive ocean and meets the infinite variety of other streams from which its own course has been hitherto shut away.

This elevation of the mind of Jesus above the

[1] Mark x. 46. [2] John iii. 1–21. [3] John iv. 7–26.

region of social differences is further indicated when one considers his relation to that view of poverty and wealth which was current among his own people and in his own time. There still survived about him a national tradition that piety should bring with it prosperity; yet, in spite of their piety, his people were plundered and oppressed by the unsanctified Romans, and the prophecy of an external reward for righteousness seemed far from fulfilled. Here was a social condition contrary both to their religious hope and to their national instinct of money-getting, and the Hebrew people were filled with bitterness and wrath toward those who were, at the same time, unholy and prosperous. "To pass through their literature," it has been justly said, "is like passing through Dante's Inferno, except that nowhere appears any trace of that Divine pity which the great Italian permits." [1] There came to exist among them what has been called a "genius for hatred" of the rich. "Woe unto you," says the book of Enoch, "who heap up silver and gold and say, We are growing rich and possess all we desire." "Your riches shall not remain for you, but shall suddenly disappear; because you have gained all unjustly, and you yourselves shall receive greater damnation." [2]

Into this social environment of embittered poverty and cultivated hate, with no solution

[1] Rogge (op. cit.), s. 34, with many illustrative citations.
[2] Enoch xcvii. 8 ff.

at its command for the paradox of poverty and piety, enters the new comprehensiveness of the teaching of Jesus. Prosperity, he preaches, is no sign of Divine acceptance; on the contrary, it is one of the most threatening obstructions of the spiritual life. The desire of the nation, therefore, should be turned altogether away from the thought of wealth as a sign of piety, or of poverty as a sign of Divine disfavor. Let the poor take heart again. They have no reason to envy or to hate the rich. Let them rather realize how hard it is for a rich man to enter into the kingdom. There is but one supreme end for the life of rich and poor alike, — the service of the kingdom; and there is but one fundamental decision for all to make, — the decision whether they will serve God or Mammon. In short, in striking contrast with the tradition and literature of hate with which he was undoubtedly familiar, Jesus surveys the relation of the rich and the poor from above, in the light of his ideal of the kingdom; and a new sense of hope and self-respect springs up in many a perplexed and questioning mind as Jesus summons it to a way of life of which neither wealth nor poverty is the key, and of which, on the other hand, neither wealth nor poverty is an absolute obstacle. "Lay not up," he says, "for yourselves treasures upon the earth, . . . for where thy treasure is, there will thy heart be also." [1]

Thus the teaching of Jesus is, in one sense, extra-

[1] Matt. vi. 19, 21.

ordinarily detached from the problem of social distinctions and commercial prosperity. Jesus is not a social demagogue ; he is a spiritual seer. He is not concerned with the levelling of social classes, but with the elevating of social ideals. He welcomes a life for its own sake, not for its circumstances of wealth or of poverty. Does this characteristic of the teaching of Jesus, however, render his message to the rich as a special class any less distinct or solemn or profound ? On the contrary, out of his fragmentary utterances and occasional parables there issues a teaching quite as radical in its character and quite as searching in its demands as any modern arraignment of wealth, but with a touch of wisdom and a balance of judgment which make it a teaching, not for a special age or class, but for all conditions and all times.

The scattered utterances of Jesus about the problem of wealth fall into two distinct classes. On the one hand is the series of sayings which deal with the faithful use of one's possessions ; and, on the other hand, are the passages which plainly demand the abandonment of such possessions. In the parables, for instance, of the talents [1] and of the pounds,[2] as in the stories of the unjust steward [3] and of the foolish rich man,[4] there seems to be indicated, not the intrinsic evil of wealth, but the duty of fidelity, watchfulness, and fore-

---

[1] Matt. xxv. 14–30.
[2] Luke xix. 13–27.
[3] Luke xvi. 1–13.
[4] Luke xii. 16–21.

sight in administering wealth. "Watch therefore,
for ye know not the day nor the hour."[1] "This
night is thy soul required of thee."[2] "Well done,
good and faithful servant."[3] "If therefore ye
have not been faithful in the unrighteous mammon, who will commit to your trust the true
riches?"[4] In such passages money appears to be
regarded as a test. Faithfulness in the few things
prepares for mastery over the many things. The
mammon of unrighteousness may make friends
who will receive one into the everlasting tabernacles. The same teaching is conveyed in that
doctrine of cumulative returns which appears in
the parable of the talents.[5] Jesus is here as far
as possible from the position of a social leveller.
He discerns with extraordinary clearness the inevi-
tably cumulative results of the wise use of possessions, and announces a law of distribution,
which is not only fundamentally opposed to the
programme of the modern revolutionist, but is also
far more in accord with the method of nature.
"For unto every one that hath shall be given,
. . . but from him that hath not, even that which
he hath shall be taken away."[6]

On the other hand, there remains a class of
passages which no softened interpretation can
render as teaching anything less than the abne-
gation of possessions. "Whosoever he be of you
that renounceth not all that he hath, he cannot

[1] Matt. xxv. 13.   [3] Matt. xxv. 21.   [5] Matt. xxv. 14–30.
[2] Luke xii. 20.   [4] Luke xvi. 11.   [6] Matt. xxv. 29.

P

be my disciple." [1] "Sell all that thou hast, and distribute unto the poor, . . . and come, follow me ; " [2] and "they left all, and followed him." [3] " Thou in thy lifetime receivedst thy good things, and Lazarus in like manner evil things : but now here he is comforted, and thou art in anguish." [4] Concerning some passages of this nature, it may be with justice urged that these absolute commands seem to have been laid, not on all men, but on that immediate group of disciples who were bidden in a peculiar degree to share their Master's wandering life, and to detach themselves from the ties of business and home.   Further, in the case of Dives and Lazarus, it is not unreasonable to infer that there must have been more involved in the original contrast of their destinies than a mere distinction of prosperity and pauperism. [5]   Even if Dives be condemned to anguish simply because he is rich, it is not easy to believe that Lazarus should be taken to heaven for no other reason than because he was poor.   Yet, after all possible mitigation has been thus proposed for the severity of such sayings, there remains in many of them an unmistakable note of renunciation.

The most conspicuous instance of this *motif* of renunciation is in the touching interview of Jesus with the rich young ruler ; [6] an incident recorded at length in all the first three gospels, as though

---

[1] Luke xiv. 33.   [2] Luke xviii. 22.   [3] Luke v. 11.
[4] Luke xvi. 25.   [5] Rogge, s. 66.
[6] Matt. xix. 16–22 ; Mark x. 17–23 ; Luke xviii. 18 ff.

specially treasured among the early tradition of
the Master's words. This young man is both
impulsive and reverent. First he runs to Jesus,
and then he kneels before him, and Jesus, looking
on him, loves him.[1] It is a beautiful meeting of
fair, frank youth with a wise, calm teacher; an
offering of spontaneous loyalty on the one hand
and an immediate impulse of affection on the
other. Yet the charm of the youth does not
soften in any degree the judgment of the Teacher.
On the contrary, precisely because he loves him
Jesus demands of him a great renunciation. One
thing stands between that winsome youth and his
service of the kingdom. It is his wealth. What
can one who loves him propose but a heroic remedy? It is a case where alleviating treatment
must fail, and where the wise physician must with
apparent cruelty counsel a capital operation. It is
a situation familiar in modern life. A young man,
well born and well bred, winsome and gallant, is
withheld from the effective use of his life by the
weight of his possessions. If he could only forget
that he was rich and give himself to strenuous
work, he might do gallant service. If some dramatic summons like that of an actual war is heard
by him, the follies of his luxury and self-indulgence
drop away from him, and he becomes the most
enduring and daring of soldiers. Meantime, however, here he is, with hardly a fair chance for a
useful life, turning play into work, and sinking into

[1] Mark x. 21.

a false and foolish estimate of life and happiness. What hope is there for such a young man except through some radical change, curative though cruel, like the surgeon's knife? It was thus that Jesus, loving the young ruler, demanded much of him; and one can imagine the loving pity with which Jesus, when the young man shrank from the only operation which could save him, "looked round about, and saith unto his disciples, How hardly shall they that have riches enter into the kingdom of God!"[1]

Here, then, in the teaching of Jesus, are two views of wealth which are apparently in conflict, — the thought of wealth as a trust to be used and the thought of wealth as a peril to be escaped; the physician's prescription for social health, and the surgeon's remedy from social death. Does this variation indicate any inconsistency or ambiguity in the teaching of Jesus? On the contrary, the very essence of his message to the rich is to be found in its twofold quality. It is not impossible for Jesus to unite severity with love. He perceives with perfect distinctness that the most immediate and insidious peril to the Christian life is to come from the love of money. Vulgarity, ostentation, envy, ambition, self-conceit, material standards of happiness — the qualities which make people unspiritual, unteachable, unresponsive to the light — are the attendants of the god Mammon. The issue is therefore undisguised. No

[1] Mark x. 23.

man can serve two masters ; no man can have two Gods. The service of the kingdom demands the whole of a man, his possessions as well as his mind and heart. The teaching of Jesus permits in no case the sense of absolute ownership. No man can say, "Is it not lawful for me to do what I will with mine own ?"[1] A man does not own his wealth, he owes it. Precisely as a business man says to himself, I must invest and distribute a certain sum with special scrupulousness because I administer it as a trustee, under a law which demands of me a special reckoning, so the disciple of Jesus acts in all concerns of his life as a servant who has heard the great word, "Be ye also ready : for in an hour that ye think not the Son of man cometh."[2]

If, then, such a listener to the teaching of Jesus has to confess to himself that he is in any degree owned by his money, if the thought of trusteeship tends to fade and the thought of a right to his possessions has crept in, if he is excusing the unrighteous gain of money by the benevolent use of money, or if he has come to a tacit contract with his soul that his superfluous means shall be the Lord's, and that with the rest he may say, "Soul, thou hast much goods laid up for many years ; take thine ease, eat, drink, be merry,"[3] — then, according to the teaching of Jesus, the absolute and immediate renunciation of wealth is better than any self-deception. "It is

[1] Matt. xx. 15.　　[2] Luke xii. 40.　　[3] Luke xii. 19.

profitable for thee that one of thy members should perish, and not thy whole body go into hell."[1] "For what is a man profited, if he gain the whole world, and lose or forfeit his own self?"[2] In short, the doctrine of Jesus is one of solemn alternatives, in the presence of which each man must test the secrets of his heart. Is he able to look up into his Lord's face at some sudden coming and say, "Thou deliveredst unto me five talents : lo, I have gained other five"?[3] Then his wealth has been his friend to lead him into the eternal tabernacles ; and the Owner of his wealth welcomes him with the word, " Enter thou into the joy of thy Lord."[4] Or must there be, on the other hand, a hiding from so searching a judgment, as of one who has worshipped another god and has left his trust uninvested and unfruitful? Then the quicker and the more rudely the altar of Mammon is overthrown, the safer is that man from the overwhelming rebuke, " Cast ye out the unprofitable servant into the outer darkness : there shall be the weeping and gnashing of teeth."[5]

Let no one fancy, then, that in translating this twofold teaching of Jesus into the language of the modern world he can make of it a more moderate or more tolerant message to the rich than the coarser utterances and more radical programmes of modern agitation. Jesus does not sentimentalize about the duties of wealth ; he sets forth

[1] Matt. v. 30.   [2] Luke ix. 25.   [3] Matt. xxv. 20.
[4] Matt. xxv. 21.   [5] Matt. xxv. 30.

with tranquil severity the alternatives which lie before the rich. If in any case riches obstruct the complete dedication of the life, then Jesus has no objection to offer to the most sweeping of modern demands for the abolition of rich men. Indeed, he goes beyond most of these demands. The modern attack on wealth would content itself if the share of profit which falls to the capitalist class could be greatly reduced. The teaching of Jesus, however, is not a doctrine of economic justice and equitable distribution; he does not ask of a man a fair proportion of his personal profits; he asks the whole of one's gains — and the life which lies behind the gains — for the service of the kingdom; and the problem of economic distribution expands in his teaching into the greater problem of spiritual regeneration and preparedness.[1]

Such is the message of Jesus to the rich. He does not present a scheme of economic rearrangement; he issues a summons to the kingdom. He confronts a man, not with the problem of his commercial rights, but with the problem of his own soul. To many a man, ensnared in the complex and intense conditions of modern life, to many a man and woman tempted almost beyond their strength by self-indulgence, narrow interests, and practical materialism, the message of Jesus comes

[1] See the passage in Paulsen, " Ethik," s. 69, " Wealth is of no worth to the Christian. . . . But wealth is not only without worth; it is a per   Property is in itself not a sin, but to the property-holder it is an immense peril."

with convincing force. Such persons know well that it is hard for those who have riches to enter into the kingdom. They know how difficult it is to maintain religious ideals, genuine simplicity, and breadth of sympathy among the exotic and artificial circumstances of a prosperous life. They see how frequently the possession of riches becomes a curse, and how often the children for whom the father has labored are but the worse for the abundance which he has secured, as though they had asked him for bread and he had given them a stone. They have to confess that it is easier for the poor than for the rich to be poor in spirit. Such persons, however, when they look once more at the world of modern life, observe that the stern demand of Jesus is sometimes met ; that—hereand there— riches are deliberately and consistently held as a trust from God, and the way of service is made broad and straight through the ministry of wealth ; and they recognize the wisdom of Jesus, when, having said so unreservedly, "How hardly shall they that have riches enter into the kingdom of God!"[1] he is still able to say of the man who had faithfully used his many talents, "Blessed is that servant, . . . Of a truth I say unto you, that he will set him over all that he hath."[2]

If, then, on such terms there is a place in the kingdom for the rich, one is led to ask, finally, how wealth, thus regarded as a trust, may be legimately used. Does the teaching of Jesus give an indica-

[1] Luke xviii. 24. [2] Luke xii. 4.44.

tion of those employments of money which make for the purposes of the kingdom?

There seem to be at least three ways in which Jesus welcomes the ministry of wealth as a part of Christian service. First, there is the use of wealth in almsgiving. "Distribute unto the poor, and thou shalt have treasure in heaven." [1] It is important, however, to note that almsgiving, though assumed by Jesus to be a habit of his followers, does not receive from him a high place among Christian virtues. Jesus takes for granted that the consecration of life will lead to the distribution of possessions; but he gives his chief attention, not to the stimulating of almsgiving, but to the correcting of its mistakes and of the false estimate of value often attached to it. Almsgiving must be free from ostentation. "But when thou doest alms, let not thy left hand know what thy right hand doeth." [2] Acceptable almsgiving must be measured, not by the amount of the gift, but by the cost of the gift to the giver. "Verily I say unto you, This poor widow cast in more than all they which are casting into the treasury." [3] Jesus himself, so far as the record shows, gave no alms, unless it can be accounted almsgiving to feed the multitude that they might be attentive to his spiritual message. In the wonderful picture of the Judgment, [4] the commendation of the righteous is not bestowed because they distributed of their abundance to the poor, but because they

[1] Luke xviii. 22.
[2] Matt. vi. 3.
[3] Mark xii. 43.
[4] Matt. xxv. 35 ff.

gave of their personal service to the stranger, the prisoner, and the sick. While, therefore, it is true that almsgiving is accepted by the teaching of Jesus as a self-evident characteristic of his service, it has in itself nothing of that primacy among the virtues which through a great part of Christian history has been attributed to it, and which has made it often a sufficient cover for a multitude of sins.

Very different from the teaching of Jesus concerning expenditure in almsgiving are his allusions to a second use of money, — its ministry to happiness and to beauty. It is only here and there in the gospels that the sense of the beautiful finds expression in the sombre and strenuous life of Jesus, as slanting sunbeams strike through a clouded and threatening day ; but when these rare flashes of æsthetic pleasure slant thus through his teaching they illuminate a side of his character which has been from many devout Christians almost concealed. Jesus looks about him, at the birds of the air and the lilies of the field, and the sheer prodigality and loveliness of their lives make them fit illustrations of the method of God. Jesus sits among the happy guests at a wedding feast and enters joyously into the festive spirit of that scene. He is called a winebibber and publican because he does not sternly shun occasions of genial hospitality and happy companionship. More impressively still his appreciation of non-utilitarian expenditure is exhibited in the story of the woman

with the box of ointment, — a story which fastened
upon the minds of those who heard it so strongly
that it appears in various connections in all four
gospels.[1] The incident presented a clear issue
between the use of money for imaginative symbolism and the use of money for almsgiving. The
disciples "had indignation, saying, To what purpose is this waste? For this ointment might have
been sold for much, and given to the poor,"[2]
Jesus, however, perceives that there are other needs
of human life to be considered besides mere maintenance of life. "Man shall not live by bread
alone."[3] As the woman pours out her prodigal
offering it is as if in answer to the deep human
demand for the beautiful, the suggestive, the sac-
rificial; and Jesus greets her gift as he greeted
the beauty of the lilies, with their suggestion of
that Divine completeness which he desired to reveal.
"Verily I say unto you, Wheresoever this gospel
shall be preached in the whole world, that also which
this woman hath done shall be spoken of for a
memorial of her."[4] Here is the charter of all
undertakings which propose in the name of Christ
to feed the mind, to stir the imagination, to quicken
the emotions, to make life less meagre, less animal,
less dull. "The limit of luxury," a modern worker
among the poor has remarked, "is the power of

---

[1] Matt. xxvi. 7; Mark xiv. 3; Luke vii. 37; John xii. 3.
Compare Stopford Brooke, "Christ in Modern Life," Sermon
XVIII, "Art Expenditure."

[2] Matt. xxvi. 8, 9.   [3] Luke iv. 4.   [4] Matt. xxvi. 13.

sharing." [1]   Expenditure of wealth on art, on education, on music, on the opening of the resources of nature to the weary life of cities, on the emancipation of mankind from commercial standards, on the provision of humanizing and symbolic ways of pleasure, — is not only justified through its elevating and educative effect, but it rests also on the explicit authority of the teaching of Jesus Christ.   It is not always better to spend for such ends than to give to the poor, but it is equally legitimate.   The Christian life would be meagre indeed if it could offer no welcome to the unreflecting and spontaneous sacrifice of the heart.

Both of these services of money, however, — its benevolent and its æsthetic use, — recognized as they are by Jesus, are subordinated in his teaching to a third use which receives from him repeated commendation.   One is almost startled to discover that this most Christian employment of possessions is simply their scrupulous and honorable use in that special work which one is called upon to do. The Christian world has become familiar with a double standard of ethics.   It has refrained from scrutinizing closely the methods by which men get their money, and has reserved its judgment for the methods by which they spend their money. A man in the world of affairs may engage in questionable occupations or undertakings if he redeems himself by the consecration of his spoils. The world's work, it is often felt, demands one

[1] Barnett, " The Service of God," p. 99.

standard of business, and what is described as
"Christian work" demands another standard.
The service of Mammon brings such large returns that it may come to seem contributory to
the service of God. Probably nothing so degrades
the Christian religion in the view of men of the
world as the conformity of Christian churches or
Christian believers to this doctrine of ethical bi-
metallism. To see a man of the double standard
accepted among the saints and a distinction permitted between the principles of the business
world and of the Christian Church, is enough to
drive from the influence of religion many a man
who has no rule of life but to be consistent and
incorruptible in his daily work. He cannot believe
that a debased coinage is valid for religious use.

With this judgment of men of affairs the teaching of Jesus precisely coincides. Jesus has nothing but condemnation for the divided life. The
fundamental principle of his teaching about wealth
is the principle that there cannot be two masters
or two gods. His severest sayings are directed
against the hypocrites, who in their business "de-
vour widows' houses," and in the synagogues
"make long prayers."[1] Consistency is, to Jesus,
the beginning of the Christian life. His judgment, therefore, is not primarily pronounced on
a man as he is praying or giving alms or performing what are technically called religious duties, but as the man is engaged in his common,

[1] Mark xii. 40.

unsanctified, daily business. The pictures of the religious life which the gospels most frequently present are drawn from scenes of the commercial world. A man, going into another country, calls his servants and delivers unto them his goods.[1] A nobleman calls his ten servants and gives them ten pounds, saying, "Trade ye herewith till I come."[2] A man leaves his home and gives "authority to his servants, to each one his work," commanding also "the porter to watch."[3] A man plants a vineyard and lets it out to husbandmen, "that he might receive from the husbandmen of the fruits of the vineyard."[4] Who are these servants, these traders, these porters, these vine-dressers? They represent the persons whom Jesus desires for his disciples; and they are performing precisely that kind of service which he wishes his disciples to render. Who, on the other hand, are the persons who receive from him his most solemn warnings or most terrific condemnation? They are the servants who neglect their trust;[5] the porter who sleeps at his post,[6] the husbandmen who fancy there is to be no reckoning,[7] the trader who deals with his Lord's money less scrupulously than he would with his own.[8] "Out of thine own mouth will I judge thee, thou wicked servant."[9] "What therefore will the lord of the vineyard do? he will come and

[1] Matt. xxv. 14.	[4] Mark xii. 2.	[7] Mark xii. 1–11.
[2] Luke xix. 13.	[5] Matt. xxv. 24–30.	[8] Luke xix. 20–24.
[3] Mark xiii. 34.	[6] Mark xiii. 34.	[9] Luke xix. 22.

destroy the husbandmen, and will give the vineyard unto others." [1] More characteristic, that is
to say, of the Christian life than the most generous almsgiving or the most suggestive æstheticism
is the manifestation of consistent fidelity in the
conduct of one's own affairs. The first searching
of a man's heart should not concern the Christian distribution of his gains, but the Christian
getting of his gains. The highest commendation
of Jesus is given, not to the munificent alms-
giver, but to the faithful steward, the watchful
porter, the scrupulous servant. It was once said
of the Messiah that "his voice should not be
heard in the street"; but, if we may translate
those words into the language of modern business,
it is precisely "in the street" that the message of
Jesus to the rich is delivered; and no self-deception of the prosperous can be greater than the
belief that this judgment of Jesus on the conduct of one's daily business can be mitigated or
transferred.

Who, then, is the Christian rich man? It is he
who recognizes that in the management of his
wealth he is in the presence of a constant and
subtle temptation; that, as Jesus said, there is in
the nature of increasing wealth a peculiar quality
of "deceitfulness," so that the money which is at
first one's servant is at any moment likely to
become one's master. The Christian rich man
knows well that it is hard for him to enter the

[1] Mark xii. 9.

kingdom of God. He observes the characters of many men shrivel in the flame of prosperity. He sees that conditions of luxury, ease, and lack of the friction of life contribute to a slackening of moral fibre. He holds before himself, therefore, the solemn alternatives of Jesus, — the mastery of wealth, or the abandonment of it. Thus the wealth of the Christian rich man becomes to him a trust, for the use of which he is to be scrupulously judged. He administers his affairs with watchfulness over himself and with hands clean of malice, oppression, or deceit. He does not hope to atone for evil ways of making money by ostentatious benevolence in spending it. He is to be judged according to his ways of accumulating wealth as rigidly as for his ways of distributing wealth. He is not hard in business and soft in charity, but of one fibre throughout. His business is a part of his religion, and his philanthropy is a part of his business. He leads his life, he is not led by it. His five talents produce other five. And who is the Christian rich woman? It is she who finds it not impossible to be rich in purse and poor in spirit. She accepts her opportunity watchfully. She knows herself a servant of whom much is required. In the midst of a world of foolishness and vanity she maintains simplicity and good sense. She is equally at home among the rich and the poor. No severer test of the Christian life than this can be proposed for any woman, and no fairer type of character is to be met than that which issues from such a test, having passed through the needle's eye. If Jesus Christ should come again, he would know what it has cost a man to put under his foot the lust of riches, or a woman to keep her heart clean from the temptations of self-indulgence. Into the homes of such men and women, however splendid their homes may be, Jesus would enter gladly, as he entered the home of Zacchæus or that of Martha and Mary. On such a man, on such a woman, he would look with a peculiar love, as he looked on the young man with great possessions. The conflict with Mammon has prepared for such a soul the way to eternal habitations. The servant stands ready for the Master's reckoning, and the Master comes and says: "Well done, . . . enter into the joy of thy Lord."

CHAPTER V

THE TEACHING OF JESUS CONCERNING THE CARE OF
THE POOR

Then shall the righteous answer him, saying, Lord, when saw we thee an hungered, and fed thee? or athirst, and gave thee drink? And when saw we thee a stranger, and took thee in? or naked, and clothed thee? And when saw we thee sick, or in prison, and came unto thee? And the King shall answer and say unto them, Verily I say unto you, Inasmuch as ye did it unto one of these my brethren, even these least, ye did it unto me.

WHEN one turns from the problem of the existence of the rich to the problem of the care of the poor, he enters a region of thought and duty much more familiar to the follower of Jesus Christ. From the first days of Christian history until now the duties of compassion for the unfortunate and of help for the helpless have been among the elementary virtues of the Christian life. The transition made by the ministry of Jesus in the history of philanthropy is hardly less remarkable than the transition made in the history of theology. With the new thought of God came a new love for man. The "Caritas" of the Christian was a fundamentally different quality from the "Prodigalitas" of the Roman.

This statement, however, must be at once

relieved of a common but unjustified form of exaggeration. Modern apologists of Christianity are in the habit of describing the contrast between pre-Christian philanthropy and the charity which followed the teaching of Jesus as a contrast between absolute darkness and dazzling light, a revolution in human relationships which for the first time in history disclosed the meaning of the great word Love. "The world before Christ came," it is freely affirmed, "was a world without love;" "Egoism was the ruling spirit of antiquity;" "The human race had forgotten God;" "The family and marriage were only political institutions;" "Without the gospel society would have been dissolved, humanity would have perished hopelessly in a bottomless abyss;" "Poverty was considered a disgrace that could only be endured by low and bad men."[1] These defenders of the Christian religion err through excessive zeal. It is not only inherently improbable that the virtues of Christianity should have been thrust upon a wholly unresponsive world, as though a flower stuck into a sterile soil should come to bloom, but it is also a superficial scholarship which discovers in the ancient world no good ground for the sowing of such virtues.

[1] Uhlhorn, "Christian Charity in the Early Church," 1883, Ch. I; Schmidt, "The Social Results of Early Christianity," 1889, pp. 107, 115, 139. See also, for further social apologetics of Christianity, C. L. Brace, "Gesta Christi," 1884. Compare the more discriminating treatment in Lecky, "History of European Morals," 1870, Vol. II, Ch. IV.

On the one hand, the Jewish tradition, which Christianity inherited, abounded not only in noble utterances of the sentiment of compassion, but also in elaborate arrangements for the practical relief of the poor. "Blessed is he that considereth the poor;"[1] "He that hath pity on the poor, happy is he;"[2] "Thou shalt surely open thine hand unto thy brother, to thy needy, and to thy poor, in thy land;"[3] "Is not this the fast that I have chosen? . . . to deal thy bread to the hungry, and that thou bring the poor that are cast out to thy house?"[4] — these exhortations represent not only the principles of Old Testament religion, but the actual conduct of the devout. The Hebrew race, throughout its entire history, has been endowed with a peculiar sense of responsibility for its weaker brethren, and in modern life is excelled by no element in any community in thoroughness and munificence of organized charity.[5]

When, on the other hand, we turn to the Roman civilization in which the Christian religion found its expansion and stability, we are confronted, it must be admitted, by conditions of the gravest social corruption and moral decline. These excesses of a debauched and decadent aristocracy, however, do not constitute a complete record of

---

[1] Ps. xli. 1.   [3] Deut. xv. 11.
[2] Prov. xiv. 21.   [4] Is. lviii. 6, 7.
[5] *Charities Review*, Vol. II, p. 21 ff., F. G. Peabody, "The Modern Charity-worker" (addressed to the United Hebrew Charities of New York City).

the social life of the Roman world. By fixing attention on the immorality of the ruling class, and by utilizing such evidence concerning it as is contributed by the Satirists on the one hand, and by the Stoics on the other, it is possible to describe the social life of Rome as one of the most flagrant domestic looseness and most hopeless social decadence. The historical romances which reproduce these conditions of the Augustan age join with the apologists of Christianity in portraying this moral bankruptcy, and the collapse of Roman power through loss of moral virility is the most solemn proof which history provides that righteousness alone exalteth a people. Yet such a judgment, if passed upon the mass of Roman life, would be as extravagant as a judgment of American civilization derived from the literature and the newspapers which find their material in the follies and sins of the luxurious, pleasure-hunting, and unbridled rich. Beneath the depravity of Roman aristocracy and the corruption of Roman government there still survived, especially in the provincial towns, an atmosphere of unspoiled social life in which the ideals of Christianity might naturally unfold.[1]

[1] A just picture of the characteristics of Roman social life may be derived from Friedländer, "Sittengeschichte Rom's," 6. Aufl., 1888–1890, esp. III, 514 ff. ; Keim, "Rom und das Christentum"; Mommsen, "History of Rome," V, Chs. XI and XII ; Pearson and Strong, "Juvenal" (Introduction, chapter on Roman life); Reville, "La Réligion à Rome sous les Sevères " ; Coulanges, "The Ancient City," 1884 ; Church, "The Gifts of Civilization," 1880, 147 ff.

Conclusive evidence of this survival may be derived, for example, from the monuments which
recalled the virtues of the dead. At the very
period when licentiousness and brutality were cor-
roding the life of the luxurious, these silent witnesses testify that in the great body of the population a way of life still prevailed which was tranquil,
domestic, compassionate, unostentatious and calm.[1]
It was in this soil of the surviving traditions of
Rome and the still flourishing traditions of Israel
that the philanthropy of the Christian religion
took root. Without such a soil Christian charity
would have been a seed sown by the wayside.
The expansion of the range and depth of philanthropy accomplished by Christianity was beyond
doubt a mighty transition in the evolution of
human character, but it was not a miraculous
transformation of human character. God had not
left himself without witnesses in the pre-Christian
world. Legal and ostentatious as was the philanthropy of the scribes and Pharisees, the Hebrew
race still maintained in many devout homes its
national virtue of compassion, and in such a home
Jesus was born. Prodigal as were the vices of

(Civilization before and after Christianity); and the striking essay
by Bosanquet on " Paganism and Christianity " in his " Civilization
of Christendom," 1893.

[1] *E.g.* Wilmanns, " Exempla inscriptionorum Latinarum," 1873,
pp. 71, 147, 150, 168, and the touching eulogy of the girl Minicia
Marcella, by the younger Pliny (Ep. V, 16), translated, with a
description of the newly discovered tomb, by Lanciani, " Ancient
Rome in the Light of Recent Discoveries," p. 282.

Roman rulers, the Roman world had not wholly abandoned its ancient ways of domestic integrity and social peace, and among such Roman homes, in cities of the Roman provinces, there was a welcome for the missionary preaching of St. Paul.

Yet, if one may fairly call the perfected rose a different flower from its wayside progenitor, it remains true that the "Caritas" of the Christian spirit was a new virtue, with an aroma of its own. "Christianity," said Mr. Lecky, "for the first time made charity a rudimentary virtue." [1] It is not, however, its rudimentariness which gives to Christian philanthropy a peculiar beauty and fragrance ; it is the scope of its sympathy, the dimensions of its giving, and its recognition of fellowship with lives hitherto ignored or rejected by the world. The worship and the fraternal relations of the first Christians abound in a quality of comprehensive tenderness quite unparalleled either in Rome or in Israel. In the earliest forms of Christian worship are special prayers for the poor, the outcast, the prisoners. "Save among us," concludes the first epistle of Clement of Rome, "those who are in tribulation, have mercy on the lowly ; lift up the fallen ; show thyself unto the needy ; heal the ungodly ; convert the wanderers of the people ; feed the hungry ; release our prisoners ; raise up the weak ; comfort the faint-hearted." [2] The same spirit of tender and self-effacing service

[1] "History of European Morals," II, 84.
[2] Lightfoot, "Clement of Rome," Appendix, p. 376.

is repeated in all the early liturgies, adorns the conduct of the primitive congregations, and illuminates the dark period of theological controversy in which the first fair visions of the Christian Church were so soon to be eclipsed. From century to century this vast enterprise of Christian charity has expanded with the growth of the Church; has atoned for many superfluous or cruel controversies; has brightened the sombre history of monasticism and of the mendicant Orders; and has drawn to the influence of the Christian religion millions of persons who could not have been compelled by threats of perdition, but who could not turn from the witness of love. Never was this sense of responsibility for the poor so profoundly felt by the Christian Church as at the present time. No body of Christians, however humble, can maintain its self-respect without an elaborate organization of compassion and relief. The Church welcomes for itself not only the test of truth, but the test of public utility. "I by my works will shew thee," it says, "my faith." [1] The giving and doing of Christians has become a vast and elaborate form of business. Special churches are established to be agencies of philanthropic work as much as places of preaching and prayer. To many a modern mind which dismisses the claims of Christianity to dogmatic truth, its maintenance is abundantly justified as an instrument of human pity and brotherhood.

[1] James ii. 18.

To all these manifestations of the Christian spirit may be added many vast undertakings of secular charity, which, even when dictated by social and political prudence, depend for effectiveness in large degree on the extraordinary power of the Christian tradition. Official relief is tempered by Christian tenderness, the homes of the poor are brightened by Christian visitation, and many an institution or "settlement" from which Christian teaching is formally excluded is in its effect an instrument of Christian love. Were it not for the general acceptance of this Christian teaching of social responsibility, the burden which the relief of the poor lays upon the self-supporting would not be uncomplainingly borne. Few persons reflect on the enormous sums annually devoted in all civilized countries to works of charity. Public relief in the United States taxes the entire population not less than two dollars per capita for the care of the dependent classes; private benefaction through societies and individuals probably costs the community an equal sum; and when to this is added the amount contributed by the churches for their own poor, and for all forms of philanthropic service, we have a bewildering total to represent the charity of the present age.[1] The same munifi-

[1] Details and statistics of charity in the United States are given in : "Jahrb. für Nationalökonomie und Statistik," 1897 ; C. R. Henderson, "Armenwesen in den Vereinigten Staaten Nord Amerika's" (with many references); and in : Conrad, " Handwörterbuch der Staatswissenschaften," 2. Aufl., 1898; F. G. Peabody, art. "Armenwesen in den Vereinigten Staaten."

cence prevails in other Christian countries. A prodigality of generosity has been reached which the history of philanthropy has never witnessed before, and for which the command of Jesus, " Distribute unto the poor," [1] is in a very large degree responsible. Whatever other teachings of the gospel - may still appear to be impracticable or Utopian, this one command, it would seem, has at last become adequately obeyed.

It is precisely at this point, however, where the Christian conscience might seem to find some satisfaction, and where at least one social problem might seem to approach its solution, that the real problem of charity in its modern form first comes into view. We have already noticed the eagerness and absorbing interest with which the modern social question in all its illustrations turns from the study of effects to the study of causes, from the alleviating of conditions to the examination of those conditions themselves. Here, also, is the mark of modern charity. This prodigious movement of sentiment and compassion is now very generally observed, not with undiscriminating admiration, but with a high degree of suspicion and criticism. What, it is asked, does this vast enterprise of Christian generosity in reality accomplish beyond the selfish satisfaction of the pious givers and the temporary protection and peace of the State ? Is it certain that this enormous expenditure of sympathy and of money is doing more good

[1] Luke xviii. 22.

than harm? Has the volume of poverty grown
distinctly less? Is this prodigality of relief a
matter for self-congratulation and pride, or is it to
be regarded as in many respects a social peril?
Is not a distinguished critic of social tendencies
justified in saying that "the next most pernicious
thing to vice is charity in its broad and popular
sense"?[1]

And if this arraignment of the total effect of
modern charity is in any degree just, should it
not be brought with even more severity against
the special charity of the Christian Church?
Where do hypocrisy and fraud find so many cred-
ulous victims as among the pious? Who are so
emotional in their philanthropy and so hard to
convert to self-restraint and to scientific methods
as the religious people? Where does divided
effort so often duplicate relief and encourage de-
ception as in the schismatic generosity of the
divided Church? Is it not true that Christian
philanthropy has in large degree utilized charity,
not primarily for the good of the receivers, but for
the good of the givers, "simply and exclusively," as
Mr. Lecky remarks, "for their own spiritual benefit"?[2] Was it not this emphasis on almsgiving as
a virtue which soon induced Christians to regard
mendicancy and asceticism as the marks of a saint;
and must not the monastic system, in spite of all

[1] W. G. Sumner, "What Social Classes owe to Each Other,"
1883, p. 157.
[2] "History of European Morals," II, 99.

its noble traits, be described, from the point of view of social progress, as a colossal mistake? Did it not, as Mr. Lecky goes on to say, "withdraw multitudes from all production, encourage a blind and pernicious almsgiving, encourage habits of improvidence among the poorer classes, paralyze all energy, and prove an insuperable barrier to material progress"? Are there not still surviving in many branches of the Christian Church this false estimate of poverty and this morbid satisfaction in pious zeal? Are there not even more radical criticisms which open from this reconsideration of Christian charity? Should a social order which has thus failed to eradicate poverty be permitted further trial? Is not the continued distinction of wealth and poverty, which gives to Christian philanthropy its opportunity, an outright confession that Christianity is a failure? Is not the whole work of charity an insult to those who claim, not a share in the rich man's bounty, but a right to the rich man's possessions? Ought there to be any poor? Is not this alleviating service of Christian charity rightly described by the modern revolutionist as an anæsthetic administered to the poor to keep them from realizing their condition?

These questions lead us beyond the problem of charity to the problem of industrial revolution and reconstruction, and must be for the moment postponed. It is enough to notice that in the relief of the poor we are confronted by the most serious and searching scepticism concerning both the methods and the spirit of charity as commonly administered. There must be, it would seem, a reconsideration of the first principles of Christian compassion. Is this beautiful and bountiful obedience to the instinct of Christian love in which, as has been believed, the Christian spirit most perfectly utters itself, on the whole, doing more good than harm; and may it not soon be regarded, as the history of monasticism is now commonly regarded, as the witness of a splendid mistake, of which the future will say, as was said of the charge of Balaklava, that it was magnificent, but not war?

If, then, an issue of this nature presents itself between the modern conception of social progress and the common practice of Christian charity, what are we to conclude concerning the authority of Jesus as a guide for our philanthropy? Must we regard his teaching as unadapted to a scientific and complex age, the beautiful survival of a remote and Oriental world? Is it possible for the poor man of the present time to receive with gratitude such a message as, "Be not anxious for your life, what ye shall eat";[1] and is it any more possible for the rich man of the present time to obey the saying: "Give to him that asketh thee, and from him that would borrow of thee turn not thou away"?[2]   One who would answer these questions cannot content himself with a general impression derived from the habits of philanthropy which have prevailed among the followers of

[1] Luke xii. 22.   [2] Matt. v. 42.

Jesus, but must return, with closer scrutiny, to the teaching of Jesus himself; and such reëxamination of that teaching discovers it to be by no means so impracticable as its critics have often assumed it to be, or so demoralizing as its adherents have often forced it to appear. On the contrary, the teaching of Jesus, when considered, not in its letter, but in its dominating spirit, has extraordinary applicability to the needs and problems of modern philanthropy, and provides in itself the best corrective for those grave errors in charity which have been committed by Christians in their Master's name.

As one thus approaches the teaching of Jesus concerning the care of the poor, he is first of all struck by its peculiar tenderness and consideration for all who are unfortunate or distressed. Jesus bears the burden of the poor always on his heart. When he sends word to the Baptist of the signs of his ministry, he uses the words of Isaiah, "The poor have good tidings preached to them"; [1] and when, again, in Nazareth he reads the same passage, and "the eyes of all in the synagogue were fastened on him," he says of himself, "To-day hath this scripture been fulfilled in your ears." [2] Throughout his teaching Jesus enforces an extraordinary principle of moral classification. He is amazingly merciful to all burdened lives, even when those lives are sinful; and, on the other hand, he is peculiarly severe in

[1] Matt. xi. 5.   [2] Luke iv. 20, 21.

his judgment of the arrogant, the self-satisfied,
the purse-proud, or the consciously holy. "Come
unto me," says his message of comfort, "all ye
that labour and are heavy laden;"[1] "Blessed are
the meek,"[2] "the poor in spirit,"[3] "ye poor;"[4]
"Him that cometh to me I will in no wise cast
out."[5] The care of the poor is thus a self-evident and elementary part of Christian discipleship.
Such sayings as: "Give to the poor,"[6] "Distribute
unto the poor,"[7] "The poor ye have always with
you,"[8] represent a corollary of the gospel, a way
of life which will necessarily happen as one seeks
the kingdom of God. If the "little flock" of
his disciples obey his teaching they will "give
alms," and make for themselves "purses which
wax not old," for "where your treasure is, there
will your heart be also."[9]

It should be observed, however, that in these
beautiful utterances of comprehensive pity, and
these categorical demands for the relief of the
poor, there is not at once indicated the precise
manner in which this relief is to be conveyed.
"Give to him that asketh thee,"[10] is indeed a
dictum of the gospel, but the duty it enforces
does not carry with it a positive declaration as
to what one shall give, or with what intention
he shall give, or under what limitation or prin-

[1] Matt. xi. 28.   [5] John vi. 37.   [8] John xii. 8.
[2] Matt. v. 5.   [6] Matt. xix. 21.   [9] Luke xii. 32–34.
[3] Matt. v. 3.   [7] Luke xviii. 22.   [10] Matt. v. 42.
[4] Luke vi. 20.

ciple his giving shall occur. The teaching
of Jesus concerning the poor is, therefore, not
exhausted in this undiscriminating demand for
almsgiving. Many a giver, carelessly distributing to the poor, fancies that he is satisfying the
demands of Jesus Christ; and many a more conscientious disciple, refusing to be prudent or self-
controlled in giving, leans on the words of his
Master, "Give to every one that asketh thee";[1]
when in reality these acts, which intend to express
obedience to the teaching of Jesus, may be absolute disloyalty to its true intention. Here, as in
so many other instances, the easy acceptance of
the letter of the gospel obscures the larger doctrine of the spirit. For the prosperous to imagine
that thoughtless almsgiving satisfies the demand,
"Give to the poor,"[2] is as superficial an interpretation of the gospel as it is for the poor to
imagine that mendicancy is endorsed by the saying of Jesus, "Ask, and it shall be given you."[3]
The teaching of Jesus, in its essential unity, lies
quite behind these scattered utterances which
seem to encourage heedless and hurtful relief. It
is a teaching which must be drawn, not only from
his many sayings about the poor, but also from his
habitual way of dealing with the poor; and, thus
collated and summed up, it is a teaching much
more profound, and very much more difficult to
obey, than his followers have been on the whole
inclined to believe.

[1] Luke vi. 30.　　　[2] Matt. xix. 21.　　　[3] Matt. vii. 7.

In tracing this inner spirit of the teaching of Jesus there must be first recalled two general principles of the gospel which have been already observed as governing the conduct of Jesus toward the rich. One of these is his relatively low estimate of almsgiving as a virtue. He assumes this form of charity, as we have said, to be a corollary of the religious life; he is ready with his praise of the man who can say, "The half of my goods I give to the poor";[1] he even sets forth as a test of God's acceptance, not theological correctness or ecclesiastical conformity, — but loving and humble service. "Come, ye blessed of my Father," he says, "inherit the kingdom prepared for you. . . . Inasmuch as ye did it unto one of these my brethren, even these least, ye did it unto me."[2] Yet, praiseworthy as Jesus assumes the habit of almsgiving to be, his allusions to it are in many instances not in terms of commendation, but in terms of solemn warning. He observes the abuse, the ostentation, and the commercialism of much which passes as charity. "When therefore thou doest alms," he says, "sound not a trumpet before thee;"[3] "Let not thy left hand know what thy right hand doeth."[4] In the story of the Good Samaritan[5] the disbursing of money for relief appears to be one of the least important incidents. The priest or the Levite might have subscribed for the care of the sufferer without

<hr />

[1] Luke xix. 8.   [2] Matt. xxv. 34, 40.   [3] Matt. vi. 2.
        [4] Matt. vi. 3.   [5] Luke x. 30–36.

R

proving himself thereby a "neighbor." The rich
men, "casting their gifts into the treasury," [1] were
viewed by Jesus with a lofty scorn because "these
did of their superfluity cast in unto the gifts," [2] but
his face lighted up with joy when he saw one poor
widow bring an offering which was to be, not commercially counted, but spiritually weighed. "Of a
truth I say unto you, This poor widow cast in more
than they all." [3] Meeting, as Jesus did, from day
to day all forms of suffering and mendicancy, there
is no record of his giving alms. When he announced the signs of his ministry he did not
open the book where it is written, "Thou shalt
surely open thine hand unto thy brother;" [4] he
turned to the greater, though to many a poor
man the less welcome, message of the prophet,
"The poor have good tidings preached to them." [5]
In the story of the Last Supper there seems to
be, beneath the conversation of the Teacher and
his friends, a difference of mind concerning almsgiving. The disciples, we read, thought, because
Judas had the bag, that Jesus had said to him
"that he should give something to the poor," [6]
while in reality it was of something infinitely
removed from almsgiving that Jesus spoke to
Judas. Indeed, it seems probable that the traitor
was more inclined to almsgiving than Jesus, for
it was Judas who, but a few days before, had said
to his Master, "Why was not this ointment sold

. . . and given to the poor?"[1] In short, Jesus
regards almsgiving as a virtue, but as a virtue
demanding constant watchfulness, discipline, and
humility. Charity, in this form, is one of the most
elementary, yet one of the most misleading, traits
of Christian character. Its rank among the virtues of the kingdom depends, not upon its munificence, but upon its conveying the spirit of sacrifice
and consecration. "Woe unto you," Jesus goes
so far as to say to the Pharisees, . . . your inward
part is full of extortion and wickedness. Ye
foolish ones, . . . give for alms those things which
are within."[2]

The second aspect of the teaching of Jesus — to
be recalled in connection with the problem of charity
as in connection with that of wealth — is the doctrine of stewardship. What is true of the whole
conduct of life is true of the special duty of benefi-
cence. While there are many other possible direc-
tions of consecrated activity, that on which Jesus
most repeatedly dwells is the conscientious devotion of life to that special trust which the individual finds committed to his hands. Here is a sphere
of charity of which the philanthropist, as a rule,
takes slight account. It is entirely possible to
manifest the scope and beauty of Christian love
without going beyond one's daily business or one's
commercial opportunity. Indeed, the special commendation of Jesus, bestowed upon the faithful
servant,[3] the diligent steward,[4] and the watchful

[1] John xii. 5.   [2] Luke xi. 39–42.   [3] Matt. xxv. 21.   [4] Luke xii. 42.

porter,[1] seems to indicate that, to his mind, the best opportunity for Christian service is provided by the business of daily life. This is a conception of business behind which many persons might be inclined to hide, as though the processes of investing and bartering and employing made up the sum of Christian benevolence. It is not, however, a gospel of Mammonism which is taught by the gospel of Christ. He finds no intrinsic dignity in buying and selling. He views the world of trade, on the contrary, from above, in the light of his clear distinction, "Ye cannot serve God and mammon." [2] To the self-considering and grasping man of business he speaks one of his most solemn warnings, "When ye shall have done all the things that are commanded you, say, We are unprofitable servants ; we have done that which it was our duty to do." [3] Stewardship, in the teaching of Jesus, is not mere shrewdness, or enterprise, or success; it is the superadded and uncommercial fidelity which discovers among the interests of Mammon an opportunity for the generous and personal service of God. A business man may so administer his affairs that they shall be either a social peril or a social advantage, an obstruction to the general welfare or a channel of Christian benevolence. If the business principles to which one conforms are honorable ; if his dealings with his employees are just, consistent, and personal ; if he anticipates the tidal nature of industry and provides for con-

[1] Mark xiii. 34.   [2] Matt. vi. 24.   [3] Luke xvii. 10.

tinuity of employment ; if his prosperity brings reward to all concerned in procuring it ; if his adversity is shared by employer with employed, and the distinction of hands and head is merged in the corporate responsibility of all, — such a person may not be known as a philanthropist but merely as a working-man with whom one wants to work, and his stewardship may not be charity in its technical sense, and may, indeed, lose much of its worth if it becomes tainted with the patronage or condescension of charity. Yet, even if such conscientiousness in business is not charity, it at least makes unnecessary much of what is known as charity, and corrects, in its own sphere, those derangements of the business world which bring as their consequences poverty and the need of its relief. Thus, the roots of charity lie in the larger problem of the industrial order, and the most unquestionable and most effective philanthropy is to be found in industrial justice, progress, and peace. The doctrine of stewardship does not exclude other ways of caring for the poor, but it lays as the foundation of judicious charity the scrupulous administration of one's own business as a contribution to the kingdom of God.

Nor is this teaching of Jesus for men alone. Many a woman in the modern world needs to learn that Christian charity, in a very different sense from that commonly accepted, begins at home. It is a mockery of Christian obedience to be zealous in the care of the poor who are at a distance, and to fail in considerateness to those who are in one's own employ. It is more uncharitable to yield to the mania for cheapness in one's commercial purchases, than to refuse alms to a beggar in the street. To do the latter is to feel a temporary twinge of personal self-inquiry ; to do the former is to become in so far responsible for cheap work, cheap wages, cheap morality, cheap disease, and death. It is a still graver offence to obey the saying of Jesus, " Distribute unto the poor," [1] and to leave unfulfilled that command of the apostle, " Owe no man anything." [2]   The mark of the unrighteous steward was that he was set to render an account for his master,[3] and used the money for spurious philanthropy. The same condemnation should be passed on one who figures on subscription lists of charities, and delays the payment of just commercial dues. "These ye ought to have done, and not to have left the other undone." [4]   The doctrine of stewardship has many branches, but its roots are to be sought in the elementary opportunities of the shop and the home.

Such are some of the preliminary aspects of the teaching of Jesus concerning the care of the poor. It is a teaching which subordinates almsgiving and weighs the general conduct of life. The teaching has a distinctly modern note. It is in unison with the precept of organized charity,

[1] Luke xviii. 22.   [3] Luke xvi. 2.
[2] Rom. xiii. 8.   [4] Matt. xxiii. 23.

"Not alms but a friend"; it counts as the first principles of the relief of the poor, the bettering of industrial conditions and the abandoning every form of industrial injustice. Yet that which seems a modern note is in reality its note of universality. Jesus, here as elsewhere, is looking at the world from above, with his hope set on the comprehensive principles of the kingdom of God, and from this point of view the special problem of the care of the poor is seen to be, not circumscribed by schemes of temporary relief, but a part of the universal problem of redeeming and renewing human character. If the mind of Jesus had been turned from its supreme intention even by his compassion for the beggars who flocked about his path, he would have scattered alms among them with as short-sighted and prodigal a generosity as many of his modern followers have permitted themselves in their Master's name; but being primarily concerned with the revelation of God in the souls of men, Jesus surveys the problem of charity in its larger relations; and that broader horizon of his teaching gives him reserve, sanity, and comprehensiveness of view.

These preliminary considerations, however, do not lead to the conclusion that the teaching of Jesus has no immediate and positive instructions to offer about the care of the poor. On the contrary, as one draws nearer to his actual dealing with specific cases of relief, and observes his conduct in its practical details, the word which has been preserved to us by the loving hand of Paul proves itself characteristic of the method of Jesus, "It is more blessed to give than to receive." [1] These specific instructions issue for the most part from the second social principle of Jesus, while his general view of the care of the poor, as we have just seen, proceeds from his first social principle. His wisdom in charity comes of his viewing the problem from above, his method in charity comes of his approaching the problem from within.

It is difficult to overestimate the significance of the fact that in the relation of Jesus to the poor he deals almost exclusively with individuals. He had compassion, it is true, on the multitudes and fed them, but this was explicitly announced by him to be "because they continue with me now three days and have nothing to eat: and I would not send them away fasting, lest haply they faint in the way." [2] His compassion for the beggars, the blind, the poor, the sick, is, almost invariably, an individualized, painstaking pity, with special adaptation to each separate case. It does not seem to occur to him that he might multiply the effect of his power, and by a single effort heal or comfort many. He knows no other way of relief than that the giver should put himself in loving and vital relation with the receiver, and establish the contagion of the strength-communicating life.

The summary of this teaching of individualized relief is to be found in the story of the Good

[1] Acts xx. 35.   [2] Matt. xv. 32.

Samaritan,[1] — a story of such exquisite completeness that one is tempted to study it as a work of
art and to prize each phrase as a separate gem.
The fundamental beauty of the story, however,
lies in the setting of all these details round one
central lesson. The lawyer, after quoting from
the earlier social legislation the saying, "Thou
shalt love thy neighbour as thyself,"[2] goes on
to ask from Jesus an interpretation of this law
of friendliness. Jesus replies that the test of
friendship is in the painstaking quality, the wise
adaptation, and the continuity, of friendly service.
There lies by the roadside what modern charity
would describe as a "case," a stranger, stripped,
half dead, and in need of a friend. Neither the
priest nor the Levite, it may be believed, are
brutal. They hurry by because they know that
the friendship which the case demands means an
expenditure of more time and trouble than they
can afford. Both are on their way to important
duties. Either of them would gladly report the
"case" to the proper authorities at Jerusalem, but
their own time and their own personal service
are precisely what they cannot spare, and they
pass by on the other side. The Samaritan also
is in haste. Up that hot and shadeless valley
he is driving his beast, laden with oil and wine
for the Jerusalem bazaars. His compassion, however, conquers his prudence. He halts, goes to
the stranger, assuages his wounds, lifts him on

[1] Luke x. 30–35.   [2] Lev. xix. 18.

his own beast, brings him to a wayside inn, provides for his care, and gives assurance that he shall not be forgotten. Nothing can describe with more precision the exact programme which scientific charity has by degrees worked out to guide the visitation of the poor — first, friendly compassion, then the relief of temporary necessity, then the transfer of the case to restorative conditions, finally the use of money, not as alms for the helpless, but to maintain continuity of relief. It was to the "host," not to the "case," that the "neighbour" gave his money, saying, "Take care of him ; and whatsoever thou spendest more, I, when I come back again, will repay thee." [1] Here is a method of relief which may appear elementary and archaic among the vast organizations and instrumentalities of modern charity. It may seem as if this simplicity of method could have no place in the complex conditions of modern life. This view, however, was precisely the view of individualized charity which was, in all probability, held by the Pharisee and the Levite. They too were involved in so many and such serious interests, that the help of the helpless must of necessity be deputed to others, and they trusted for the provision of relief to the elaborate organizations of charity which existed in their nation. The chief obstacle, that is to say, to Christian charity, now as then, is the preoccupation of the individual with his own affairs

[1] Luke x. 35.

and the consequent dependence upon impersonal methods of relief; and the reform in method now proposed in the name of scientific charity is, in reality, nothing else than a return to the principles of the Good Samaritan.

Two words sum up the change of method advocated at the present time by scientific charity. The first word is classification; the second is anti-institutionalism. In the first place, it is observed that the relief of the poor under modern conditions has become too complicated and varied an affair to be dealt with in any single way. In the homogeneous social life which once prevailed in small and isolated towns, charity was simply the helping hand of a neighbor held out to the unfortunate or disabled by his side. In the great modern city, on the other hand, charity deals with many distinct types; and a method which deals with these types indiscriminately leads to social demoralization and disaster.[1] Of such distinct types the most conspicuous are three. In the first place there are what may be called the "can't-works," the aged, sick, and defective, who must receive gentle and continuous consideration; in the second place there are the "out-of-works," able to labor but temporarily unemployed, for whom work must be found; and to these two separate classes must be added as a third and distinct type the "won't-works," the professionally idle, vagrant,

[1] *Charities Review*, March, 1897, F. G. Peabody, "The Modern Charity-worker."

mendicant poor. To deal with these three types under one method is to do harm to all. To house the worthy poor with criminals is to insult them; to provide the out-of-works with alms instead of with work is to degrade them; to maintain the won't-works in idleness is to become responsible for the permanence of a vagrant class. Classification, the discrimination of types, flexibility and adaptability of method, — these are the elementary principles of scientific charity. Pity for one type, work for another, correction for the third, must be offered; and these three distinct demands call for three distinct ways of administration. The non-effective and the willingly idle must not be permitted to hang about the necks of those who have both the capacity and the desire to rise. The movement of social life is like the movement of an army in the field. There is the march of the effective troops, and there is also the merciful attendance of the Red Cross nurses, caring for the wounded, tending the sick, and mitigating the hardships of battle. One cannot say that nursing is less noble or less essential than fighting; but one must say that it ought not to impede or embarrass the fighting capacity of the army. After all, the campaign must be fought through, not nursed through; and the central problem is not to relieve those who fall by the way, but to maintain the fighting army in effectiveness and discipline.[1]

[1] *Charities Review*, July, 1897, F. G. Peabody, "Developing the Up-draught,"

Here enters the second principle of charity reform, — that of anti-institutionalism. Institutions are almost necessarily undiscriminating in method. They deal with masses of poverty under general rules of administration, and even if the mass be of varied stuff when it enters the institution, it is likely to be, when it comes out, of one type, and that the lowest. The levelling effect of institution life is peculiarly threatening, as we have already noted in speaking of the family, to the character of children. To throw the infinitely varied types of childhood, good and bad, promising and depraved, into the uniformity and homelessness of an institution is to level the best with the worst, and to lessen in all the spirit of self-control and personal initiative. "The institution boy," said one of the most observant students of child life, "makes the poorest kind of apprentice. He is saved from becoming a tough to become an automaton." [1] A good institution is, it is true, better than a bad home; but while on that account institutions must exist for the rescue of the degraded, it is precisely this contact with the degraded which threatens the morals of the better type. Thus, for children first of all, and as far as possible for all cases of need, the hope of permanent amelioration of life lies in the escape from mass treatment and in the adaptation of relief to the individual case. The right place for a child is in a home, where he can

[1] J. A. Riis, "The Children of the Poor," 1892, p. 277.

be dealt with as a separate individual; and right relations with any home or any life among the poor can be established only as each case is approached as a new problem, making a new demand on the giver's insight, patience, and love. The vast and costly experiments which have been undertaken in wholesale relief have brought us at last to the most elementary principles. The new charity proceeds from consolidation to individualization. The elevation of the poor is not to be accomplished by mechanical devices of legislation or organization, as though poverty were a solid mass under which social jack-screws might be inserted to lift the whole; it is to be accomplished only as one life reaches down and lifts up another life by the communication of strength and the contagion of personality. Individualization of relief, in other words, means simply that a busy man or woman of the modern world halts, lifts, tends, cares for, and is continuously responsible for that definite person who must be cared for or redeemed. The last word of scientific poor-relief is a reiteration of the teaching of Jesus.

Why is it, then, it may be asked, that this natural and Christian method of relief has been so largely supplanted by complex and vicarious arrangements of charity, so that, instead of being neighbors to a poor man, we are subscribers to a society for his relief? It is obviously because the Christian ideal of social service demands more time, thought, and care than we are for the most part either able or inclined to give. To most persons it appears, as it appeared to the priest and the Levite, impracticable to interrupt the business of life by personal service of the unfortunate. The special offering which is demanded — the offering of one's self — is a gift which is in many instances already mortgaged to other duties; and the second best contribution — that of indirect and deputed help — seems all that can be made. For many persons this is a legitimate self-defence. There are circumstances in many lives where one cannot be at the same time both a faithful steward and a Good Samaritan. This admission, however, does not lessen the significance of the teaching of Jesus. That teaching still enforces the truth that vicarious, official, institutional relief, however well administered, is in its very nature a substitute for that which in a perfected society would be done by individuals for individuals in the name of Christian love. Impersonal and deputed care, even if well designed, is but an artificial makeshift for personal and continuous service; and the only justification of vast and elaborate arrangements of public and private charity is the proof that they provide an adequate substitute for that personal offering which individuals are not prepared to make.[1]

[1] Compare, on this point, the English and the German theories of poor-relief: Fowle, "The Poor Law," 1881; Aschrott, "The English Poor Law System," 1888, and his "Die Entwicklung des Armenwesens in England seit dem Jahre 1885," 1898; Mackay,

From this principle of individualization, then, are to be derived the two corollaries which give to the relief of the poor its direction and its discretion. In the first place, it becomes evident that the more scrupulously this substituted relief is disentangled from officialism, routine, and anonymousness, and the more directly it is made an instrument of wise and loving personality, the nearer it approaches both to scientific charity and to the teaching of Jesus. The friendly visitor among the poor, bringing neither patronage, nor alms, nor self-consideration, nor religious propagandism, but sunshine, courage, refinement, employment, patience; the social settlement set in the squalor and dulness of the great city, not for exhortation or condescension, but for sheer neighborliness; the beautiful union which is sometimes witnessed of official duty with loving and personal care, — these are the finest products of modern philanthropy. We speak, in commercial language, of the "plant" of a modern enterprise of charity, but the plant of charity grows for no other purpose than that there may issue from it the flower of personal devotion. We devote much time to devising the mechanism of charity, but that mechanism revolves for no

"The English Poor," 1889 ; and "Parliamentary Report on the Elberfeld Poor Law System," 1888 (see the evidence of C. S. Loch, p. 88 ff., "We cannot have an out-relief policy in London — the German experience shows. We have not citizenship enough to administer it ") ; Böhmert, " Armenwesen in 77 deutschen Städten," 1886 ; Münsterberg, " Die Armenpflege," 1897 ; *Forum*, December, 1892, F. G. Peabody, " How should a City care for its Poor ? "

other purpose than to communicate the power of personal love.

The second corollary from the principle of individualization is still more important. If the machinery of relief is to be substituted for personal service, it must be so organized as to be a real, even if not a perfect, substitute. The only excuse which can justify a prosperous life for declining in its own person to undertake the part of the Good Samaritan is, that it has at its command an alternative which is likely to be more judicious and persevering. When a beggar confronts a Christian in the street, there are presented to the Christian but two alternatives. Either he must himself, with painstaking and continuous devotion, deal with the case; or else there must be already provided by the community an adequate substitute for his own time and service. The third possibility, — that of blank refusal of friendly aid, — does not present itself to the mind of any person who has once heard the great command, "From him that would borrow of thee turn not thou away." [1] When a pious giver refuses to dismiss even the probably fraudulent beggar without relief, lest here and there one worthy mendicant shall suffer, that giver is obeying a perfectly legitimate instinct. The Good Samaritan asked no questions of the stranger before helping him. The word of Jesus, "Give to him that asketh thee," is a word which modern science must obey.

[1] Matt. v. 42.

s

Obedience to the instinct of compassion, however, is not inconsistent with common sense. The demand laid on one to give does not involve the necessity of foolish giving. Much time and money may be wisely spent in devising ways of administration which shall legitimately relieve the individual from the obligation of personal service. The problem of judicious relief is not to suppress the instinct of benevolence, but to redeem that instinct from pernicious employment in indiscriminate aid; and to this end it is absolutely essential that the substitutes for personal aid which the organization of charity may offer shall be accessible, discriminating, sympathetic, safe, and easy to understand.

By these steps we are brought to that method in charity which is most clearly indicated by the teaching of Jesus. If, as we have seen, it is not almsgiving which Jesus primarily inculcates, and if, nevertheless, he desires to establish a personal relationship between giver and receiver, what is the special gift which, according to his teaching, is to pass from the strong to the weak? It is the gift of power. The life of Jesus, as it touches the lives of the degraded, the defective, or the despairing, communicates to them new courage, hope, and self-respect. Jesus, when approached by persons crying for deliverance from some temporary trouble, often leaves the trouble itself unrelieved, in order to reach some permanent and underlying need which they had never dared to think of satisfying. The blind beggar [1] had sat, it seems, daily on the curb in Jerusalem, where the devout had tossed him their alms; and the beggar had come to hope for nothing more than that he might receive more alms. Jesus gives him no alms, but bends over him, anoints his eyes, and communicates the power of sight for which he had not asked, so that the man is no more a beggar, and the people say, "Is not this he that sat and begged?" Other blind men cry to Jesus, "Have mercy on us, thou son of David"; [2] and again his mercy is shown, not in pity alone, but in the communication of power. "Believe ye," he says, "that I am able to do this?" They say unto him, "Yea, Lord." And he answers, "According to your faith be it done unto you." [3] It is the same with the compassion of the followers of Jesus.[4] The gift of Paul to the impotent man is not of help to the helpless, but of help to self-help. "Stand upright on thy feet," [5] says the apostle, "and he leaped up and walked." The word of Peter to the palsied man is, "Arise, and make thy bed." [6] With still more accurate reiteration of their Master's intention Peter and John meet the man at the Beautiful Gate. He has been "laid daily at the door of the temple," [7] for no other purpose than to ask alms of those that entered into the temple, and seeing Peter and

[1] John ix. 1–12.
[2] Matt. ix. 27.
[3] Matt. ix. 28, 29.
[4] Acts ix. 34.
[5] Acts xiv. 10.
[6] Acts ix. 34.
[7] Acts iii. 2.

John, "he gave heed unto them, expecting to receive something from them," but Peter answers : "Silver and gold have I none; but what I have, that give I thee. In the name of Jesus Christ of Nazareth, walk." [1] In other words, the teaching of Jesus considers primarily, not a man's apparent needs, but the man himself. The mind of Jesus is ever on that kingdom which is to come through the consecration of personality. In each case, therefore, the fundamental problem is that of converting helplessness, self-distrust, and conscious incapacity, into the courage, power, and initiative of a life contributory to the kingdom. Rise; stand upon thy feet; open thine eyes; walk,— such are the great words of Christian charity. The gift it desires to impart is not a temporary contribution of relief, but a permanent increase of opportunity and capacity. Christian charity is not the "Prodigalitas" of the classic world; it is, "Caritas," the love which, for the sake of others believeth, hopeth, endureth all things.

This is a teaching most fruitful in its consequences for the charity of every age. The relief of destitution by the provision of food and shelter still remains a duty of any well-ordered State. "Every society," as a historian of the English Poor Law remarks, "upon arriving at a certain stage of civilization, finds it positively necessary for its own sake . . . to provide that no person . . . shall perish for want of the bare necessaries

[1] Acts iii. 5, 6.

of existence." [1] Such provision of the necessities of life, however, even when made on the most liberal terms, does not bring us within the region of Christian charity. It is simply a political and social necessity, insuring public peace and decency. Christian charity begins where political prudence halts. Its task is not that of quieting the restless poor by the anæsthetic of relief; it is the task of quickening the discouraged life with the stimulant of individualized love. Christian charity takes account not merely of conditions, but of capacity. Its problem is not that of relieving destitution, but of developing possibilities. Its aim is to convert a shut-in, stunted, spiritually defective life into a healthy, effective, contributory factor of the kingdom.

Here, then, is the hierarchy of charity. Essential but most elementary is its maintenance of physical life. Food, drink, and shelter are for the poor, precisely as they are for the prosperous, essential preliminaries of a humanized life, but, considered as ends of charity, they are as inadequate as when, in more luxurious forms, they are regarded as ends of life by the self-indulgent and ostentatious rich. A rich man's life consisteth not in the abundance of things which he possesseth, and a poor man's poverty does not consist wholly in the lack of such possessions. Beyond the provision of these necessities in the life of the poor, as in the life of the prosperous, lies the demand

[1] Fowle, "English Poor Law," p. 10.

for the communication of capacity. The need of the poor man is not bounded by relief under his conditions; he needs also courage to better his conditions. The aim of charity is to give, not only comfort, but power; not merely a greater equality of circumstances, but a greater equality of opportunity. The problem of the prosperous, as we have already seen, is to own one's wealth instead of being owned by it, and to make of money the instrument of social service; and with the same end in view charity should approach the problem of the poor. How can a life, it asks, weak, ignorant, and beset by grave temptations, be endowed with self-mastery and self-respect, and become an instrument of the kingdom of God? Thus, in the hierarchy of charity, above the work of the food-kitchen and the temporary refuge, is to be set the elevation of the poor through industry, in the farm and the shop; through education, in the gymnasium and the trade school; through the home, under conditions where a home can be realized; through employment, such as can be fairly called a living; through the glimpse of beauty and the purifying of love. Much of the charity most in vogue even among Christian churches is but slightly in accord with the teaching of Jesus. It does not, indeed, give stones when asked for bread; but it gives bread when asked for hope, power, pleasure, life. Man lives indeed by bread, but not by bread alone. It is no just appreciation of the poor which leads one to imagine that they want most of all to be fed. They want, precisely as the prosperous want, that life which is more than meat, — the sense of capacity, of joy, of hope ; and of all the sources of their degradation the most perilous is the loss of their courage and faith. "The highest ambition of the beneficent," said Mr. Spencer, unconscious perhaps that he was reiterating the teaching of Jesus, "will be to have a share—even though an utterly unappreciable and unknown share — in the making of man." [1]

How is it then, one may finally ask, that this quality of power is communicated ? It is communicated, answers the teaching of Jesus, not chiefly by legislation or by organization, but by contagion. It is not a mechanical, but a vital, force. The power of Jesus and his disciples to be obeyed when they say, "Rise, stand upright, walk," proceeds from the contagious quality of the good life. And why is our poor-relief, even when conscientious and scientific, so often without this communicative power ? It is because we are not, as a rule, good enough to do much good. A stream cannot satisfy thirst if its springs are dry. The best intention to lift the poor must fail if there is no lifting power to apply. The poor can not be pushed up, they must be drawn up. "I, if I be lifted up from the earth," said the Master, "will draw all men unto myself." [2] The lifting force of social life is not compulsion, but, like that of the planetary world, attraction. "If I bestow

[1] "Principles of Ethics," II, 433.   [2] John xii. 32.

all my goods," says the apostle, "to feed the poor,
. . . but have not love, it profiteth me nothing."[1]
Indeed, the goods thus bestowed are likely to be
so foolishly bestowed as to profit the poor also
nothing. In short, the problem of being good
and that of doing good are not two problems, but
one; and many a disheartening experiment in
well-intentioned charity forces a community or
an individual to a reëxamination of their own
hearts.

What, then, is Christian charity? It is certainly
not that haphazard and ostentatious giving which
is seen of men and has its own reward of praise
and self-esteem; nor is it a prodigal giving for
distant needs, atoning for neglect in one's own
immediate cares; nor is it emotional compassion
posing as more pious than intelligent method.
Christian charity is, first of all, rational, prudent
and wise. It surveys its problem from above,
with detachment, perspective and horizon. It
begins with its nearest duties of business and
of home. It satisfies itself, not by offering temporary relief, but by the permanent elevation of
the level of desires. It is educative, disciplinary,
comprehensive, just. Christian charity, therefore,
deals primarily with the individual. It may employ large methods, but it is not lost in them. It
seeks the one sheep that is lost. Its aim is not
the perfecting of a system, but the saving of a
soul. It looks behind conditions for the person

[1] I Cor. xiii. 3.

who is ensnared in them. It expects, not to make
the world soft, but to make characters strong
enough to live in a hard world. It judges all
undertakings of poor-relief by their contribution
to virility, initiative, and self-help. Its care is
devoted, not to providing crutches for the weak,
but to providing ways in which the weak shall
be able to obey the command, " Rise up, stand
upon thy feet, walk." Finally, Christian charity
finds its instrument for this educative and permanent relief in the communicative power of
Christian personality. "Only he who has," said
Emerson, "can give, he on whom the Soul de-
scends alone can speak." The complex mechanism of modern charity is but a medium through
which works with security and effectiveness the
power of a good life. The mechanism of charity
is economic; its motive power is spiritual. The
science of charity is a work of organization, the
sentiment of charity is a work of contagion. The
first step toward doing good is in being good.
The elevation of the poor is retarded by many
faults of social mechanism, but it is much more
retarded by ignorance, impatience, self-regard and
injustice, in those who help the poor; and one of
the keenest joys of human life is felt by those
who, dismissing great schemes of social improvement, give themselves to the patient service of a
few discouraged lives, and discover that power
may be communicated to those lives and may
lift them into self-respect and hope. To these

self-effacing servants of the common good Jesus spoke his most unmeasured praise: "Come, ye blessed of my Father, inherit the kingdom prepared for you from the foundation of the world: Inasmuch as ye did it unto one of these my brethren, even these least, ye did it unto me." [1]

[1] Matt. xxv. 34, 40.

CHAPTER VI

THE TEACHING OF JESUS CONCERNING THE INDUS-
TRIAL ORDER

𝔗𝔥𝔢 𝔖𝔬𝔫 𝔬𝔣 𝔪𝔞𝔫 𝔠𝔞𝔪𝔢 𝔫𝔬𝔱 𝔱𝔬 𝔟𝔢 𝔪𝔦𝔫𝔦𝔰𝔱𝔢𝔯𝔢𝔡 𝔲𝔫𝔱𝔬 𝔟𝔲𝔱 𝔱𝔬 𝔪𝔦𝔫𝔦𝔰𝔱𝔢𝔯.

In all that has been thus far said of various
social questions there has been a sense of incompleteness and fragmentariness, as though in each
case we were dealing with one aspect of a more
inclusive problem. The problem of the family
expanded as it was considered, until it was seen
to involve further issues of economic and social
life; the problems of wealth and of poverty opened
into larger questions of ownership and occupation,
of work and idleness, of the distribution of products and the utilization of leisure. Wealth, we
observed, should contribute, first of all, to economic justice; charity must provide, first of all,
for economic self-help. Round these inner circles
of social relationship which hold the family and
the community sweeps the larger circle of the
industrial order. If we extend the radius of the
family circle, we enter the sphere where men
meet as employers and employed. If we follow
the circumstances of wealth and poverty out to
their margin, we pass into consideration of the
use, or the misuse, or the incapacity to make

267

use, of industrial opportunity. The philosophy of socialism, it is true, grossly exaggerates this truth when it announces that this relation of concentric circles is a relation of cause and effect, as though the key of every social question must be sought in the industrial problem. The family is more than an economic unity, and is modified by other motives than those of economic interest; wealth and poverty spring from many other causes besides industrial conditions. Yet it is none the less true that the industrial question environs like an atmosphere the whole body of social life. The integrity of the family is profoundly affected by economic changes and defects ; wealth and poverty are inevitable social facts under the prevailing conditions of ownership and of industry.

What, then, is this industrial problem in which all other social questions are thus deeply involved ? The problem has two aspects. On the one hand is the form which it assumes, on the other hand is the spirit which it represents. These two aspects of modern industry must be carefully distinguished and may be considered in turn.

The form of the industrial problem has become determined by the amazing expansion of modern industrial methods, the vast combinations of employers and of employed, and the enormous prizes which reward strategy or good fortune. These characteristics of modern industry have brought the factors of industry to a situation which appears not unlike a state of war. The forces of production are maintained on a war footing. The modern "captain of industry" is of the same stuff which makes great generals. He is a farsighted, determined leader of men, with his mind fixed on a single end, and with an industrial army at his command. Over against him are many opposing forces, — the force of his immediate competitors in business, the remoter hostility of competing nations, and, more than all, the spirit of industrial disaffection stirring in his own troops and inciting to mutiny. More and more the industrial world finds itself occupied by two armed camps, — the force of the employed combined to meet what seem the aggressions of the employers, and the force of the employers combined to resist what seem the unreasonable demands of the employed. Strikes and lock-outs are temporary raids across the enemy's frontier; organization on both sides disciplines and drills the contending armies ; industrial arbitration, like international arbitration, offers itself as a last substitute for battle ; while, hanging on to the skirts of the two forces, threatening the employers with violence, and weakening by its competition the power of the employed, is that unorganized and shifting mass which we call the army of the unemployed. Even international diplomacy is now concerned quite as much with questions of industrial warfare as with political issues, and the treaties, the competitions, and the territorial expansion of nations have become more and more the weapons of the warfare of trade.

If this is a true picture of the competitions of industry, then the present form of the industrial question becomes plain. It is a question of adequate substitutes for economic war. It is the problem of industrial peace. This peace may be sought in many ways. Sometimes it is temporarily secured by the sheer superior force of one party in the conflict. Such peace, however, in industrial, as in political life, is unstable and disturbed. The force that has been crushed waits for its occasion to renew resistance. Industrial slavery, like political slavery, prophesies revolution. Again, industrial peace is sought by retreating from the field of industrial conflict into the uncompetitive tranquillity of some communistic society, as pious souls in other days retreated from the conflicts of the world to the monastic life. Such peace, however, is even at its best for the few only. The hurrying world of modern industry passes by these undertakings, as a railway train in Italy sweeps by some lingering monastery on its secluded height. Sometimes, again, industrial peace is actually established within a limited circle, as in the substitution of mutual interest for commercial antagonism in the coöperative system. Finally, such peace is sometimes dreamed of as universal and permanent, within a coöperative commonwealth of common ownership and industrial democracy. All such schemes and dreams assume that the present war footing of industry, like that of nations, is both extravagant and unnecessary ; all are wit·

nesses of a widespread desire for industrial disarmament. The labor movement of the present day is in its form an industrial peace-crusade.

It may be urged, indeed, that to picture the field of economic activity as a battle-field is grossly to misconceive the nature of modern industry. Employers and employed, it may be pointed out, are in reality, not hostile forces, but allies and partners in production. They prosper or suffer in the end together, and to assume a discord between their interests is not only unjustified, but suicidal. Is it not, it may be asked, a strange form of peace-movement which begins by exaggerating the antagonisms of industry, and proposes as its end a social revolution which shall completely abolish the capitalist class ? These are reasonable criticisms. There is nothing in the nature of industrial life even under present social conditions which necessarily involves it in war, or which forbids the most idyllic relation of mutual confidence and affection. Here and there such a relation in industry actually exists, and instead of a state of war we have an " industrial partnership," or an " *Institution patronale*," or a "*Famille ouvrière*." Such an admission, however, only brings more clearly before us the real nature of the prevailing industrial warfare. It is not an antagonism which is inherent in economic life. In fact, it is at bottom not an economic antagonism at all. Like most declarations of war it proceeds, as a rule, from unanticipated and emotional causes.

The industrial conflict of the present day is simply the form assumed by that profound sense of moral distrust which is stirring in the hearts of the hand-working class, and expressing itself in a passionate demand for industrial justice.

At this point we observe the second aspect of the industrial question. Its form is determined by economic conditions, but its spirit expresses a moral protest. Fifty years ago the great body of hand-workers were ignorant and unobservant; now they have eaten of the fruit of the tree of knowledge and their eyes are opened. They look about them at the prodigious productiveness of modern industry, and it seems plain to them that the division of profits is unjust. That which incites them to revolt is not that they earn less than before, but that they know more than before, and feel and desire infinitely more. That which makes them dissatisfied is not that their economic condition grows worse, but that their emotional and intellectual life is wakened and demands new satisfactions. They observe that in the general progress of economic prosperity the relative gain which falls to them seems slight when compared with the enormous accumulations of superfluous wealth which fall into the hands of the few. Thus they find themselves the agents in producing wealth of which they obtain but an insignificant share, and they cry out with passionate indignation as against a grievous wrong. No one gets any just impression of what is called the labor movement who does not thus recognize the interior spirit which expresses itself in these demands for industrial change. The economic programme proposed by an agitator may be so demonstrably speculative or Utopian that one can hardly imagine it as commanding the loyalty and self-sacrifice of plain and practical minds; but that which sustains the programme is the emotion to which it gives a form. Many a misdirected and indefensible enterprise becomes significant when one hears the ethical undertone which it is trying to express. Beneath the tossing and conflicting waves thrown up upon its surface are the profounder movements of emotion which rise like great rollers out of its depths.

Here, then, are the two aspects of the industrial problem—its economic form and its ethical spirit; its form, a search for industrial peace; its spirit, a demand for industrial justice. What, then, we go on to inquire, has the teaching of Jesus to do with these things? Has he any instructions to give concerning the form of the industrial order? Has he any suggestions to offer concerning the spirit of industrial life?

To the first of these questions a general answer may be given without delay. It is impossible to imagine that any specific instructions concerning the form of modern industry shall be derived from the teaching of Jesus. The social horizon of that teaching was as remote from the problems of modern industrial life as though it were

T

in another planet. To turn to Jesus for categorical instruction concerning industrial organization, individual initiative, or social control, is as preposterous as to inquire into his views concerning modern inventions or modern politics.[1] Such phrases as Christian economics, in the sense of organizing modern life under the direct regulation of Jesus, or Christian sociology, as a science of modern society directly defined by Jesus, or Christian socialism, as a form of government prescribed by Jesus, are as much without justification in the teaching of Jesus as it would be to speak of Christian astronomy or of Christian science.

To the obvious fact that Jesus could not have given specific legislation for a social situation which was undreamt of in his day, there must be added the fact that he for the most part declined to give such legislation even for those social problems which were actually brought before him for judgment. The Pharisees take counsel "how they might ensnare him in his talk,"[2] and bring to him the question of tribute. Does he teach submission to Rome, or is he a political revolutionist? Jesus, however, perceives their

---

[1] H. Holtzmann, " Die ersten Christen und die soziale Frage," s. 21, "To speak of the economics of the New Testament is, in my opinion, as impossible as to speak of its dietetics (Acts xv. 20, 29), its hermeneutics (I. Cor. ix. 9, 10), its astronomy (Matt. ii. 9, 24, 29), or its meteorology (Matt. xvi. 2, 3 ; Luke xii. 54, 55).

[2] Matt. xxii. 15 ; Mark xii. 13 ; Luke xx. 20.

craftiness, and dismissing their specific question, solemnly announces to them his higher law. You show me, he says, this coin with the image of Cæsar on it, the symbol of your obedience to him; but show me also whether there is stamped upon your hearts the mark of an equal loyalty to God. At another time Peter brings to him the social question of the temple tax.[1] Are the followers of Jesus ecclesiastical reformers who are to consider themselves free from the Mosaic law? Again Jesus refuses to be entangled in such a question. He and his friends, he says, are like the sons of kings, who are free from the obligation of tribute, but whose freedom from such obligation makes tribute no burden. Let us not lower ourselves, he teaches them, to such a controversy, but let us discharge ourselves of non-essentials so as to cause none to stumble, and then use our freedom for the work of the king's sons. Still again, there is brought to him the problem of the distribution of property. "Master," says one, "bid my brother divide the inheritance with me;"[2] and, as before, Jesus first refuses to deal with the question as though he were a social reformer, and then proceeds to translate the question of inheritance into a question of the spiritual life. "Man," he first sternly answers, "who made me a judge or a divider over you?" and then, looking about him at the listeners eagerly awaiting his views on the distribution of property, he passes from the ques-

[1] Matt. xvii. 25.   [2] Luke xii. 13–15; compare Ex. ii. 14.

tion which had been asked him to the motive which prompted the question. "Take heed," he says, "and keep yourselves from all covetousness." "A man's life consisteth not in the abundance of the things which he possesseth." Finally, and with still greater candor, Jesus, at the close of his life, declines jurisdiction in social and political affairs.[1] The authority which he claims for himself is not that of a ruler, but that of a revealer. "My kingdom," he says to Pilate, "is not of this world." "Now is my kingdom not from hence." "To this end am I come into the world, that I should bear witness unto the truth." These solemn affirmations completely distinguish the mission of Jesus from that of a social legislator or revolutionist. No specific form of industrial arrangement can fairly claim to reproduce a design prescribed by him.

Yet it by no means follows from this conclusion that the teaching of Jesus has no bearing on modern industrial life. On the contrary, when one recalls the social principles of the gospel, they are at once seen to involve decisions concerning many economic schemes of the present day. Jesus, in the first place, surveys industrial life, as he does all other human interests, from above, as a means to that spiritual education of the race which is to have its end in God's kingdom. The world of business affairs is to Jesus not an isolated sphere of human activity, for it lies within the

[1] John xviii. 36, 37.

large horizon of his spiritual purpose. This point of view, however, involves two judgments concerning industrial life, which at first sight appear to be not wholly consistent. On the one hand, the view from above removes Jesus from all primary concern with questions of economic profit or loss. His teaching concerning industrial life is moved by a great desire to direct the forces of ambition and emulation away from economic satisfactions toward spiritual ends. "Lay not up for yourselves," he says, "treasures upon the earth, . . . but lay up for yourselves treasures in heaven."[1] "Be not therefore anxious for the morrow:" "Seek ye first his kingdom and his righteousness."[2] The rich man, according to Jesus, says to his soul, "Soul, thou hast much goods laid up for many years;" but God answers him, "Thou foolish one, that layest up treasure for himself, and is not rich toward God."[3] On the other hand, this distinct subordination of economic interests and gains does not carry with it, in the teaching of Jesus, a note of asceticism. Over against his assurance that the "true riches" are not mere products of industry must be set the no less obvious fact that he moves with sympathy and appreciation through the world of industrial activity, and finds in it, not material for censure, but for example and praise. The sower in the field,[4] the shephe[l] with his flock,[5] the merchant buying pearls,[6] the fisher

[1] Matt. vi. 19, 20. [3] Luke xii. 19–21. [5] John x. 2–5.
[2] Matt. vi. 33. [4] Matt. xiii. 3–8. [6] Matt. xiii. 45, 46.

casting his net,[1] the laborer waiting to be hired,[2] the householder digging his winepress,[3] even the tax-gatherer[4] and the soldier[5] doing the duty assigned to them, — these are not types of conduct to which Jesus alludes in words of admonition or regret, but are, on the contrary, types which he naturally utilizes as texts of his discourse. The persons whom he most sternly rebukes are not those who are deeply absorbed in the world of work; they are those who, having work given them to do, shirk it or leave it half done. The servant who trades with his master's talents[6] is commended; but the rebuke of Jesus is for him who did not put his money at the banker's, whence he might have received his own with interest. The praise of Jesus is for the shepherd who scours the hillside to find the one missing sheep;[7] for the scrupulous housekeeper who lights her lamp and diligently sweeps her house until she finds the one lost coin.[8] Jesus, that is to say, while announcing that the real treasure is in heaven, and while describing the man who looks for it on earth as a fool, none the less repeatedly teaches that scrupulous fidelity in one's daily business commands the commendation of God. "If therefore ye have not been faithful in the unrighteous mammon, who will commit to your trust the true riches ?"[9]

---

[1] Matt. xiii. 47, 48.
[2] Matt. xx. 6.
[3] Matt. xxi. 33.
[4] Matt. ix. 9.
[5] Matt. viii. 5–13.
[6] Matt. xxv. 16, 17.
[7] Luke xv. 4–6.
[8] Luke xv. 8, 9.
[9] Luke xvi. 11.

Is there an inconsistency between these two aspects of the teaching of Jesus, — its subordination of industrial results and its commendation of industrial fidelity? On the contrary, it is precisely the union of these traits which marks the Christian view of industrial life. The Christian moves through his experience in the world as the judicious traveller passes through an interesting country. Such a traveller does not permit himself to be altogether absorbed in the routine or discomfort or mechanism of his journey, but recognizes the resources and charms which disclose themselves along his way. He finds delight in incidents which to many would be irksome. He deals cheerfully with the details of travel for the sake of those ends of travel which he desires to attain. He is laying up treasure which cannot be lost, and where his treasure is there his heart is also. It is this problem of uniting alertness with repose, devotion to details with perception of an end beyond details, which, for great numbers of persons, represents the personal aspect of the industrial question. How to combine delight in work with deliverance from the despotism of work is to many an unsolved problem. If they give their hearts to industrial activity they become its slaves ; and if they give their hearts to spiritual interests, then they become unprofitable servants in the world of work. How is it, then, that peace of mind and a sense of unity are to be attained in these divided and discordant lives? They are to issue, according to the teaching of Jesus, from the discovery of spiritual significance in that work which one is called to do, and this discovery is made when one looks at his experience from above. The religious point of view is not one which distracts the mind from its work, but one which gives the mind insight into its work. The world of industry abounds in resources and satisfactions, well worth attaining at the cost of much dull routine along the way, and the larger end justifies the painstaking fidelity. Details which might seem irksome when viewed from below, become dignified and honorable when viewed from above. The man who trudges through his work without a thought beyond his dusty road, and the man who will not go that way at all because the road is dusty, equally miss the lesson of industrial life. The view of that life from above finds a place for its activity and fidelity within the horizon of a Christian ideal. The Christian is faithful in that which is least, and through that fidelity enters into the joy of that which is much.

To the doctrine of horizon as applied to industrial affairs must be added the Christian doctrine of industrial progress. Jesus not only surveys the world of business from above, but approaches it from within. His method begins with the individual. His supreme intention is that of making persons who shall in their turn make the kingdom of God. Here, then, is a test to be applied to any form of industrial life. Instead of estimating the economic advantages or disadvantages of a form of industry, the teaching of Jesus weighs it as a contribution to character. Of any industrial programme or proposition Jesus asks, not whether it will pay, or will be extravagant, or difficult to administer; but rather, what sort of people will it be likely to produce. In the making of goods will it make good characters; or, while making cheap products, will it also make cheap men? This is a point of view from which any commercial system may be fairly considered. We may apply the test, for example, to the industrial order now prevailing, and we have already observed one type of character developed by such a system — the character of the alert, audacious, commanding personality, the "captain of industry," the Napoleon of finance. These are qualities worth producing. No new economic arrangement can permanently supplant the present industrial order unless it tends to produce an equally virile and forcible type of man. At this point, however, a new series of questions begins. Are these qualities of leadership, it is asked, the finest moral product of which the present order of industry is capable? If this is true, is it not possible that a better arrangement of economic life might produce a more generous and noble type? When, still further, we pass from the character of the captains of industry to that of the privates in the industrial army, what, under our present commercial system, do we find to be the normal product of moral virility? Does the method of the great industry tend to develop initiative, intelligence, and versatility in the great mass of subordinates, or does it rather develop a stunted, dehumanized, mechanical type? Is it true that the private in the great factory, as in a fighting army, is often the better soldier when he is no longer a free person, but more completely a part of the machine? Questions like these make the burden of that social complaint which expresses itself in what we call the labor movement. Unreasonable and misdirected many of these industrial demands may be, yet they utter a cry from the ranks of industry for a more human, free, and reasonable life. They are the passionate writhings of suppressed and defeated personality, buried under the mountain of overwhelming routine, as the struggling Enceladus lay beneath the heaving Ætna. The pathos and the dignity of the labor movement is to be found in this reiteration of the teaching of Jesus, that economic schemes are to be estimated by their contribution to personality. The economic order is an instrument for the making of men; and a struggle which, like the present labor movement, brings forth, even through much travail, more thoughtful and loyal men, is the birth struggle of a better social world.

This principle of Jesus which subordinates profit to personality may be applied as a test of any industrial scheme. Indeed, the principle sometimes interprets industrial movements whose economic success would be on other grounds inexplicable.

An interesting illustration of this truth is provided by the coöperative system of Great Britain. It is a movement which has had a most chequered history of economic success and economic failure. Under some conditions the extraordinary expansion of the coöperative system would lead one to conclude that those plain weavers of Rochdale had discovered a panacea for economic ills ; under other conditions, apparently not less favorable, coöperation has met with immediate disaster. What is it which makes the coöperative plan at one point so fruitful and at another point so barren in its results ? It is the fact that the system is not merely an economic device, but much more fundamentally a moral movement. Coöperation depends for its success, not only on its commercial principles of cash payment and deferred benefit, but on the moral qualities of patience, thrift, and loyalty, which make that character known as the "coöperative man." "The cardinal doctrines of its faith," said Professor Marshall at the Coöperative Congress of 1889, "are . . . firstly, the production of fine human beings, and not the production of rich goods, as the ultimate aim of all worthy endeavor. Secondly, he who lives and works only for himself, or even only for himself and his family, leads an incomplete life ; to complete it he needs to work with others for some broad and high aim." [1] The achievements of the coöperative system in Great Britain are moral victories. Millions of plain peo-

[1] A. Marshall, "Inaugural Address at Ipswich," 1889, p. 2.

ple have been trained in the instincts of coöperative life, and the industrial profits have been the
natural results of the coöperative sentiment. Yet
this ethical quality of the coöperative system is at
the same time its limitation. Where the coöperative man is lacking, the economic scheme fails.
What has wrecked many sanguine enterprises in
coöperation has been, as a rule, not their business
difficulties, but the lack of patience, self-sacrifice,
or honor among the coöperators themselves. The
passage of Cæsar across the Alps, Mr. Holyoake
once said, was most seriously delayed by the number of asses accompanying the troops, and the progress of coöperation is retarded by the same animals.
Thus the coöperative system is a striking illustration of the teaching of Jesus. The first condition of success in coöperation is a constituency of
self-respecting and loyal persons. A few plain
people associate themselves in a coöperative enterprise, quite unconscious that they are in any degree bearing witness to the social principles of the
gospel; they apply themselves to the simple problem of conducting a shop or factory with fidelity,
self-sacrifice and patience; and as their work expands they seem to themselves to have made a
good commercial venture, while in fact, in one
corner of the great industrial world they are illus-
trating the principle of the Christian religion, that
industrial progress begins from within.

Such is the point of view, and such is the way of
approach, which are indicated by the teaching of

Jesus in its relation to forms of industry. Those methods and programmes are most consistent with the gospel which enlarge the horizon of work, and which make work more personal, responsive, originative, and human. All ways of education which enlarge the scope and significance of industrial life are justified and suggested by the teaching of Jesus. Such education is economically justified because it provides the community with better artisans, mechanics, printers, plumbers, and carpenters; but it is much more fundamentally justified because it enriches and strengthens personality, teaches respect for honest work, and illuminates work with the sense of beauty and the love of truth. Whatever thus converts a machine into a man, permitting the worker to look at his work from above, and to interpret it from within, has a place in the Christian programme of industrial life. It not only contributes to economic stability, but it perpetuates the teaching of Jesus Christ.

There still remains to consider in this connection the third social principle of the gospel, which, in fact, dominates and interprets the other two. The doctrine of social horizon and of social origin meet in the social ideal of Jesus Christ. He surveys the world as the field of the kingdom of God, and inspires individuals to become instruments of that kingdom. When one thus recalls this central and commanding hope of Jesus concerning the future of the world, and the language he habitually used concerning it, there is certainly in his ideal a striking likeness to many a hope and dream of the modern industrial world. The kingdom of God, according to Jesus, is to be found in the gradually realized, and finally perfected, brotherhood of man. This kingdom is to come in ways which the wise and prudent do not anticipate. It is by no means certain that it will come through a peaceful process of social evolution. "I came not to send peace, but a sword!"[1] It may be ushered in even by force: "The kingdom of heaven suffereth violence, and men of violence take it by force."[2] It will be a kingdom hard for the rich to enter, but the poor, the blind, the maimed, and the lame will be welcomed into it.[3] It is a kingdom already potentially existing in the world, like a seed already planted which will soon grow up to overshadow all the herbs.[4] Finally, it is a kingdom in which a new system of labor will prevail;[5] a system in which the workers will be paid, not according to their service, but according to their needs. "It is my will to give unto this last, even as unto thee. . . . So the last shall be first, and the first last."[6] Is there not in these varied descriptions of the coming kingdom of God an extraordinary anticipation of many modern prophecies of industrial revolution, and of an international and universal brotherhood where there shall be no rich and no poor, where from each shall be demanded according to his powers, and to each shall be given according to his needs? Is not

[1] Matt. x. 34. [3] Luke xiv. 21. [5] Matt. xx. 1–16.
[2] Matt. xi. 12. [4] Matt. xiii. 31. [6] Matt. xx. 14, 16.

this hope of comprehensive social unity even now expanding like the mustard seed, unobserved by many of the wise and prudent of the world? May it not be said of the fulfilment of this social programme, "Watch therefore, for ye know not the day nor the hour;"[1] and again, "This generation shall not pass away, till all these things be accomplished"?[2] How are we to interpret the obvious likenesses of these two social ideals, that of the modern teaching of collectivism and that of the teaching of Jesus concerning the kingdom of God?

We have already more than once recalled one answer which is frequently given to this question. These likenesses, it is said, are so obvious and striking that the two social ideals must be regarded as practically identical. Jesus was a socialist. If he had lived in our day he would have been a Messiah of this new gospel which defends the poor against the rich, and opposes the domination of capitalism with an ideal of industrial justice. "There can be no manner of doubt," remarks a German theologian, "that the fundamental ideals of socialism are to be referred back to Jesus."[3] Much as there is, however, in the language of the gospels to encourage this view, such an identification of the teaching of Jesus with modern socialism has never thoroughly commended itself even to socialists themselves. The more thought-

[1] Matt. xxv. 13.   [2] Matt. xxiv. 34.
[3] O. Holtzmann, "Jesus Christus und das Gemeinschaftsleben der Menschen," 1893, s. 14.

ful and scholarly advocates of radical reform have felt, though they have not always analyzed their feeling, a subtle difference, as of a change of atmosphere, when they passed from the region of their social schemes and approached the spirit of the teaching of Jesus. One breathes in the gospels a climate of tolerance, mercy, and many-sidedness, which is far from stimulating to the socialist's temper, and moderates the bitterness of his indictment of the world. Glad as organized socialism might be, therefore, to appropriate for its programme the spiritual forces of the modern world, it has never felt quite secure in accepting as an ally the impulses of the Christian religion. It has permitted the religious sentiment to exist "as a private affair," but there has been little inclination to a formal alliance. The undivided allegiance demanded by the socialist ideal would be, it is felt, less heartily rendered if at the same time one were encouraged to be loyal to the ideals of Jesus Christ.

The suspicion thus manifested by the thoughtful socialist proceeds from a sound instinct. When one passes from the level of the social-democratic programme to the level of the teaching of Jesus, there may be indeed much likeness in the landscape which one surveys, but a difference of elevation is immediately perceptible, and a change is felt which is nothing less than climatic. A new quality of social feeling, a new flora, as it were, of social virtues, a new diversity and comprehensiveness of social judgments, prove that, though the outlook be the same, we stand at a greater height. Thus it happens that to those who habitually look at life in terms of the socialist creed the teaching of Jesus is full of surprises. Sympathy with the socialist aim Jesus constantly exhibits, yet he cannot be regarded as a safe teacher. The socialist never feels quite sure what Jesus may say next. Many of his sayings read like orthodox socialist doctrine; but, of a sudden, there is uttered something quite destructive of the socialist creed, and it is as if among familiar plants one should come suddenly upon a flower which belonged to quite another and a sunnier zone.

Consider, for instance, that saying of Jesus which has received much commendation from socialist writers, — the principle of remuneration proposed for the laborers in the vineyard.[1] All who are ready to work are, it is announced, to be paid an equal and a living wage. The fact that one man has a better chance in life does not guarantee him a better compensation. "It is my will to give unto this last, even as unto thee."[2] Was ever a parable of industry more prophetic of the modern programme? Does it not almost anticipate the new formula: "Man for man, time for time; from each according to his capacity, to each according to his needs"? Was it not this

[1] Matt. xx. 14, and xix. 30; Mark x. 31; Luke xiii. 30.
[2] Matt. xx. 14.

U

saying of Jesus which made the text of Mr. Ruskin's splendid indictment of the economics of competition and the basis of his doctrine of a non-competitive, just exchange ? [1]

If this saying, we must answer, were the whole of the teaching of Jesus concerning industrial life, we should certainly have a most sweeping doctrine of social revolution. No sooner, however, do we turn a few pages of the gospel, than we find a conception of social life apparently in complete opposition to the doctrine of equality, — a law of essential and cumulative inequality. The servant, we read, who has been trusted with five talents doubles them in trade, and his master says to him, " Well done, . . . for unto every one that hath shall be given," [2] and on the other hand, the servant to whom least was intrusted receives the rebuke, " From him that hath not, even that which he hath shall be taken away." The same principle of cumulative returns is applied by Jesus not only to gain in money, but also to gain in knowledge. To the disciples who have already learned something of the new gospel it is given to know more. They shall learn of the " mysteries of the kingdom of heaven," [3] but to others it is not given ; so that one man in his spiritual knowledge shall have " abundance," and from another

---

[1] " Unto this Last " (concluding paragraph), " Go forth, then, weeping, bearing precious seed, until the time come and the kingdom when Christ's gift of bread and bequest of peace shall be Unto this Last as unto thee."

[2] Matt. xxv. 23, 29.   [3] Matt. xiii. 11.

"shall be taken away even that which he hath." [1] The same law is applied again to the capacity of observation or of judgment. The man who takes heed "how he hears," finds his capacity of hearing and of judging enriched, while he who covers his lamp with a vessel or puts it under a bed finds secret things less and less manifest, until even that discernment which he seems to have is by degrees taken from him. [2]

What is to be said of this principle of cumulative returns and cumulative losses, in money, in learning, or in capacity? The first thing to say of it is, that it is a principle which is unquestionably and profoundly true. The whole experience of life testifies to the enlargement of capacity through its use, and to the shrinking of unused faculties as of unused limbs. One of the most effective spurs of human effort is the assurance that energy once set in motion gets momentum; that it is the first accumulation of money, or of skill, which costs; that returns of money or of work are like seeds, which, when once planted, grow while man sleeps; and that such acquisitions, once attained, may be even transmitted from parents to children and prolong the action of the law of cumulative returns. The opposite aspect of the truth is no less obvious. A world of cumulative gains must be one of cumulative losses. It is a world, therefore, where inequality is an essential aspect of human life, in

[1] Mark iv. 25.
[2] Luke viii. 16–18; Mark iv. 25; compare Rev. ii. 5.

which unused capacity declines, and undeveloped resources shrivel into weakness and impotency. The poor man often grows poorer for no other reason than because he has not that little which would give him his chance to get more; the evil life propagates itself from generation to generation until it passes from ignorance to vice, and from vice to sheer degeneracy; trouble breeds trouble; mistakes lead to further mistakes; one lapse from virtue tempts to deeper sin, until they which have not seem stripped even of that which they have. Here, however, is a social law which seems absolutely inconsistent with the socialist ideal,— a law, indeed, which represents that view of the world against which the socialist most hotly contends. When, therefore, the socialist reads no less than six times in the first three gospels that this is a world of essential inequality, must he not hesitate to claim for his cause the support of the teaching of Jesus, and may he not fairly wonder how this assurance of cumulative returns could have come from the same lips which announced equality of payment as the law of the Lord's vineyard?

How is it, then, that there can legitimately exist within the teaching of Jesus two principles of industrial life which seem so completely irreconcilable? To announce at one moment that the last comer shall be first, and at another moment that he who has shall have more, is from the point of view of economic teaching sheer self-contradiction.

Jesus, however, is not thinking of economic profits or losses, but of the education of human souls for the kingdom of God ; and he observes that in God's training of men the two principles coexist, — the principle of cumulative returns and the principle of proportionate judgment. On the one hand, a man is led to do his best because he has perceived that capacity, power, and resources either develop or shrink, so that to him who hath is given and from him who hath not will be taken away. On the other hand, the same man is aware that the judgments of God will be determined, not by absolute achievements, but by proportionate fidelity. "To whomsoever much is given, of him shall much be required ; "[1] and of him whose opportunity has been least, but who has been faithful to it, the great word may be spoken, "It is my will to give unto this last, even as unto thee."[2] Thus the two principles which are economically inconsistent are spiritually allied. At the evening, when the Lord of the vineyard comes, saying, "Call the labourers, and pay them their hire,"[3] the man who has achieved little may hide himself behind his successful brethren, saying, "I am but an unprofitable servant ; my opportunity has been slight, and my gains are few," but the principle of a proportionate judgment gives him the place which his desire and his fidelity have won.

"'Tis not what man does which exalts him, but what man
    would do," —

[1] Luke xii. 48.   [2] Matt. xx. 14.   [3] Matt. xx. 8.

says Browning's David; and the same note is struck by Rabbi Ben Ezra,

> "What I aspired to be
> And was not, comforts me."

The true relation between the social ideal of Jesus and the social ideal of the modern revolutionist comes then, at last, into view. The Christian doctrine of the social order holds the programme of the socialist, and holds much more. There is a place in the gospel for the principle of equal compensation; but there is also a recognition of the opposite truth of unequal endowment. The relation, therefore, between the two social ideals is like that of two parallel lines lying in different planes. There is the same direction in both, and, if one regards their direction only, the one line of social movement may be easily mistaken for the other. The two lines lie, however, on different levels of experience; they have different starting-points and different ends, and their paths can never meet. The motives from which the two proceed, and the ideals toward which they lead, are in different zones of human desire. The socialist programme begins with the observation of economic needs and ends in an ideal of economic change; the teaching of Jesus begins with the sense of spiritual need and ends in the ideal of a spiritual kingdom. Both social teachings move through the life of the real world, giving laws to its industry and direction to its energy; but the aim of the one is to make the poor rich, and the aim of the other is to make the bad good. The socialist philosophy finds in economic transformation the cause of character; Jesus counts on character to bring about economic transformation. The one plan builds up social life from below, the other derives it from above. The coöperative commonwealth is to rise out of a new arrangement of production; the New Jerusalem is to descend out of heaven from God.

Here are two ideals of the social order which, parallel though their lines may be, are by no means identical. It is one thing to think of industrial change as a means of spiritual education, and it is quite another thing to think of industrial change as a means of abolishing private property. The socialist programme proposes an industrial system which must depend for its perpetuation on unselfishness, magnanimity, and simplicity of character; but it makes no adequate provision for the training of these virtues.[1] Nationalize the means of production, it is said, abolish the capitalists, and then the same persons who are to-day ambitious, competitive and self-seeking will become public-spirited, generous, and self-controlled. Cleanse the outside of the cup and platter, and the inside will be purified of ravening and wickedness. Extend the line of economic development, and it will run up into the qualities of

[1] Compare, 3ter Evang.-soz. Kongress, 1892; A. Wagner, " Das neue sozialdemokratische Programm," s. 96 ff.

the kingdom of God. The teaching of Jesus looks at the world of industry from precisely the opposite point of view. It passes no judgment on economic programmes, however radical those programmes may be. It affirms, however, that, until industrial life is lifted to the level of a moral opportunity and taken in hand as a trust from God, no economic scheme, however promising it may be, has the assurance of effectiveness or permanence. There may be grave difficulties to be overcome in the existing machinery of industry, but the chief difficulty with industrial life, according to the teaching of Jesus, is not mechanical, but moral. The devil has tempted modern men as he once tempted Jesus, showing them all the glories of the world, and saying, " All these things will I give thee, if thou wilt fall down and worship me ; " [1] and many a modern man has accepted the terms. According to Jesus, the root of the industrial question is not in conditions, but in character. It has become a threatening social question, not because the economic system is bad, but because people are. Its solution is to be reached, not primarily through good machinery, but through good men. No arrangement of industry can be devised which is beyond the possibility of being utilized for evil by unscrupulous and designing men ; and if, on the other hand, the control of industry were in the hands of conscientious and generous men, then almost any economic system — even the present

[1] Matt. iv. 9.

one — might perhaps prove itself sufficiently effective and just, and the industrial revolution, which now appears to many minds imperative, might come to seem superfluous.[1]

Through this contrast of ideals, then, we are brought into sight of the practical problem of modern industry. Here is the upper level of social development, as traced for us in the teaching of Jesus; and here is the lower level of economic change, as indicated to us by scientific socialism. Above, is the conception of industrial life as moving toward the kingdom of God; below, is the pursuit of happiness to be attained through better economic distribution. In this condition of things the present industrial alternatives may be perhaps thus stated, — that if the social movement does not proceed along the higher plane of progress, it is extremely likely to proceed along the lower plane. A problem so intensely felt as is the industrial question of the present day is bound to find some channel of expression, and if this stream of passionate feeling does not follow the line marked out for it by the teaching of Jesus, then the channel which seems, for the time, most ready to receive the stream is that of the socialist transformation. In fact, these alternatives are already indicated by the spirit of the

[1] On the tendency of the institution of private property to develop altruism, see the remarkable admissions of L. Stein, "Die soziale Frage im Lichte der Philosophie," s. 105 ff., and comments thereon in *International Journal of Ethics*, April, 1898, p. 364 ff.

modern agitation. The creed of social revolution has become, in many minds, a distinct substitute for a spiritual religion. It has drawn to itself the same emotional loyalty and zeal which are commonly associated with a religious faith. Men go to the scaffold for the cause of revolution as they once died for Christ, and with a spirit akin to that of Christian martyrs give their lives for the creed of the social democracy. When one remembers that this creed, which commands such devotion, is in its form an economic programme, and that the articles of this religion deal, not with supernatural realities, but with questions of wages and taxation, the passionate attachment of socialists to their faith may well seem surprising. Why is it that such extraordinary devotion is offered to an industrial programme, and indeed to a programme which by many of its adherents is but very vaguely understood? It is because this creed, unspiritual though it seems, represents to millions of people a religion, and provides a substitute for that teaching of the Christian Church which they have been led to reject. In short, the acceptance of social revolution as a religion is a practical indictment of the religious teaching of the Christian Church. The religious emotion demands some way of utterance even in those who reject religion, and the socialist movement provides a way of utterance for many persons who have lost faith in the purposes of Christianity. The socialist programme, in other words, represents the penalty which the modern world is paying for its insufficient obedience to the social teaching of Jesus. If social progress had proceeded steadily and firmly along the higher level of spiritual education, there would have been little provocation to transfer this progress to the lower level of industrial revolution. Failing, however, to find in religion anything real, what could plain people do but make of socialism a real religion? It is a question of alternatives. The revolt of the laboring classes is a pathetic attempt to find a substitute for religious faith, and the only effective way to meet that revolt is to prove that the Christian religion is rational, practicable, socially redemptive and economically justified.[1]

Such, then, appears to be some suggestion of the teaching of Jesus in its relations to forms of modern industry. He surveys economic problems from above, and perceives that fidelity in the affairs of industry opens the way to the kingdom; he approaches economic problems from within, and finds their key in character; finally, with a triumphant hope, he pictures this eager life of the world of trade taken up into the Divine process of spiritual education, and moving along the higher level of his social idealism toward the realization of the kingdom of God. It was pointed out, however, at the beginning of the present chapter, that the

[1] Compare also, "The Kernel and the Husk" (Am. ed. 1887), p. 326 ff. : "It appears, then, that what is called 'Socialism' is really nothing but a narrow and unwise form of Christianity."

problem of form in industry constituted by no means the whole of the industrial question, but that behind the economic forms now proposed there lay the ethical spirit of the present agitation, giving power and passion to many a scheme which in its form might be misdirected or immature. It remains therefore to consider the relation of the teaching of Jesus to the prevailing spirit of modern industrial life, and to observe the motives and passions on which he relies for industrial progress.

The first spiritual quality in the teaching of Jesus which is thus applicable to modern industry has been already noticed in his utterances concerning the kingdom of God. This fulfilment of his ideal is anticipated by Jesus with a persistent, and, as it must have seemed to many who were with him, a Quixotic, hope. In the face of the gravest obstructions and misapprehensions he proclaims that the kingdom is at hand: "The kingdom of God is come nigh unto you;"[1] "The kingdom of God is within you;"[2] "There be some . . . which shall in no wise taste of death, till they see the kingdom of God."[3] Jesus, that is to say, is the most unfaltering of optimists. He sits with his friends by the well of Jacob, watching the peasants as they plough the fertile field in the early spring, and he contrasts the slow process of the seasons with the immediate ripening of his own work. Say not of our mission, he tells his disciples, as the farmer says of his task, that

[1] Luke x. 9.   [2] Luke xvii. 21.   [3] Luke ix. 27.

months must pass before the harvest comes; lift up your eyes beyond this valley to the field of the world, which is "white already unto harvest." [1] How unreasonable and exaggerated such optimism must have seemed to many a judicious observer of the signs of the times! How meagre, in fact, was the welcome which the teaching of Jesus practically received! How quickly it was to meet with defeat and blight, like a seed that had been planted in sterile sand! How soon that field of his mission which Jesus had prophesied should be white with harvest was to become Aceldama, a field of blood! Yet, how unswervingly, at every step of his ministry, Jesus was guided by his unconquerable optimism! He believed in people who did not believe in themselves. He discerned good in people who seemed to themselves irretrievably bad. He forgave people whom the judicious had condemned. He inspired people to be what he desired them to be. The wavering and unstable Peter must have seemed to himself much more like shifting sand than like solid rock; but Jesus discerns within that feeble discipleship an underlying quality of strength, and calls on Peter to be the rock which his name implies, and the character of the disciple grows firm and consistent under the touch of the Master's confidence and hope. Finally, Jesus, with a transcendent optimism, trusts his entire teaching to followers who, as he well knew, understood but imperfectly what

[1] John iv. 35.

they had learned from him. He is sure that the
Holy Ghost will some day guide them into all truth,
and bring to their remembrance all that he had
said to them.[1] He is not discouraged by the
waste of much precious seed,[2] by the growth of
tares among the grain,[3] by the unfaithfulness of
stewards,[4] by the unresponsiveness of the wise and
prudent,[5] or even by the disloyalty of friends.[6]
Sometimes the splendor of his hope blazes out in
Oriental images of mighty triumph. "The Son of
man," he says, "shall come in the glory of his
Father with his angels."[7] "As the lightning
cometh forth from the east, and is seen even unto
the west; so shall be the coming of the Son of
man."[8] "From henceforth shall the Son of man
be seated at the right hand of the power of God."[9]
In short, through all the obstacles of bigotry,
stupidity, hardheartedness, hypocrisy and ecclesiasticism which confronted him, Jesus remains a
consistent optimist, confident that the world about
him is ready for his message, and that the fulness
of time is come.

When we turn from this quality of the teaching
of Jesus to the prevailing spirit of modern industrial agitation, we find a curious mingling of traits.
On the one hand is an optimism quite as thoroughgoing as that with which Jesus surveyed the signs
of his own time. There are, indeed, observers

---

[1] John xvi. 13; xv. 26. [4] Matt. xxv. 24–28. [7] Matt. xvi. 27.
[2] Matt. xiii. 4–7. [5] Matt. xi. 25. [8] Matt. xxiv. 27.
[3] Matt. xiii. 25, 26. [6] Matt. xxvi. 21. [9] Luke xxii. 69.

who find in the present social order no ground whatever for social hope. The feverish haste and tumultuous agitation of the present time are, to such persons, signs of social bankruptcy and approaching chaos. They retreat from this decadent civilization to the monastic life of some communistic society, or register their protest against the whole tendency of modern society, or sit on the bank of the hurrying stream of modern life and plan some impossible diversion of its current or some restriction of its flow. This frame of mind, however, — the spirit of social reaction or despondency, — is as far as possible from the spirit of the scientific socialist. He has no desire to retreat from the tendencies of modern economic life, or even to counteract their effects. On the contrary, he welcomes the increasing complexity of industrial life as a prophecy of his gospel. His creed is taught in a spirit of the most buoyant optimism. The social conditions which for the present exist are regarded by him, not as signs of increasing evil, but as essential preliminaries of that better future which is soon to come. They are a phase of social evolution which is essential to progress, but which is now in its turn destined to disappear. Even those economic tendencies which many reformers regard with alarm are, from the point of view of the consistent socialist, contributory to the one great end toward which social evolution works. The vast combinations of capital which seem to threaten industrial democracy are in reality only the forerunners which prepare its way. Let centralization of control, it is said, proceed, let trust be joined to trust, until industrial life becomes one vast monopoly, and then the time will be ripe for the coöperative commonwealth; the producers will at last take control of the mechanism which was devised to crush them, and out of a world of seeming evil there will issue a world of perfect good. Social evolution will be fulfilled when the democracy, which has already learned to govern itself, will at last come to produce for itself. The socialist is sustained by a vaster hope of social transformation than the world has known since the days of the optimism of Jesus, and may be tempted to repeat his confident prophecy, "Lift up your eyes and look at the fields, for they are white already unto harvest."

Yet, on the other hand, beneath this strain of optimism in modern socialism there is often a curious and jarring note of social pessimism. The mood of morbid despondency and reckless cynicism which is blighting so much of modern literature seems to be peculiarly attracted by schemes of social revolution. An affinity may be observed between literary and social iconoclasm.[1] The

---

[1] *E.g.* Ibsen, Letter to Georg Brandes: "The State must be abolished. In a revolution that would bring about so destructive a consummation I should gladly take part. . . . Changes in the form of government are nothing else than different degrees of trifling — a little more or a little less absurd folly." Compare also, H. Van Dyke, "The Gospel for an Age of Doubt," 1896, Lecture I (and citations in Appendix).

belief that modern morals are but disguised animalism and modern society is but a tissue of conventional shams induces the further belief that the social order is doomed and that a social catastrophe is at hand. This social pessimism is fostered by preachers of the socialist creed. If all social hope is to be set on the one great end of revolution, why, it is asked, should one concern one's self with efforts to better the world as it now is? Shall we not rather permit the present social order to go from bad to worse until, at last, by the pressure of its own inherent evil, it is shattered from within, and upon its ruins rises the democracy of labor?

Among the early Christians there were many who, in a mood akin to this, awaited the "end of the world." [1] A cataclysm, they believed, was soon to occur in which the entire fabric of civilization as it then existed was to disappear; and those who so believed concerned themselves little with passing phases of political or social reform, but withdrew from a perishing world and made ready for the great day of the Lord. There is, however, one characteristic of the new social pessimism which sharply distinguishes it from the spiritual anticipations of the early Christians. They lived in the light of their Lord's return, and had no doctrine of social destruction or of positive antagonism to the social order; the modern revolutionist is, first of

[1] Matt. xxiv. 3.

x

all, an enemy of things as they are, and may, indeed, follow his creed but little beyond its destructive teaching. Social reconstruction is too remote
and vast a dream to make an effective appeal to
the imagination of plain people, but social obstruction, and the destruction of the present social
order with its obvious defects and wrongs, make a
programme which can be easily understood. The
first lesson, then, in the catechism of industrial
revolution is a lesson in class hatred. No permanent good, it is taught, can be expected from the
employer class, however excellent its members
may be; no social adjustment which may follow
a social catastrophe could be worse for the working-man than is the present order. "Civilization,"
it is, with profound emotion, said, "denies to
man the right to live a guiltless life. . . . Whatever I do, whichever way I turn, I can neither
feed nor clothe my family, nor take any part in
public affairs as a citizen, nor speak the truth as
I conceive it, without being stained with the blood
of my brothers and sisters." [1]

In this wail of social pessimism, however,
great numbers of intelligent hand-workers detect
a false note. They are perfectly aware that, in
spite of many industrial hardships and injus-
tices, the standard of life and the purchasing
power of the wage-earning class are unmistak-
ably and progressively improving. The age of

[1] *The Industrialist*, July, 1898; G. D. Herron, "The Social
System and the Christian Conscience."

machinery has made it possible to secure a livelihood in fewer hours and with less labor than was ever possible before. The general tendency of industrial life is to thrust competent workmen, not down, but up, and to fill the lower places with the less competent, who in their turn feel the up-draught of economic progress.[1] An industrial programme which assumes that the present order is hopelessly evil cannot command the loyalty of those whose experience justifies social hope. To them it seems by no means certain that an industrial catastrophe would be a greater blessing than that which may come through the slow processes of industrial evolution. In short, those who have any stake in the present order hesitate to commit themselves to a gospel of social decadence and despair, and leave the creed of social pessimism to be preached by the disaffected, the unscrupulous, the ignorant, or the academic.

The spirit of the present industrial agitation, then, has in one aspect a remarkable likeness to the spirit of Jesus, while in another aspect it is radically opposed to that spirit. In its intention there is the same confident idealism, but in its method there is little of that faith in individual initiative and in the possibilities of the world as it now is, which gave to the teaching of Jesus its sanity.

[1] Compare C. D. Wright, Address at Mt. Holyoke, March 13, 1899; and the eloquent essay of F. Naumann, "Der Christ im Zeitalter der Maschine," in his "Was heisst Christlich-Sozial?" s. 30.

Thus the programme of the socialist alternately attracts and repels the followers of Jesus. Its dream of an industrial world of greater justice and larger opportunities seems but a renewal of the vision of the kingdom of God; but its spirit, sedulously fostering social distrust and despair, has no place in the gospel of the kingdom. It is difficult for persons trained in the Christian tradition to imagine the reign of human equity and brotherhood introduced through the free play of passion and hate, or to believe that a bad world can be transformed by one external device into a world of love and beauty. Social pessimism is not easily combined with social hope. The optimism of Jesus, on the other hand, is consistent and unfailing. It transforms the world because it hopes for the world. Socialism blackens the character of the real world to heighten the contrast with its ideal; Jesus illuminates the real world and makes it the instrument of his ideal. The heart of man naturally responds to the message of the optimist, for he brings that which is better than social prosperity, — the gift of hope. The fulness of time came in the teaching of Jesus, because Jesus had such fulness of hope for his own time.

What was it, then, we go on to ask, which justified in Jesus this hope for the world? It was, as it has been the main purpose of our inquiry to show, the confidence which Jesus had in the capacity of the human soul. If he can stir but a few individuals to positive loyalty to him and his hope, the world and its redemption are, he believes, secure. "All things are possible," he says, "to him that believeth." [1] "This is the victory that hath overcome the world, even our faith." [2] His most anxious inquiry of his disciples is this, "Do ye now believe?" [3] The gift which his followers soon learn to ask of him is the gift of faith. "Lord," they say, "Increase our faith." [4] The instrument which he would use for the overturning of the world is the power of personal faith: "If ye have faith, . . . ye would say unto this sycamine tree, Be thou rooted up, and be thou planted in the sea; and it would have obeyed you." [5] Here is the second quality in the spirit of Jesus which affects his social teaching. He looks upon the world with hope, because he acts upon it through faith. We have already seen that his social teaching begins with the individual and finds the key of circumstances in the growth of character. Now, however, we must consider this characteristic of his teaching, not as a method or programme, but as a spiritual dynamic, a guiding passion, an instrument of social service. What Jesus desired to communicate to his followers was, first of all, a moral initiative, a sense of spiritual capacity. He was moved by what the author of "Ecce Homo" accurately calls "the enthusiasm of humanity." He had a passion for personality. The contagion

[1] Mark ix. 23.   [2] 1 John v. 4.   [3] John xvi. 31.
[4] Luke xvii. 5.   [5] Luke xvii. 6.

of his spirit disclosed men to themselves, from the
time when it was prophesied of him that through
him the "thoughts out of many hearts may be
revealed,"[1] to the time when the disciples, walking to Emmaus, said, "Was not our heart burning
within us, while he spake to us in the way?"[2]
Social redemption, according to the teaching of
Jesus, begins in this communication to human
lives of the spirit of an active faith.

What is the relation of this second characteristic of the spirit of Jesus to the spirit of modern industrial life? Does the teaching of Jesus,
because it is primarily addressed to the individual,
depreciate or ignore the efforts which the modern
world devotes to the improvement of external conditions? On the contrary, the teaching of Jesus,
as we have already seen, welcomes every industrial
change which makes in any way for the making of
men, which gives greater scope for personal initiative, or which discovers and confirms personal capacity. Jesus, however, is a teacher, not of industrial
mechanics, but of spiritual dynamics. The adjustment of economic conditions is, in each new age,
a new problem of social mechanism, to be solved
by new devices concerning which Jesus can have
nothing to say; but the end for which these vary-
ing forms of social mechanism are devised is in all
ages the same. It is the production of personality,
the making of men.

Each economic proposition finds itself, sooner

[1] Luke ii. 35.　　　　[2] Luke xxiv. 32.

or later, confronted by this test, and at this point meets the teaching of Jesus.[1] Consider, for example, the effect of this test on a minor question of economic life. There has been, of late, much discussion of the value of thrift. Thrift, in less advanced days, was held to be an elementary social virtue. Young persons were encouraged to this virtue by praise and reward, and adults by the establishment of banks for savings. Now, however, we are told by radical reformers that the habit of saving is by no means to be regarded as an unquestionable social advantage, but rather as a serious social peril. He who learns to save from what he is now able to earn is, it is said, less likely to demand larger earnings. He is inclined to be satisfied with things as they are and grows less disposed to a radical change of social conditions. As his savings increase, he grows more conservative in his social creed, detaches himself from the interest of the wage-earning class, and goes over to the side of those who are perpetuating social injustice. "We teach our people," recently said a labor leader, "that thrift is no virtue." "Thrift," said John Burns, at the Trades Union Congress of 1894, "was invented by capitalist rogues to deprive honest fools of their proper

---

[1] So Ruskin, "Fors Clavigera," Letter 70. "Property must consist of good things, not bad ones. It is rightly called a man's goods, not a man's 'bads;'" and "Munera Pulveris," § 34, "We must distinguish the accidental objects of morbid desires from the constant objects of legitimate desires."

standard of comfort, so that their balance in the bank would be in proportion to the capacity of the workers to allow themselves to be deprived of their share of the national wealth." What may be inferred from the teaching of Jesus concerning his judgment in an industrial question like this? Jesus, it must be answered, being not a deviser of social programmes, does not enter into the question of the economics of thrift; but, as an inspirer of personal lives, offers a teaching which has a distinct bearing on the ethics of saving. The reason which that teaching would emphasize for encouraging the saving of money is not that it makes more money, but that it makes better men. The first justification of thrift is not that it makes a bank account large, but that it makes people thrifty. The children of the prosperous as well as the children of the poor may be taught, through habits of thrift, lessons of foresight, self-respect, and wise generosity. If an economic programme does not encourage frugality, prudence, and self-control, it can have no important place in the future of society; for no industrial future can permanently prosper which is to be ushered in by imprudent or spendthrift habits. The man who had not on a wedding garment found no satisfaction in the wedding feast.

Here, then, is one of many industrial propositions in which are disclosed both the likeness and the contrast between the teaching of Jesus and the modern tendencies of economic life. The teaching of Jesus regards not comfort but character as the object of economic change. It is not so much concerned with making the world soft and easy, as with making moral fibre hard and strong. Where many reformers point, with entire justice, to an effect on character of improved economic conditions, the teaching of Jesus recalls attention to the marvellous conquests of unpropitious economic conditions which have been achieved by men of faith. Not those regions of the earth where nature has been kindest and labor least compulsory have been economically most prosperous, but those which, by extorting struggle, have developed manhood. Not the sunny slopes of Italy and Spain, or the incredible fertility of Egypt, or the spontaneous harvests of the tropics, have been the guarantees of industrial prosperity, but the incessant battle of Holland with the sea, and of Germany with superior enemies on every side, and the insular necessities of Great Britain, and the rugged soil and climate of New England. "What do you raise here?" asked a traveller in the land of the Pilgrims, " from this sand and these rocks?" And the answer was, "We raise men." [1]

Such is the spirit of the teaching of Jesus. He

[1] On the influence of a hostile environment on " social fibre," see the striking view of Bagehot, in his " Physics and Politics," Ch. II, "The Use of Conflict." Compare also, *Spectator*, April 8, 1899, p. 479, on the Labor-Socialist Conference, " The competitive struggle has many drawbacks, but at least it produces men, and it is men we want to make, not great associations of consumers of food."

is not indifferent to the amelioration of circumstances; on the contrary, it is the inspiration of
his teaching which has suggested most of the enterprises which have introduced into industrial life
the sentiments of compassion or justice. These
industrial enterprises, however, when undertaken
in the spirit of Jesus, begin, not as mechanical
devices, but as spiritual desires. The individual
dreams of an industrial relation which shall verify
the teaching of Jesus, and then proceeds to show
his faith through his works. The commercial
scheme expresses the personal ideal. Back of the
system is the man of faith.[1] When the Son of
man cometh, he will look, first of all, not for a
method of economic distribution, but for "faith on
the earth."[2]

How then, one finally asks, shall this spirit of the
teaching of Jesus practically manifest itself? When
a man is stirred by the optimism of Jesus to a new
quality of hope, and quickened by the method of
Jesus to a new capacity of faith, what does that
man want to do? The answer to this question
brings us to the last command of the social teaching of Jesus, — the great word "service," or to
that other word, corrupted by the usage of
Christian sentimentalism — the still greater word

[1] So Leclaire, in his first experiment of the system of profit-sharing: Sedley Taylor, "Profit-sharing," 1884, p. 25, "I cannot believe
that this consummation will ever be reached through the conflicts
of opposing interests; it can only be from economic science enlight-
ened by the Spirit of the Gospel."

[2] Luke xviii. 8.

"love." "I am in the midst of you," says Jesus, "as he that serveth."[1] "The Son of man came not to be ministered unto, but to minister."[2] "Whosoever would be first among you shall be your servant."[3] "By this shall all men know that ye are my disciples, if ye have love one to another."[4] According to the teaching of Jesus, the evidence of what is now called success, or of what the gospel calls "glory," is to be found in the capacity and the willingness to serve. When Jesus knows that "the Father . . . hath given all things into his hand,"[5] and that he has "come from God and goes to God," what does he offer as the witness of this transcendent leadership? He lays aside his garments and washes his disciples' feet, and when he has done this lowly service he says, " Now is the Son of man glorified, and God is glorified in him."[6] Side by side with the symbolism of the Lord's Supper there should be set this other symbolism of the Christian life— the symbolism of service. The one is the sign of power derived from Jesus ; the other is the sign of service inspired by Jesus. The final test of Christian discipleship is in its capacity to stoop and serve. " For I have given you an example, that ye also should do as I have done to you."[7]

We turn, then, with this last quality of the teaching of Jesus to the methods of modern industrial life,

---

[1] Luke xxii. 27.
[2] Matt. xx. 28.
[3] Matt. xx. 27.
[4] John xiii. 35.
[5] John iii. 35.
[6] John xiii. 31.
[7] John xiii. 15.

and it seems at first sight as if there were no common ground on which the two might meet. What place is there, one asks, for such words as service or love among the scrambling competitions of the business world? What, indeed, is the world of business but a vast battle-field of organized self-interest, a gambling-table with enormous stakes, a lottery where a few great prizes tempt a hundred feverish victims to venture and lose? How strangely it would sound if in some business centre the great words were spoken, "Whosoever would be first among you shall be your servant!"[1] What a curious motto for a business office would be the words, "By this shall all men know that ye are wise men of business, if ye have love one to another." Is there not, on the other hand, abundant justification for that passionate hopelessness which cries out in the name of Christ: "It is only the densest ethical ignorance that talks about a Christian business life, for business is now intrinsically evil; . . . there is no such thing as an ethical bargain, . . . there are no honest goods to buy or sell; . . . the hideous industrial war . . . makes the industrial system seem like the triumph of hell and madness on the earth"?[2]

It is quite true, one must answer, that the world of industry abounds in persistent and subtle temptations of self-seeking, ambition, cruelty, and bad faith. Business life in the modern world is to many persons what the exceeding high mountain

[1] Matt. xx. 27. [2] *The Industrialist*, July, 1899, G. D. Herron.

was to Jesus, — the place where the devil exhibits the kingdoms of this world and their glory, and says again, "All these things will I give thee, if thou wilt fall down and worship me."[1] No man, it must be fully admitted, deals prudently with his business affairs who does not daily recognize that he is likely to be at any moment tempted of the devil. All this, however, is by no means to say that the business world is in its nature irretrievably depraved, or that there is no such thing as a Christian business life or an ethical bargain. On the contrary, there are many aspects of the business world — and aspects of which the social reformers as a rule take small account — where both ethics and religion have an important part in shaping and directing modern industry.

In the first place, if we can detach ourselves for a moment from the motives and passions of individuals in business, and observe the organization of business as a whole, considering its total working and results, it is seen to be, not — as is often asserted — a scheme of destructiveness and social piracy, but a vast and complex movement of social service. Crookedness and greed enough there are on the surface of the business world, as the surface of a stream bears along much scum and froth; but the stream itself, as it sweeps through the life of the time, bears in its current, not a means of poisoning the age, but a means of satisfying its needs. The creation of new forms of business proceeds,

[1] Matt. iv. 9.

as a rule, not from the desire to rob the community, but from the desire to serve it; and, in the main, the most rewarding forms of business are those which are based on the discernment of real needs and the supplying of real benefits. The amazing multiplication of production through modern machinery works, on the whole, to the same large end of social service. Tragedies enough there are of personal loss created by the introduction of improved mechanical methods, as though machinery were designed to grind in pieces the workmen who are caught in its wheels; yet nothing is more obvious than that machinery, through its marvellous cheapening of production, is the poor man's friend rather than his enemy. Startling, therefore, as may be the temporary successes achieved in defiance of the natural laws of business, the movement of industry on the whole is a movement toward good. The achievement of the arctic explorer Nansen was accomplished by committing himself to the polar current and letting it carry him along its course. The wise business man commits himself in the same way to the great current of human need and makes himself a laborer together with God. Indeed, there are many ways in which the moral end of the industrial order is reached through unconscious or even unwilling instruments, as though with a sort of providential irony. Many a man who is involved in business affairs is quite unconscious that he is performing any social service; he may even be attempting to get the better of the social world, or to do it a wrong ; yet the principle of service often utilizes the self-interested or rapacious spirit, and makes the wrath of man to praise it, so that an undertaking devised for the meanest ends is over-ruled in its intention and contributes finally to the general good.

Still more noteworthy than this ministry of service, consciously or unconsciously fulfilled, is a certain distinctively ethical quality which may be observed in the business world. It is quite true that the prevailing standards of industrial life fail in many of the finer and tenderer traits of social morality, but it is none the less true that a certain moral code, with characteristics of its own, exists in business affairs and demands of business men the most scrupulous conformity. Business life is often harsh and even merciless in its methods, but it makes much of such qualities as truth, honor, fidelity, and loyalty. In fact, when one looks below the surface of business life, it is most impressive to observe that its very existence and continuance depend on certain moral assumptions, and that it trains men in some ethical qualities which do not seem to be developed in the same degree anywhere else. People who are proposing to reform social morality are not infrequently deficient in certain virtues which are absolutely fundamental in commercial life. The reformers are apt to classify as the highest of moral traits the softer sentiments of sympathy, generosity and self-sacrifice, but they are not always scrupulous in measuring words and in discharging business obligations; men, on the other hand, in the business world are often limited in their moral horizon, and slow in their moral emotions, but they are the chief agents in maintaining certain of the most elementary of social virtues. For multitudes of such men the law of the good life is practically bounded by the maintenance of their credit and the speaking of the truth. Thus it happens that business transactions of vast dimensions are determined by a word or even by a sign, and that vast systems of communication are trusted for their security to the absolute fidelity of some obscure servant at the telegraph table or the railway switch. The more elaborate business becomes the more dependent it is on these moral qualities. More fidelity and sobriety are required of the motorman than of the horse-car driver ; greater trustworthiness of the modern mechanic than of the hand-worker whom he succeeds. For the vast majority of workers in the business world it is better capital to be morally incorruptible than to be intellectually clever. The first question which most employers desire to ask concerning a person seeking employment is not : Is he shrewd, unscrupulous, pliant ? but : Is he of clean character, can he be trusted, does he drink ? So far, at least, the moral life has become a distinct element in the industrial problem, and must be reckoned with in any organization of industry which intends to meet the needs of the age.

Modern business is not, as it is so often pictured, the work of a horde of pirates and wreckers watching for a chance to entrap and despoil the unwary; it is much more like the legitimate traffic of the high seas, where there are many perils of storm and collision, and many disasters wrought by treachery or rashness, but where on the whole strong men are trained and the work of the world is bravely done.

In spite, then, of the insidious temptations in which the world of industry abounds, the spirit and intention of business life have some contact with the spirit of the teaching of Jesus. The law of service which he announces for his disciples is not a wholly unknown principle in the world of competitive trade. It governs the organization of industry regarded as a whole, and it tests great numbers of individual lives even when they are unconscious of its judgment. What then becomes the duty of the follower of Jesus in his relation to the industrial world? His duty is, not to deny himself this way of expressing the spirit of service, or to permit himself scepticism concerning the possibility of such expression, but to give himself with confidence and joy to his business affairs as to that opportunity for the Christian life which lies nearest to his hands. The problem of the Christian in the world is not to escape from the world, or to be on his guard against the world, but to overcome the world. Confronted by the kingdoms of this world, he does not hide from

Y

their temptation, but rebukes the tempter and proceeds to rule the world through serving it. He converts, as the book of Revelation says, the kingdom
of this world into the kingdom of our Lord and of
his Christ.[1]

Here is a test which any man may apply to
his own business life. Am I, in my own place
and degree, moved by the spirit of service? Am
I contributing to that general movement of industry which lifts and ameliorates the life of my
time; or am I, on the other hand, either a social
parasite or a social highwayman? Am I so producing, distributing, administering, as to be a
laborer together with God; or am I thwarting the
generosity of nature and fattening on the misfor-
tunes of the weak? These are hard questions for
many men, corrupted by the passion of commercialism or by the opportunity for gain; but they are
questions which for the vast majority of plodding
business lives lead to the restoration of self-respect
and hope. Great numbers of such persons are
sorely disheartened and perplexed by the inconsistency which appears to exist between devotion
to their business and loyalty to their Christ. They
want to be followers of Jesus, but they have to
struggle for a living in the world of industry, and
their religion and business, their worship and
work, seem hopelessly set apart. This is the spiritual struggle which in earlier ages drove thou-
sands of conscientious souls into the monastic life.

[1] Rev. xi. 15.

They could not find the way to be at once about their own business and about their Father's business. What is it that can restore the sense of unity to such divided lives? It is the spirit of service. To be able to look up out of the dust and uncleanness of the business world and honestly say, "I am here as one that serveth; I am not being ministered unto, but I am ministering; I accept my business responsibilities and my business limitations as indicating the place in this world where I am wanted, and the work in this world which I am called to do," — that is what gives to many an obscure and tempted life its tranquillity, significance, and dignity. The soldier in the thick of the battle does not expect to know the whole plan of the campaign, nor has he enlisted for any dainty service. He is set in his own place, perhaps alone on the skirmish line, perhaps in the solid front of the main body, perhaps, like the centurion of the gospel, as a man of authority having soldiers under him, but in any case with the movement of the whole army depending at one point on him. When he is thus in the midst of active warfare he is just where a trained soldier desires to be, and he gives his life to his work with a high and solemn joy.

Is such a figure of speech merely a preposterous idealization of the scramble and greed of the world of industry? On the contrary, it is precisely such a campaign of human ingenuity and skill, enlisted to subdue and utilize the forces of nature, which industrial life in reality represents; and it is in such a field of service that the good soldier of Jesus Christ finds his opportunity. Base stratagems and barbarous methods still abound in the campaign of industrial war and have their inevitable consequences in stirring disloyalty and revolution in the ranks; but these abuses of industrial opportunity only serve to indicate what the task of the follower of Jesus must be. The Christian man in the business world is not bewildered by its confusion or overcome by its temptations. He is held to his post by the spirit of service. He looks at business affairs from above, and perceives beneath their strenuous competitions the signs of a possible brotherhood of industrial peace. He approaches industrial problems from within, convinced that any economic millennium must be reached, first of all, through the consecrated initiative of competent individuals. Thus, in the world of business he sees one of the most effective agencies for perpetuating the teaching of Jesus, — a place where integrity, fidelity, patience, thrift and consistency have immediate justification and large utility. He is alert for every sign of a more just organization of industry, but he is equally alert to make the most of those moral opportunities which are already in his hands. He views the economic world with hope and his fellow-men with faith, because he approaches both in the spirit of love.

Is such a habit of mind extremely rare in industrial life? Have the kingdoms of this world been so persuasively presented by the devil to this generation that business men have as with one consent fallen down and worshipped him? On the contrary, behind the insatiable and unscrupulous commercialism which disfigures the face of modern industry there is a great mass of faithful life doing the real work of the world with unobserved and untempted devotion. The business world is like a building whose front is defaced by such conspicuously bad work that the whole structure seems to totter. Fortunately, however, the columns which support the whole are undisturbed. There may be grave reasons for shame that the building is not more consistent or beautiful, but there is no reason to believe that it will fall. The pillars of modern industrial life are securely set in the moral stability of the vast majority of business lives. Millions of such persons, as they scrupulously discharge their business obligations, are meeting the demand of Jesus, "Whosoever would be first among you shall be your servant";[1] and as they stoop to their obscure duties are obedient to his example, "If I then, the Lord and the Master, have washed your feet, ye also ought to wash one another's feet."[2] The Christian problem of the industrial world is to multiply lives like these. If any revolution in the industrial order is to overthrow the existing economic system, the new order must

[1] Matt. xx. 27.   [2] John xiii. 14.

depend for its permanence on the principles of the teaching of Jesus ; but if the principles of the teaching of Jesus should come to control the existing economic system, a revolution in the industrial order would seem to be unnecessary.

CHAPTER VII

THE CORRELATION OF THE SOCIAL QUESTIONS

Because J live, ye shall live also.

WE have considered several of the modern social
questions under the form of concentric circles environing the individual life. The radius of personal inquiry is prolonged until it reaches, first
the problem of the family, then that of wealth and
poverty, and finally that of the industrial order; and
the area of each problem in succession is seen to be
an essential part of a more comprehensive problem
with larger circumference and content. This figure
of speech, however, though convenient for consecutive chapters and entirely justified in point of fact,
gives by no means an adequate picture of the real
relationship among the various social questions.
It is quite true that the problem of the family
expands as one considers it until it is seen to be
in large part a question of the uses of wealth or
the effects of poverty; it is true again that wealth
and poverty cannot be dealt with as independent
or fixed conditions, but must be interpreted in
terms of economic organization, progress, and
reform ; yet it is not less true that these outer
circles of social relations change under our hands

into the inner problems, so that the radius which measures them contracts as easily as it has been prolonged. The industrial agitation, for example, is but one form of the revolt of the poor against the rich ; the extremes of wealth and poverty are alike in threatening the existence of domestic ideals and of family seclusion ; the programme of the socialist forces us to reconsider, first, the distribution of private property, and then the nature and place of the family group.

Thus the relation of the social questions with each other is not that of mere sequence or expansion; it is one of mutual dependence and transferability. Each problem which we have considered turns out to be, in one or another aspect, another problem in disguise, and it becomes impossible to speak of any one as wholly cause or as wholly effect. Shall we say, for instance, that it is the ill-ordered and ambitious home which leads to poverty, or shall we say that it is the strain of poverty which shatters the peace of the home ? Is it the industrial order which creates the sins of the rich, or is it the unscrupulous rich who pervert the industrial order? In neither case can we affirm that at one point the social malady invariably begins and that all other symptoms come of contagion. Each problem may begin anywhere. The diseases which we have considered are epidemic rather than contagious. Lack of industrial opportunity may involve, first, poverty, and then the shattering of the home. An ambitious home may lead first to wealth and then to industrial crookedness. In short, we come upon a relationship analogous to that which has been discovered to exist between the various forces of the physical world. What once appeared to be the isolated and disconnected action of heat, light, motion, or electricity, is now associated with all other physical forces under the doctrine of correlation. I strike two stones together and the motion is converted into heat or into light. I rub my sealing-wax and the motion is converted into electricity. I change heat into light in the lime light; heat into electricity in the electric light; and finally, electricity into light and heat and motion in that wonderful combination of discoveries which has become familiar in the electric railway. Here is the most fruitful doctrine of modern science. The varied modes of action in the physical world are not to be interpreted or utilized in isolation; they are convertible, interpenetrating, correlated.

Something like this is the truth which underlies the whole series of the social questions. For practical convenience, each may be hypothetically isolated; there may be specialists in charity or in economic reform, and even specialists in some subsection of one social problem, such as charity for children, or trades-unionism; there may be special organizations for divorce-reform or the building of dwellings or the promotion of coöperation; yet, in all this diversity of operations, it must not be forgotten that these varied enterprises are funda-

mentally correlated and convertible social forces.[1]
The gentle charity-visitor begins her apparently
simple task of relieving some destitute home, and
suddenly finds herself confronted by other social
problems which seem quite beyond her capacity
to solve. The real question presented to her turns
out, perhaps, to be one of domestic cruelty, involving a decision on her part concerning the unity
of the family ; or, more probably, the destitution
which she is called to relieve is but a sign of irregu-
lar employment, for which the permanent remedy
is, not alms, but work. Thus the problem of relief
is abruptly transformed into that of domestic integrity or into the complex economic question of the
glut of labor ; and the kindly visitor to the poor is
bewildered as she perceives the scope and relations
of her lightly assumed task. Or, again, the judicious philanthropist, applying himself to improving
the dwellings of the poor, discovers that the first
principle of this new science lies — as we have
already observed — not in generosity or charity,
but in provision for domestic seclusion and for
economic independence. Many such enterprises
have failed because the poor prefer a home, however squalid, to a barrack, however convenient ;
and many other such enterprises have failed because the poor have declined to be even generously
patronized or deprived of liberty. Wisdom in

[1] In the same sense, Professor Clerk-Maxwell describes what he
calls the " cross-fertilization of the sciences." (Iles ; Flame, Electricity and the Camera, 1899, p. 74.)

this apparently detached form of philanthropy comes of recognizing the correlation of the social questions.

The doctrine which thus issues from our considerations appears, it must be admitted, in its first statement to be a somewhat disheartening truth. If it is true that no social question can be thoroughly interpreted without involving one in remote and often much more comprehensive questions, how can one hope to reach any satisfying conclusion? Who can deal adequately with all these correlated aspects of social life? When one finds some special and limited inquiry ramifying into so many complex considerations of social philosophy, is he not naturally tempted to abandon a task which he has neither the time nor the capacity to complete?

Certainly, one must answer, there is much in such reflections which is likely to check enthusiasm and even to suggest despondency. When one comes to realize the dimensions and many-sidedness of the special problem with which he is concerned, he will certainly approach it with less assurance and be less certain that a complete and final solution of it is at hand. It is, however, precisely this reserve and prudence, and the wholesome loss of self-confidence which they involve, which many social reformers of the present day most urgently need to cultivate. Each social question has become, to many zealous advocates, of such engrossing interest that it

seems to them to hold the key of social amelioration. We are met on every side by social panaceas
and social solutions. There appears to be in many
minds a sense of obligation to possess some specific for social diseases or to know some short cut
to social prosperity. "If my plan," said one expo-
nent of a problem of general redemption, "is not
sufficient, what is yours?" as though it were the
duty of any serious-minded man to have some
universal remedy to propose.

There is a splendid earnestness in this eager
devotion. It proceeds, for the most part, not from
intellectual conceit, but from moral enthusiasm.
Something, it seems to these philanthropists,
must be done and done at once, to make a better
world, and they gallantly apply themselves to the
cleansing of that little corner of the great social
order upon which the windows of their minds
happen to look. Their social outlook creates their
social creed. The special reform with which they
concern themselves seems to them comprehensive
and sufficient. If the world would but accept their
remedy, — single tax, prohibition, nationalization of
industries, Malthusianism, old age pensions, non-
resistance, communal ownership, or some other of
the panaceas so earnestly commended, — the whole
constitution of modern society would be established in permanent health. It is a gallant and,
as we shall in a few moments point out, a fruitful enthusiasm, which is infinitely more contributory to social progress than critical cynicism or

indifference. Yet it remains true that the rarest virtue in the reformer is the gift of broad and patient wisdom. The very intensity of his vision involves, as a rule, a corresponding narrowness of view. His eye is fixed on a single end, and he takes little account of outlying or qualifying circumstances. What he needs to appreciate, then, is the correlation of the social questions, — the many, and often remote, conditions which affect and sometimes transform the problem immediately before him, and the unexpected allies which may come to his aid while quite unconscious of serving him.

A striking illustration of this expansion and transformation of one social question into other forms is to be found in the later developments of the so-called temperance cause. Here is a social movement which has been very generally regarded as an isolated and specialized work. A few obvious remedies have seemed sufficient to meet the portentous evil of the drink habit. The pledge of abstinence, the prohibition of sale, the physiological instruction of children, the constant agitation of public sentiment, — these and kindred methods of direct reform have appeared to bound the sphere of temperance work. More and more, however, it has become evident that, beyond these specific agencies of reform, there are, on every side of the temperance question, influences and movements which are among its most threatening enemies or its most powerful allies. Domestic,

economic, even psychological and racial, conditions are intimately correlated with the problem of drink. Is it drink which destroys the
family, or is it the disordered family life which
tempts to drink? Is the drink habit a morbid
passion, or is it in many cases a normal and
healthy craving for recreation which drives men
to the saloon? Is it true, as one distinguished
economist has said, that the thirst for liquor
among working-men is not so much a question of
drink as of food, and that to know why a poor man
drinks one has but to look in his dinner-pail? Is
it drink which robs men of their earnings, or is it
the fluctuation of earnings which drives men to
drink? Would the drink traffic be less pernicious
if wisely converted into a municipal industry?
Is the moral tone of the community weakened by
prohibitory legislation? How does it happen that
the wine-drinking peoples of southern Europe are
temperate, and the water-drinking Anglo-Saxons
intemperate? These are but indications of the
varied inquiries which now confront any one who
looks below the surface of the problem of temperance. What seemed to be a detached question
concerning a personal habit is in fact correlated
with almost every movement of social or economic
reform. The most effective attack upon the drink
habit may come of some flank movement, in the
interest of better homes, or healthy amusement,
or regular work, or nourishing food, or State control, or the education of a new and superior desire.

A similar extension and ramification might be observed in any one of the social questions of the present time. Each has a part in the solution of all the rest, and all are in a measure dependent on the progress of each. Playgrounds, as the mayor of Boston has lately pointed out, may be regarded as an offset to penal institutions, and gymnastics may reduce the expenditure of prisons, so that it may be even urged that "crime in our large cities is to a great extent simply a question of athletics." No social problem can, in any absolute sense, be dealt with alone. It is but one aspect of the general evolution of social habits and ideals. One of the most observant of American economists has remarked, "When I hear any one bring forward a solution of the social question, I move to adjourn." There is, he means to say, no such thing as the complete and immediate solution of special problems which are inextricably involved in the general progress of social evolution. The whole social body moves together if it moves at all. The correlation of the social questions gives to the scattered movements of social reform a unity and interdependence so vast and complex that one must dismiss the notion of a panacea for each separate social ill, and content himself with an imperfect and contributory service.

Does it, however, follow from this view of progress that one must turn back to his own special problem with the despondent sense that little can be done? Is the doctrine of correlation in reality a

disheartening truth? On the contrary, the enlargement of relations, and the convertibility of power
thus acknowledged, give dignity and significance
to many a partial and discouraging effort for social reform. Modesty, indeed, the doctrine of correlation teaches. One must recognize that the
work he has undertaken is much more varied and
comprehensive than it at first appeared to him to
be. To find, however, one's own limited plan of
social service reënforced by, and in its turn reën-
forcing, other and larger plans, is to regain self-
respect and hope where one had felt discouraged
and alone. The solitary sentinel remembers that
the army is at his back; the hard-pressed bat-
talion is aware that the same battle is going on
all along the line; that defeat at one point may
contribute to the general victory, and that the effective force is often strengthened by new and
unanticipated allies. The movement against the
drink habit, for instance, of which we have just
spoken, gets new vitality and importance as it
becomes associated with the whole movement
of industrial and moral progress. Temperance
reform was in grave danger of being side-tracked
from the main line of modern interest, and given
over to the politicians and the pious. It is now
seen to be one aspect of the comprehensive social
movement of the time, and, to many careful observers, the problem of economic progress appears
to be in very large degree dependent upon the
problem of drink. The most judicious leader of

the labor agitation in Great Britain, on being asked why he advocated total abstinence, answered that it was for the economic power which could be in this way so easily saved. He believed in and practised temperance, that is to say, not primarily for the sake of temperance, but for the sake of labor reform. He was, indeed, but repeating what Professor Cairnes years ago pointed out, that the future of the laboring classes might be prophesied by an examination of the excise returns. Economists, that is to say, and labor agitators join with physiologists and moralists in calling new attention to the social significance of the drink habit; and the advocate of temperance, instead of being, as in the past, in some degree isolated in his reform and distrusted as a fanatic, finds himself, through the acceptance of the doctrine of correlation, in the very centre of the main stream of social reform.

The same enlargement of function and diversity of usefulness may be discovered in any form of honest social service, and make of the doctrine of correlation, not a discouraging, but a highly stimulating, teaching. Suppose, for instance, that a few generous-minded persons organize on an intelligent plan a working-men's club. They have, in all probability, no very definite idea of the outcome of their enterprise, but are moved by the desire to offer education and entertainment to less fortunate men. As their fraternal work proceeds in its unambitious service, how shall

z

it be classified among the social movements of the time? From one point of view it has a place in the temperance campaign, for it provides a genuine substitute for the attractions of the saloon; from another point of view it is a contribution to the labor movement, for it gives to handworkers material for study and liberty of discussion; from still another point of view it is a peacemaker between social classes, for rich and poor find in it a real democracy and come to a more just understanding of each other's ideals and faults. It may even make for the stability of the home, though it seems to withdraw its members from their homes. An intelligent working-man in such a club, being asked whether his wife did not wish him at home in the evening, answered, "Yes; but she says that when I am at home I am much more interesting." One thing such a club resolutely denies that it is — a form of charity; yet it precisely expresses that acceptable charity which brings, not alms, but friendship. One great human interest such a club as a rule excludes — the discussion of religion; yet its rule of conduct is that which Jesus himself laid down as one-half of religion, "Thou shalt love thy neighbor as thyself." Thus this unassuming undertaking has its part in at least a half-dozen of the social movements of the time, and may perhaps be contributing more to effective philanthropy and to undefiled religion than many an organization definitely created in their names.

Or — to turn the same story round — suppose

that an employer, ignorant of the real instincts and ambitions of his employees, introduces in his business a spurious though well-intended form of generosity. He feels a touch of that breeze of industrial fraternity which has sprung up in our time, but it does not really stir his nature to a new life. He wants to keep his self-respect, but he wants also to keep his profits. He looks, therefore, for ways of combining the service of God and the service of Mammon. Thus he may seem to himself to be generous when he is in fact only patronizing. He provides homes for his employees, but under terms which limit their liberty; he adjusts wages with what appears to be liberality, but under conditions which irritate and restrict; he counsels thrift and simplicity, while his own domestic life remains ostentatious and vulgar. Is this merely a commercial phenomenon, bounded by the business in which master and man meet? On the contrary, this half-hearted service has its effect all along the line of the social movement, to hinder advance and to create distrust. The instinct of the home in working-people protests against a home that is not one's own; the self-respect of the wage-earner refuses to be patronized; the commercial maxims of the employer cannot teach what his private life denies; finally, the man who had fancied himself earning the gratitude due to a generous philanthropist finds himself, to his own great surprise, responsible for industrial dissatisfaction and revolt.

Here, then, is the larger teaching of the doctrine of correlation. There is in the modern
social world no detached or isolated life, and no
one can be sure at precisely what point his life
or work may affect the life or work of the community. He may be in intention serving at one
point, and the force of his service may be transformed into quite another form of effectiveness;
or he may be quite unconscious that he has any
part whatever in the social question, while, in fact,
he has made himself a conspicuous instigator of
social revolution. When one realizes this truth,
he turns, with a new courage and self-respect, to
the special form of service which immediately in-
vites him. Any honest and generous work, he
sees, may count in unforeseen and surprising ways.
His charity may fail in the form of relief, and yet
may be communicated in the form of character;
his business may be necessarily businesslike, and
yet may be wise philanthropy. The scattered
social forces, utilized by myriads of men, are
taken up into the comprehensive unity of the
social movement, so that each separate impulse
is transmitted through the whole organic life.

Such is the correlation of the social questions;
and when we turn from this modern and scientific
analogy to the teaching of Jesus Christ, we find
the same truth foreshadowed in many striking
ways. No inquiry could be more misleading or
superfluous than to search the gospels for confir-
mation of the principles of modern science. The

harmonies of science with religion are in this sense as unreal and fanciful as the harmony of poetry with chemistry, or of art with politics. Yet as one traces the correlations of social activity and the transmission of social power, he cannot help recalling the reiterated promises of Jesus to his disciples that the humblest tasks performed by them might become effective for the greatest ends. "Whosoever," he says, "shall give to drink unto one of these little ones a cup of cold water only, . . . he shall in no wise lose his reward."[1] "Whoso shall receive one such little child in my name receiveth me."[2] "Then shall the King say, . . . Come, ye blessed of my Father, inherit the kingdom prepared for you from the foundation of the world : for . . . Inasmuch as ye did it unto one of these my brethren, even these least, ye did it unto me."[3] Jesus, that is to say, dignifies and transfigures the devotion to that which is least, not merely by the promise of that which is much as its future reward, but by the assurance that there is no distinction of least and much, that the issues of the kingdom and the service of the King may be determined by the giving of the cup of water and by the care of the little child.

Nor is it in terms of commendation only that this teaching of the conversion of social forces is set forth. Some of the most solemn denunciations of Jesus are uttered against those who slight the modest opportunity or obstruct the insignifi-

[1] Matt. x. 42. [2] Matt. xviii. 5. [3] Matt. xxv. 34, 40.

cant life. With great detail and eloquent reiteration he describes the man who omits to care for
the hungry, the naked, and the sick, and perceives
in this social neglect an essential disloyalty to
God. "Depart from me, ye cursed, . . . Inasmuch as ye did it not unto one of these least, ye
did it not unto me." [1] He deals with the mere
obstructionist in social life as one who is in reality
thwarting the ends of the kingdom and whose life
is worse than wasted. "Whoso shall cause one
of these little ones . . . to stumble, it is profitable
for him that a great millstone should be hanged
about his neck, and that he should be sunk in
the depth of the sea." [2] Even the words which
men carelessly utter, Jesus teaches, are correlated
with remote issues of thought and conduct, and
affect all the outer circles of one's social life, as
the ripples from a stone cast into a still lake go
circling out until they break upon the distant
shore. "Every idle word that men shall speak,
they shall give account thereof in the day of judgment. For by thy words thou shalt be justified,
and by thy words thou shalt be condemned." [3]
Jesus, that is to say, announces as a spiritual principle the same quality of radiation and convertibility in moral forces which we have considered in
terms of a physical analogy. There is to him no
detached duty, no isolated neglect, no lost word.
Each is transformed into new shapes of utility or
new occasions of offence, and each may come at

[1] Matt. xxv. 41, 45.   [2] Matt. xviii. 6.   [3] Matt. xii. 36, 37.

last to be the test of the whole of life in the day of judgment. The doctrine of correlation is a modern statement of the teaching of Jesus, that the fragmentary service of the least of his brethren is taken up into the unity of discipleship to him.

At this point, however, we come into view of a further aspect of this physical analogy which we have left thus far unnoticed, and which is not without new suggestiveness when applied to the social world. The transmutation of physical forces and their conservation in new forms indicate to the scientific observer that he is observing, not intrinsically different phenomena, but various manifestations of a single force. We cannot properly speak of the forces of nature. Heat, light, magnetism and the rest are in fact only the temporary expressions of one pervasive and comprehensive force. Behind the diversity of operations in nature lies the supreme fact of the unity of nature, whose action is neither originated nor increased, but only transmuted and conserved, by the forces which we see. The fundamental belief upon which physical science rests is the assurance of continuity and undiminished effectiveness in that central activity which in the transformations of the various physical forces appears to be dissipated or destroyed.

What then, one goes on to ask, is the nature of this permanent unity of power, of which the physical forces of nature are transient expressions? To this question the teaching of physical science gives no reply. We have come to the border line between that which can be observed in nature and that which must be inferred to be at the heart of nature, and we pass from the domain of physics to that of metaphysics. For the sake of clearness in distinguishing between the changeful and the permanent aspects of physical life, science has agreed to give to the underlying unity of force the title of "energy"; yet of the nature of this central energy science makes no assertion beyond the fact of its manifestation in those forces whose action we observed. Mr. Spencer, as he reaches this central doctrine of the unity of force, approaches it in language which reaches almost a lyric strain of confession, and concludes with words not unlike those of a theological creed. "Deeper," he says, "than demonstration — deeper even than definite cognition — deep as the very nature of mind, is the postulate at which we have arrived." "Amid the mysteries which become the more mysterious the more they are thought about, remains the one absolute certainty that he is ever in the presence of an Infinite and Eternal Energy from which all things proceed." [1]

Such is the doctrine of energy into which the doctrine of correlation opens; and as we have ventured to use the analogy of the latter doctrine to illustrate the transformations and unity of social

[1] "First Principles" (Am. Ed.), Ch. VI, p. 192; "Religion, a Retrospect and Prospect," p. 35.

service, we are naturally led on to ask the final question which this analogy suggests. Here are these various forms of social activity, transmuted, as we have seen, in the most surprising ways and with undiminished force into new channels of expression and effectiveness. The correlation and conservation of the social movements bind together all scattered types of social service in a sense of unity. They are not disconnected undertakings, but partial manifestations of one social dynamic, which moves the entire mechanism of the social order. What, then, is the nature of this unity which thus expresses itself in all these changeful aspects of social responsibility? What is the social energy from which all these movements which we have considered may be believed to proceed?

This question is obviously not met by the intrinsic difficulty which is presented in the case of the physical world. There is in social life no chasm to be bridged between what can be observed and measured and what lies absolutely beyond verification. The social movements are not external and mechanical changes; they are simply phases of human life and history, open to analysis by any one who can interpret the motives of masses of men. In short, in the study of modern society, we are moving altogether in the region of human motives and ideals, where the social energy which stirs the whole must be of the same verifiable quality as the social movements which it utilizes. An army may be in one aspect regarded and studied

as a machine, and in some cases the more perfectly mechanical the movement of an army is,
the better it fulfils its ends; yet there is no difficulty in recognizing that what acts like a machine
is after all an instrument and expression of the
commander's will. In the same way, the social
forces of philanthropy and reform have their mechanical laws and external conditions; but the
social energy which directs and unites them is to
be sought in the world of human desires, duties,
reasonings, and hopes.

When, therefore, we ask what it is in human life
which has inspired the extraordinary range and diversity of the modern social movements, the whole
character of our preceding inquiries indicates the reply. The social questions are, in their main scope
and intent, manifestations of the moral life of the
time. They are ethical questions. They appear
in forms which are political or industrial, but behind these diversities of form works the one spirit.
Against the lust of the flesh there rises up the instinct of chaste love and creates the social question
of the family; against the lust of riches there appear
the emotions of benevolence and pity and create
the problem of charity; against economic injustice there rises up the hope of an industrial commonwealth and creates the labor question. Thus
there is a mechanism of the social questions and
a motive power, and while the mechanism may be
externally adjusted by legislation or organization,
the motive power is to be found in human hearts

and wills. The social questions occur simply because a very large number of people are trying in many different ways to do what is right. The moral life is written across the face of the time in the language of the social questions. The social energy of the modern conscience finds its main channel of expression in the social forces of modern reform.

This truth of the fundamentally ethical character of the social questions has repeatedly presented itself in the course of our separate considerations. Now, however, when it appears once more as the outcome of the doctrine of correlation, we are led to observe more closely its implications and corollaries. If it is true that social progress is but the expression of moral energy, this is a truth of the utmost significance, both for the student of social questions and for the student of the teaching of Jesus Christ.

To the first of these students there is indicated the one absolutely indispensable element in all forms of social service. It is the supply and the control of moral motive-power. The social movements of the time have become organized on such a scale that a vast amount of time and attention are necessarily devoted to the administration of their machinery. Nothing, however, is more purposeless or more ludicrous than an elaborate mechanism which has not power enough to do its work. Social power uncontrolled by well-ordered mechanism is, it is true, often in-

effective, wasted, or dangerous, like steam escap-
ing from ill-adjusted valves ; but social mechanism
unprovided with moral power is simply dead
routine or downright self-deception, like a machine which men spend their lives in devising,
and which, after all, will not move. Here is the
practical peril which every administrator of social
reform has to meet. It is so easy to get involved
in the machinery which one has perhaps himself
created, so easy indeed to become a part of that machinery and to trust to its automatic effectiveness,
that it sometimes requires a positive spiritual
effort to remind one's self that the only justification of a social machine is its transmission of social
energy. A charity administrator accomplishes his
round of inquiry and relief, an organizer of work-
ingmen gathers the whole membership of a trade
into his union, a temperance reformer procures
the legislation which his cause seems to require,
— yet, when the test of this mechanical activity
arrives, how disheartening its results often seem
to be! The poor remain as importunate and as
ingeniously deceitful as ever ; the working-men,
when the strain is put upon their loyalty and
patience, fall away from the organization and its
creed ; the community persists in behaving, under
the best of liquor laws, much as it did when there
was no restraint. Is it then to no purpose that
poor-relief and labor-unions and temperance laws
are so laboriously devised and sustained ? On the
contrary, these channels of organization are abso-

lutely essential both to control and to utilize the social energy which they receive. The wise engineer, however, is aware that through such channels is to flow a turbulent stream of human emotion and desires, which has its sudden floods and ebbs, and for whose restraint and discipline he must provide. Charity administration, in judicious and loving hands, checks the flood of mendicancy, finds new outlets into the fields of industry, stirs and guides the motives of the poor, until the stream of poverty, broad as it remains, is held in check by the channel of relief. Labor organization, to be under control when the stream of passion runs high, must be fortified by moral education when the current of industrial life is calm. Nothing is more suicidal in such movements than to trust to sudden emotions or inflaming words or elaborate organization. These sources of power fail as suddenly as a spring freshet subsides, and leave at the best only a track of destruction behind. Permanent efficiency proceeds from intelligence, prudence and loyalty cultivated in tranquil days and providing, in time of strain, an even and trustworthy supply of moral energy. Temperance reform is but a labor of Sisyphus, and the burden it desires to remove rolls back on the community again, unless the agitation is consistently directed, not so much to the hampering of a trade, as to the disciplining of a passion. The drink habit is in very large degree the perversion of one of the most universal of human desires, the thirst for exhilaration, recreation, and joy, and to remove the only available means for satisfying this normal craving without providing adequate substitutes, is like blocking the channel where a stream does harm without observing how many new fields the same stream is likely to devastate.

Thus in every social question the problem of guiding and directing social energy lies behind the problem of developing social organization. The first inquiry of the social reformer should be: "What is the nature of the special emotion or desire or appetite with which I am now called to deal? How can I utilize it, educate it, and direct it to its proper end?" Here is the key to judicious methods. When one fairly realizes that he is concerned, first of all, not with machinery, but with life, not with "cases," but with people, not with economic schemes, but with the passions, hopes, and ideals of human beings, then his ways of social organization will become, not less painstaking, but more sympathetic, prudent, patient, and wise. There is no quality in modern life more beautiful, or indeed more heroic, than this capacity to handle social machinery without loss of moral vitality and faith. To be from day to day an official and still to remain merciful, tender-hearted, and hopeful; to be a reformer, without loss of broad sympathy or of hospitality of mind; to be an employer, and find within the field of industry room for humanity, democracy, and idealism ; to believe in a cause, but to believe still more in the courage, strength, and peace to which the cause opens the way, — these are the qualities which redeem social service from its discouragements, its small conceits and its automatism, and make it virile, healthy, happy, and sane.

This truth, however, that the social questions are expressions of moral energy is a truth which is also of special significance for the student of the teaching of Jesus. From what source, one asks himself, is there to come an adequate supply of this moral energy, this impulse of love and hope, of courage and patience, of sympathy and wisdom, which shall keep the social movement fresh and free ? What source of spiritual power can insure to the stream of service an even and abundant flow, instead of an intermittent and wasted current ? It is not necessary, in reply to this question, to insist that the teaching of Jesus is the sole source of such social energy. Many causes have conspired to make the present the age of the social question, and many influences and circumstances have enlarged the stream of sympathy and social obligation which flows through the midst of the present time. Yet it is perfectly evident that the Christian Church has at its command both a quantity and a quality of social power, which, whenever they have been fairly utilized, have had quite unparalleled effect. No sooner did the first flood of Christian feeling sweep over the ancient

world than a new harvest of philanthropy spontaneously sprang up, as a new crop springs from
a sterile field where the stream of irrigation has
flowed. The same social fruitfulness has followed
in every age each new access of genuine Christian
life. Even when such a stream has been diverted
to what seems antagonistic to the social life, as in
the development of monasticism, there have been
none the less created new social ties, with new
ways of organization for social service. Plainly
we have in the teaching of Jesus a source of social
energy which has been but scantily utilized by the
modern world.

Nor is it necessary to insist that the message
of Jesus is primarily one of social welfare. On
the contrary, it comprehends many other things;
and, as we saw at the outset of this inquiry, is
primarily, not a message to society, but one
addressed to the needs and desires of the individual soul. Primarily devoted, however, as
the message of Jesus is to the individual, it is
none the less true that with constant and solemn
reiteration he affirms the test of the salvation of
the individual to reside in his contribution to
social service. Not confession of sin alone, he
says, nor adoration, nor orthodoxy of opinion, but
the fruits of the spirit are the signs of discipleship.
If any man have not the spirit of Christ he is none
of his. "By their fruits ye shall know them." [1]
"Not every one that saith unto me, Lord, Lord,

[1] Matt. vii. 16.

shall enter into the kingdom of heaven; but he that doeth the will of my Father which is in heaven."[1] Not ecclesiastical fellowship nor theological assent separates, according to Jesus, the sheep from the goats, but the care of the hungry and the stranger and the sick.[2]   Not he who receives the water of baptism or the cup of communion has the assurance of blessing, but, "Whosoever shall give to drink unto one of these little ones a cup of cold water only, . . . shall in no wise lose his reward."[3] What irony of religious teaching, then, it is, and what a deliberate withdrawal of the influence of Christianity from any bearing on the concerns of modern life, when it is proposed to prolong the ancient controversies of orthodoxy or ritual or organization, as though they in any degree represented the ends to which Jesus devoted himself, or could be of the slightest real concern to those who are meeting the needs of the present age.   According to the teaching of Jesus, the Christian Church is to be, not a deposit of opinion, but a source of spiritual energy, a mighty social dynamic, a fountain of redemptive life.   "Because I live," he says, "ye shall live also."[4]   The gift of Jesus is a gift of life.   "I came that they may have life;"[5] and life is known by its creative, self-propagating, self-communicating power.

It follows from this truth that achievements which are often regarded as extraneous and acci-

---

[1] Matt. vii. 21.   [2] Matt. xxv. 35.   [3] Matt. x. 42.
[4] John xiv. 19.   [5] John x. 10.

dental in the work of a Christian church may be
in fact its essential and central intention and the
best justification of its existence and its claims.
A church, for instance, proceeds to enforce its
forms and tests, its theology and philosophy,
as its central duty, and as if incidentally and
by the way leavens the community about it with
the spirit of benevolence, sympathy, patience,
and hope. What a curious experience it might
be for such a church some day to wake, and
discover that these incidental achievements were
what most commended it to its Master! A
Christian mission in foreign parts lavishes its
efforts in the attempt to bring heathen to Christ,
and counts, with great self-reproach, few gains
from all its devotion; but meantime, while fulfilling its technical obligation, it comes to pass
that the spiritual climate in the neighborhood
of these devoted souls by degrees experiences a
subtle change — cruelty disappears, domestic life
grows purer, tolerance and truthfulness begin to
supplant the heathen traits of bigotry and deceit. What is this gentler air which is breathed
wherever a wisely administered mission has done
its patient work? It is the proof that the mission is accomplishing that which it was set to
do. This, and not the number of converts it can
count, may be the test of its missionary fidelity, genuineness, and power. Many a man can
teach Christian doctrine to heathen listeners, but
only a life which has been hid with Christ in God

can communicate to heathen lives the spiritual energy which proceeds through Christ from God. Or, once more, a new and sudden responsibility is laid upon a nation to convey to people at the ends of the earth the blessings of a Christian civilization ; and many are rash enough to say in the name of religion, " Let us first subdue this people by force of arms and then the way will be clear to carry to them the teaching of Jesus." The teaching of Jesus, however, is not something that waits until the social questions of aggression and war are answered. It must be communicated through the process of civilization, not after that process, or before it. It is impossible for the same nation to present itself to a heathen world, first as rapacious, commercialized, and lustful for glory, and later as an ambassador of the mercy and grace of Christ. We have seen in the making of money that it is the getting of wealth with clean hands, and not the free spending of ill-gotten wealth, which marks the Christian man of business. The same thing may be said of empire-making. It is the moral quality of the conquest itself, and not that which may happen after the conquest, which represents the Christian energy of the conquering nation ; and it is the motives which prompt and direct the original approach to a heathen civilization which are likely either to bring heathen to Christ or to repel them from him.

What is it, then, to which we are brought as the special problem which presents itself to the Christian Church in the age of the social question? It is the problem of communicating to the social movement that social energy which the teaching of Jesus originates and conserves. There are other aspects of that teaching which have met the peculiar needs of other times; and there are some aspects of it which are plainly applicable to all times and which touch the universal experience of human sin, contrition, and aspiration. Yet all these profound effects of the teaching of Jesus, its reconstruction of theology and its regeneration of individual life, are consummated and justified by being gathered up into a sense of power which can create a better world. After all, the test of religion is in what it will do. St. Paul, discoursing of Christian theology, submits even the world of knowledge to the test of power, "That I may know him," he says, "and the power of his resurrection";[1] as though even his certainty concerning the resurrection of Christ was precious to him because of the power which it conveyed. Jesus himself often defines discipleship to himself in terms of social utility. "By this shall all men know that ye are my disciples, if ye have love one to another."[2]

What, then, is the place of the Christian Church in the modern world? It is not a place where correctness of opinion is guarded and maintained; not a cold-storage warehouse for uncorrupted truth; not merely a place of religious utterance, or of religious symbolism, or a gymnasium of ritual

[1] Phil. iii. 10. [2] John xiii. 35.

for the calisthenics of the soul. It is, to use the language of our modern life, a "power-house," where there is generated a supply of spiritual energy sufficient to move the world with wisdom, courage, and peace. Let this power fail, and a church stands in the midst of modern life without adequate reason for existence, a Sunday club, an entertainment bureau, a survival of the days when religion was real. A living church communicates power. "The tree is known by its fruit."[1] "Every tree therefore that bringeth not forth good fruit is hewn down, and cast into the fire."[2]

And what, again, is the place of a Christian teacher or preacher in such a time? He is like one who has at his command some tremendous source of physical power, such as the cataract of Niagara provides, and who proposes to utilize this power in the service of the world. The stream has flowed for ages, abundant and unspent, but for the most part it has been rather a spectacle to admire than a power to use; and when, from time to time, timid ventures have been made to use it, they have come to harm by the very excess of power which they had not learned to control. At last arrives the new opportunity of the modern world. The miracles of modern invention and organization provide an adequate channel for the distribution of this mighty power through all the varied and correlated needs of men, and the task of the modern engineer, unprecedented in its

[1] Matt. xii. 33.   [2] Matt. iii. 10.

opportunity, is to direct and control the power itself. Never before has the world seen the mechanism of the social order adapted as it now is for the conveyance of social energy. The ample channel, thus provided, waits for the power of the Christian life, and as the sufficient stream leaps forth into the varied activities of the world, it sings as it flows, " I came that they may have life, and may have it abundantly." [1]

What, then, in its simplest statement, is the relation of the teaching of Jesus to the social question? That teaching is, for those who can receive it, the chief source of this spiritual power, for whose transmission the social order is prepared ; and of this transmission of power the humblest of the followers of Jesus may be an instrument. He sanctifies himself for others' sakes, and there is given to him unanticipated effectiveness for social service. He becomes an unobstructed channel for the water of life. "He that believeth on me, . . . out of his belly shall flow rivers of living water." [2] Much there may be in the teaching of Jesus which remains too exalted or obscure to command the honest conviction of the man of the modern world; yet he has found at least the secret of spiritual power. The view of life from above has given him command of the world below; the approach to life from within has made him master of himself ; and the direction of life to a spiritual ideal has given

[1] John x. 10. [2] John vii. 38.

him magnanimity, patience, and peace. It may not be for him to know the mysteries of the kingdom of heaven, but it is enough if he may prepare the coming of that kingdom, and the great words of Jesus support his ignorance and renew his hope : "Not every one that saith unto me, Lord, Lord, shall enter into the kingdom of heaven; but he that doeth the will of my Father which is in heaven." [1]

> " And I remember still
> The words, and from whence they came,
> Not he that repeateth the name
> But he that doeth the will.
> And him evermore I behold
> Walking in Galilee,
> Through the cornfield's waving gold
> By the shores of the Beautiful Sea.
>
> *   *   *   *   *
>
> " And that voice still soundeth on
> From the centuries that are gone
> To the centuries that shall be.
> From all vain pomps and shows,
> From the pride that overflows,
>
> *   *   *   *   *
>
> " Poor sad humanity
> Through all the dust and heat
> Turns back with bleeding feet
> By the weary round it came,
> Unto the simple thought,
> By the great Master taught,
> And that remaineth still,
> Not he that repeateth the name
> But he that doeth the will." [2]

[1] Matt. vii. 21.   [2] Longfellow, "The Golden Legend," Finale.

INDEX OF BIBLE PASSAGES

		PAGE				PAGE
Exodus	ii. 14	275	Matthew	vi. 33		277
	xix. 6	93		vi. 34		277
Leviticus	xix. 18	249		vii. 7		240
Deut.	xv. 11	228, 242		vii. 16		352
Psalms	li. 10	118		vii. 21	353, 359
	xli. 1	228		viii. 4		89
Proverbs	xiv. 21	228		viii. 5		77
Isaiah	ix. 6	86		viii. 5–13		278
	xi. 2	86		viii. 10		203
	lviii. 6	228		viii. 14		203
	lviii. 7	228		viii. 21		81
	lxiii. 9	86		ix. 9		278
Jeremiah	xxiii. 28	31		ix. 10		203
	xxiii. 29	31		x. 31		77
	xxiii. 32	31		x. 34		286
	xxiii. 39	31		x. 42	341, 353
	xxiv. 6	31		xi. 5	238, 242
	xxiv. 7	31		xi. 12		286
Daniel	ii. 44	93		xi. 25		302
Matthew	iii. 10	179, 357		xi. 28	70, 239
	iv. 3	114		xii. 28		96
	iv. 4	115		xii. 33		357
	iv. 9	296, 317		xii. 36		342
	iv. 18	77		xii. 37		342
	v.–vii.	88		xiii. 3–8		277
	v. 3	193, 200, 239		xiii. 4–7		302
	v. 5	239		xiii. 11		290
	v. 21	146		xiii. 25		302
	v. 30	214		xiii. 26		302
	v. 31	146		xiii. 31	100, 286
	v. 42	193, 237, 239, 257		xiii. 32		100
				xiii. 33		100
	vi. 2	241		xiii. 45		277
	vi. 3	217, 241		xiii. 46	92, 277
	vi. 10	92		xiii. 47		278
	vi. 19	188, 207, 277		xiii. 48		278
	vi. 20	193, 277		xiii. 54		86
	vi. 21	207		xv. 32		248
	vi. 24	189, 244		xvi. 2		4

		PAGE
Matthew	xvi. 3	4
	xvi. 27	302
	xvii. 1	88
	xvii. 9	89
	xvii. 15–18 . . .	108
	xvii. 25	275
	xviii. 4	94
	xviii. 5 . . . 94, 341
	xviii. 6	342
	xviii. 8	157
	xviii. 9	157
	xviii. 12	80
	xix. 3	146
	xix. 4	151
	xix. 5 . . . 150, 151
	xix. 6 . . 150, 152, 158
	xix. 8	155
	xix. 9 . . . 146, 159
	xix. 10	155
	xix. 10–12 . . .	156
	xix. 16–22 . . .	210
	xix. 21 . 193, 239, 240
	xix. 24	189
	xix. 30	289
	xx. 1–16	286
	xx. 6	278
	xx. 8	293
	xx. 14 . 286, 289, 293
	xx. 15	213
	xx. 16	286
	xx. 27 . 315, 316, 325
	xx. 28	315
	xxi. 33	278
	xxii. 15	274
	xxii. 18	146
	xxii. 20	193
	xxii. 21	78
	xxii. 28	159
	xxii. 30	159
	xxii. 33	147
	xxii. 39	56
	xxiii. 23	246
	xxiii. 26 . . 113, 179
	xxiv. 3 . . . 101, 305
	xxiv. 27	302
	xxiv. 30	92

		PAGE
Matthew	xxiv. 31	92
	xxiv. 33	96
	xxiv. 34	287
	xxv. 13 . . 209, 287
	xxv. 14–30 . 208, 209
	xxv. 14	222
	xxv. 16	278
	xxv. 17	278
	xxv. 20	214
	xxv. 21 . 122, 209, 214, 243
	xxv. 23	290
	xxv. 24–28 . . .	302
	xxv. 24–30 . . .	222
	xxv. 29 . . 209, 290
	xxv. 30	214
	xxv. 34 . 241, 266, 341
	xxv. 35	353
	xxv. 35 ff. . . .	217
	xxv. 40 . 71, 241, 266, 341
	xxv. 41 . . . 71, 342
	xxv. 45	342
	xxvi. 6	148
	xxvi. 7	219
	xxvi. 8	219
	xxvi. 9	219
	xxvi. 13	219
	xxvi. 21	302
Mark	i. 14	92
	i. 15	92
	i. 20	203
	ii. 15	203
	iv. 9	81
	iv. 25 . . 290, 291
	iv. 31	100
	iv. 32	100
	iv. 34	90
	viii. 15	95
	viii. 26	89
	viii. 36	113
	ix. 1	93
	ix. 23	309
	x. 1–12	152
	x. 11	146
	x. 17–23 . . .	210

		PAGE			PAGE
Mark	x. 21	211	Luke	xii. 13	194
	x. 23	188, 212		xii. 13–15	275
	x. 31	289		xii. 14	78
	x. 43	94, 205		xii. 15	79, 189
	x. 46	77		xii. 16–21	194, 208
	xii. 1–11	222		xii. 19–21	213, 277
	xii. 2	222		xii. 20	209
	xii. 9	223		xii. 22	237
	xii. 13	274		xii. 32–34	239
	xii. 37	204		xii. 33	193
	xii. 40	221		xii. 40	213
	xii. 43	217		xii. 42	243
	xiii. 34	222, 244		xii. 43	216
	xiv. 3	219		xii. 44	216
Luke	i. 53	194		xii. 48	293
	ii. 35	310		xii. 54–56	4
	ii. 51	148		xiii. 19	100
	ii. 52	86		xiii. 21	100
	iv. 4	219		xiii. 30	289
	iv. 20	238		xiv. 21	193, 286
	iv. 21	238		xiv. 33	210
	v. 11	210		xv. 4–6	278
	v. 14	89		xv. 8	80, 92, 278
	v. 27	77		xv. 9	278
	vi. 20	57, 188, 193, 200, 239		xv. 18	102, 117, 147
	vi. 24	57, 188, 193			xvi. 1–13	194, 208
	vi. 29	81		xvi. 2	246
	vi. 30	193, 240		xvi. 11	209, 278
	vii. 22	82		xvi. 18	146, 152
	vii. 37	77, 219		xvi. 20	194
	vii. 50	70		xvi. 21	210
	viii. 3	204		xvii. 5	309
	viii. 16–18	291		xvii. 6	309
	ix. 25	214		xvii. 10	244
	ix. 27	259, 300		xvii. 20	93
	ix. 28	259		xvii. 21	93, 300
	ix. 29	259		xviii. 8	314
	ix. 51	98		xviii. 13	117
	ix. 58	147		xviii. 18 ff.	210
	x. 9	300		xviii. 22	57, 189, 193, 210, 217, 234, 239, 246
	x. 23	96			
	x. 30–35	241, 249		xviii. 24	57, 216
	x. 35	250		xix. 2	203
	x. 42	77		xix. 7	77
	xi. 39–42	243		xix. 8	203, 241

		PAGE				PAGE
Luke	xix. 9	203	John	xiii. 14		325
	xix. 13	222		xiii. 15		315
	xix. 13–27	208		xiii. 29		192, 242
	xix. 20–24	222		xiii. 31		315
	xix. 22	222		xiii. 35		28, 315, 356
	xx. 20	274		xiv. 8		78
	xxi. 1	242		xiv. 12		87
	xxi. 3	242		xiv. 19		90, 353
	xxi. 4	242		xv. 26		302
	xxii. 12–38	88		xvi. 7		90
	xxii. 27	315		xvi. 13		82, 302
	xxii. 36	81		xvi. 31		309
	xxii. 69	302		xvii. 4		88
	xxiv. 21	90		xvii. 19		91, 104
	xxiv. 32	310		xviii. 15		203
John	ii. 1–11	76, 148		xviii. 36		94, 276
	ii. 2	81		xviii. 37		276
	iii. 1	77, 203		xix. 26		148
	iii. 1–21	89, 205		xix. 27		148
	iii. 35	315		xix. 30		88
	iv. 7–26	205		xix. 38		204
	iv. 7–29	89		xix. 39		204
	iv. 24	148		xx. 21		89
	iv. 26	148		xxi. 3 ff.		203
	iv. 35	301	Acts	ii. 4		198
	vi. 37	239		ii. 44		22, 198
	vi. 63	90		iii. 2		259
	vii. 38	358		iii. 5		260
	viii. 7–11	148		iii. 6		260
	viii. 12	74		iv. 32		22
	ix. 1	77		iv. 37		25
	ix. 1–12	258		v. 1–10		25
	ix. 8	259		v. 4		25, 98
	x. 2–5	277		vi. 1		199
	x. 10	90, 353, 358		viii. 27		199
	xi. 1–44	76		ix. 34		259
	xi. 6	81		xi. 29		24
	xi. 21–27	148		xii. 12		24
	xii. 1	88		xiii. 7		199
	xii. 3	204, 219		xiv. 10		259
	xii. 5	192, 243		xvii. 34		199
	xii. 7	148		xviii. 8		199
	xii. 8	148, 239		xx. 35		248
	xii. 32	86, 263		xxiii. 6		77, 199
	xii. 35	74	Romans	viii. 19		102, 126
	xii. 46	74		xiii. 8		246

			PAGE				PAGE
Romans	xiv. 17	. . . .	99	Galatians	vi. 10	. . . .	196
I Cor.	i. 26	. . . .	196	Philemon	iii. 10	. . . .	356
	iii. 21	. . . .	201		iv. 11	. . . .	196
	iii. 23	. . . .	201		iv. 18	. . . .	196
	xi. 22	. . . .	196	I Timothy	vi. 18	. . . .	196
	xiii. 3	. . .	196, 264	James	i. 11	. . . .	201
	xiii. 7	. . . . .	260		ii. 18	. . . .	232
	xvi. 2	. . . . .	24		v. 1	. . . . .	198
II Cor.	ix. 7	. . . .	24, 196	I John	v. 4	. . . . .	309
I Thess.	ii. 9	. . . . .	196	Revelation	ii. 5	. . . . .	291
II Thess.	iii. 12	. . . .	24		xi. 15	. . . .	322

INDEX

Abbott, Lyman, 69 *note*.
Acts of the Apostles, 197, 198.
Adler, G., 28 *note*.
Allen, A. V. G., 91 *note*.
Ananias, sin of, 25.
Arnold, Matthew, 96, 119.
Aschrott, P. F., 255 *note*.
Aveling, E. B., 141 *note*.

Bagehot, W., 135, 313 *note*.
Barnabas, the disciple, 25.
Bax, Belfort, 16, 142 *note*.
Bebel, A., 3 *note*, 16, 19, 140 *note*, 141 *note*.
Beyschlag, W., 68 *note*, 91 *note*, 93 *note*, 95 *note*, 98 *note*.
Biedermann, A. E., 103 *note*.
Bödicker, 39 *note*.
Böhmer, Julius, 68 *note*.
Böhmert, Victor, 256 *note*.
Bonar, J., 13 *note*.
Bosanquet, B., 230 *note*.
Bousset, W., 95 *note*.
Brace, C. L., 227 *note*.
Bradley, F. H., 59.
Brentano, L., 37 *note*.
Brooke, Stopford, 74, 219 *note*.
Brooks, J. G., 46 *note*.
Brooks, Phillips, 68 *note*, 90.
Browning, E. B., 114.
Browning, Robert, 293, 294.
Bruce, A. B., 68 *note*, 101 *note*.
Burns, John, 311.
Bushnell, Horace, 132 *note*.
Business, Christian conduct of, 244 ff.; pessimistic views of, 316; a system of social service, 317 ff.; ethical quality of, 319 ff.; the law of service in, 321 ff.

Campbell, Colin, 191 *note*.

Cannon, W. B., 83 *note*.
Carlyle, 31 ff.
Carpenter, J. E., 192 *note*.
Catholic Church, in the social movement, 41 ff.; social doctrine of, 45, 46 *note*.
Charity, rejection of, 6; old and new view, 8; problem of, 116; use of wealth for, 217; Christian, 226 ff.; early Christian, 231; suspicion of, 234 ff.; revolutionists' opinion of, 236; dangerous form of, 243; begins at home, 245; changes advocated in, 251; institutionalism in, 253 ff.; organization of, 257; its real task, 261 ff.; nature of Christian, 264; specialists in, 329.
Children, in the socialist State, 143; care of, 168 ff.; in a Christian home, 181; care of, in institutions, 253.
Christianity, socialist opinion of, 16, 19 ff.; relation to social question, 21; mark of modern, 29; schemes for applying to social question, 30, 36, 41, 53; essence of modern, 69 ff.; attitude toward woman, 148; root in family affection, 148 *note*; influence on work for the poor, 233; final test of, 315.
Christie, F. A., 54 *note*.
Church, R. W., 69 *note*, 229 *note*.
Church, the, relation of labor to, 15; relation of social reform to, 26 ff.; institutional, 29; to enter industry, 43, 45; no economic programme, 49; loss of influence, 56; the revolutionists' view of,

64; organization of, 72; traditions respecting Jesus, 85; transformation of, 110; danger of, 126; attitude toward divorce, 131; in Jerusalem, 200; ethical degradation of, 221; its relations to the poor, 232; abuse of charity in, 235 ff.; mistaken charity of, 262; rejection of, 298; its potentiality, 351; a source of spiritual energy, 353; true work of, 354; its place in the modern world, 356.

Club, working-men's, 337 ff.

"Columbia College Studies," 130 note.

Commercialism, danger of, 175 ff.; emancipation from, 220; in business, 322, 325.

Commissioner of Labor, report on marriage and divorce, 130 note, 164 note.

Communism, Christian, 22 ff.; nature of, at Jerusalem, 25, 199; New Testament commentators on, 26 note.

Competition, 38, 313 note.

Conrad, J., 233 note.

Contemporary Review, 64, 66.

Cook, F. G., 131 note.

Coöperation, 28.

Coöperative societies, 15, 47, 283 ff.

Coulanges, F. de, 134 note, 229 note.

Curzon, on Le Play, 39 note.

Darwin, 136.

Davies, J. Ll., 69 note.

Devas, C. L., 13 note.

Dike, S. W., 131 note.

Divorce, increase of, 129; teaching of Jesus concerning, 152 ff.; law of Moses on, 155; futility of remedial legislation, 162; in cities, 164; among the prosperous, 171, 177.

Donald, E. W., 69 note.

Drummond, J., 69 note.

Ebionism, 191 note.

"Ecce Homo," 55, 67 note, 73 note, 146 note, 148 note, 309.

Economics, relation to ethics, 13 note; of early Christians, 25; Carlyle and Ruskin as teachers of, 33, 35; study of, 36; un-Christian character of, prevailing, 38; the fundamental problem of, 105; of the New Testament, 274.

Egoism, danger of, 173; in antiquity, 227.

Elvers, R., 46 note.

Ely, R. T., 69 note.

Emerson, R. W., 265.

Engels, Friedrich, 16, 17 note.

Ethics, and the social question, 10, 12, 13 note, 346; the old, 12; and economics, 12 note; must solve social question, 40; social, of Jesus, 103; lower standards of, 172 ff.; double standard of, 220; in the labor question, 273.

Fairbairn, A. M., 68 note.

Faith, power of, 309; strength of men of, 313; need of, 314.

Family, the, value questioned, 7; place in social question, 40; open to change, 124; teaching of Jesus concerning, 129 ff.; evolution of, 134 ff.; patriarchal theory of, 135; the primitive, 137; socialist teaching about, 140 ff.; economic usefulness of, 141 ff.; a bulwark of the present order, 144 ff., 162; emphasized by Jesus, 145 ff.; its place in the thought of Jesus, 149; permanence of, 158 ff.; the hope of the world, 161; causes undermining its stability, 163 ff.; chief peril to, 174; undermined by commercialism, 175 ff.; solution of the problem of, 178; what is a Christian, 180 ff.

Fiske, John, 136.

Flint, Robert, 18 *note*, 69 *note*.
Force, transformation of social, 340 ff.; the fundamental social, 346.
Fowle, T. W., 255 *note*, 261 *note*.
France, social question in, 40 ff.
Fremantle, W. H., 68 *note*.
Friedländer, Ludwig, 229 *note*.

Garnett, Richard, 31 *note*.
George, Henry, 10.
Germany, social question in, 41 ff.; Protestant social programme in, 48; militarism in, 109.
Gibbins, H. de B., 31 *note*.
Gilbert, G. H., 68 *note*.
Girard, on Von Ketteler, 42 *note*.
Gladden, Washington, 69 *note*.
Göhre, P., 17 *note*, 29 *note*, 46 *note*, 48 *note*, 60 *note*, 62 *note*, 71 *note*, 142.
Good Samaritan, the, lesson of, 241, 249, 255, 257.
Gore, Charles, 69 *note*.
Gospel, the, nature of, 78; study of, 81; characteristics of, 83, 88; apocalyptic ideas in, 95 ff.; variations in, 152; demands family integrity, 162; distorted by literalism, 190; the fourth, disregards material things, 192; peculiarity of the third, 194; its estimate of alms, 241; tolerance of, 288.
Graham, W., 186.
Grégoire, L. (pseudonym), 37 *note*, 46 *note*.
Gronlund, L., 141.
Guilds, 45.

Hadley, A. T., 13 *note*.
Harmel, Léon, 45.
Harnack, A., 101 *note*.
Harris, George, 69 *note*.
Hart, A. B., 164 *note*.
Hasler, F., 13 *note*.
Haupt, Erich, 96 *note*.
Hegel, effect of his philosophy on socialism, 18 ff.

Henderson, C. R., 233 *note*.
Herrmann, W., 16 *note*, 18 *note*.
Herron, G. D., 26 *note*, 63 *note*, 189 *note*, 306 *note*, 316 *note*.
Higgs, H., 39 *note*.
Hobbes, Thomas, 9.
Hobson, J. A., on Carlyle, 31 *note*, 34 *note*.
Hodges, G., 69 *note*.
Holtzmann, H., 20 *note*, 27 *note*, 60 *note*, 93 *note*, 101 *note*, 191 *note*, 194 *note*, 274 *note*.
Holtzmann, O., 28 *note*, 190 *note*.
Holy Ghost, sin against, 25; will guide men to truth, 302.
Huber, Victor, 46 ff.

Ibsen, 304 *note*.
Ideal, social, of Jesus, 91 ff., 121; remoteness of the spiritual, 119; of socialism, 122; of social service, 255; the expression of, in business, 314.
Idealism, of Jesus, 104; not outgrown, 123, 128; of industrial agitation, 307.
Individual, the, 80, 89, 101, 103; responsibility of, 116; his devotion to an ideal, 119; his limitations and emancipation, 120; his development by society, 131 ff.; in the family, 173 ff.; ideals of, purified, 178; redemption of the world by, 309; his responsibility, 323; must serve society, 352.
Industrial order, 267; present condition of, 268 ff.; causes of antagonism in, 272 ff.; Christian view of, 279; its effect on men, 281 ff.; transition in, 297; different feelings toward, 302 ff.; Christian problem of, 325.
Issel, Ernst, 95 *note*.

James, Epistle of, 197, 198 ff.
Jannet, C., 39 *note*.

2 B

Jerusalem, communism among Christians at, 24 ff., 199.

Jesus Christ, his rebuke to those who cannot see the signs of the times, 3; and the socialists, 17; his gospel, 20; did not enjoin communism, 24, 26; his social teaching, 53 ff., 76 ff.; laborers' respect for, 65; of the churches and of the gospels, 66; imitation of, 70; adaptation of his teaching, 71 ff.; different views of, 72 ff.; his supreme concern, 77; social teaching not his aim, 79; method of teaching, 80 ff.; how interpreted, 81; reason for his insight, 84; his picture in art, 86; teaching universal, 87; did not systematize, 89; his social ideal, 91, 100; his eschatological sayings, 95 ff.; his philosophy of religion, 102; individualist or socialist, 103 ff.; his ministry for this life, 106; aspects of his teaching, 107 ff.; his way of salvation, 110, 111; his temptation, 114; his belief in personal responsibility, 117; his contribution to the social question, 123; his teaching concerning principles, 125; interest in his personality, 127; his leadership, 128; teaching about the family, 145 ff.; his sympathy for domestic life, 147; respect for women, 148; on marriage and divorce, 151 ff.; his answer to the Sadducees, 159; his solution of the problem of the family, 178; how to interpret, 191; his environment, 202 ff.; taught all classes, 204 ff.; teaching concerning the rich, 207 ff.; and the rich young man, 210 ff.; apparent conflict of his teachings, 212; severity of his message to the rich, 214 ff.; whom he commends, 222 ff.; his teaching concerning the poor, 226 ff.; his view of alms, 241

ff.; his doctrine of stewardship, 243; the modern tone of his teaching about the poor, 246; his method of dealing with the poor, 248, 258; did not teach economics, 273 ff.; his teaching concerning industry, 276 ff.; method of approaching the industrial question, 290 ff.; on cumulative returns, 290 ff.; reconciliation of his industrial teachings, 292 ff.; relation of his and the socialists' ideal, 294 ff.; an optimist, 300 ff.; what justified his hope of the world, 308 ff.; relation of his teaching to thrift, 312; practical application of his teaching, 314 ff.; how to follow him in business, 323 ff.; his teaching on the correlation of forces, 340 ff.; test of discipleship to him, 352.

Jodl, Friedrich, 13 note.

Jones, Henry, 103 note.

Juvenal, 229 note.

Kaftan, J., 55, note.

Kaufmann, M., 11 note, 15 note, 37 note, 42 note, 48 note.

Keane, Bishop, 46, note.

Keim, Th., 152 note, 191 note, 227 note.

"Kernel and the husk," 65, 299.

Ketteler, W. I. von, 42 ff.

Kingdom of God, 91 ff.; how it is to come, 101, 118; what it offers, 120; Christian law designed to establish, 158; thought of Jesus concerning, 285 ff.; confidence of Jesus in, 300.

Kingsley, Charles, 37 note, 38.

Köhler, Hermann, 15 note, 16 note, 18 note, 27 note.

Lamennais, 41 ff.

Lanciani, Rodolfo, 230 note.

Lange, F. A., 13 note.

Lassalle, F., 18, 42 ff.

Lecky, W. E. H., 227 *note*, 231, 235 ff.

Leclaire, E. J., 314 *note*.

Leo XIII, Encyclical of May, 1891, 45, 46 *note*.

Le Play, F., 39 ff.

Liebknecht, W., 19.

Lightfoot, J. B., 231 *note*.

Lipsius, R. A., 103 *note*.

Lloyd, A. P., 130 *note*.

Longfellow, H. W., 359.

Lowell, J. R., 8, 9.

Lubbock, Sir John, 134 *note*.

Luke, Gospel of, Ebionism in, 191 *note ;* its teaching about rich and poor, 192 ff.; peculiarity of, 194 ff.; Paulinism in, 195.

Lütgenau, Franz, 17 *note*.

Mackay, T., 255 *note*.

McLennan, J. F., 134 *note*.

Maine, Sir Henry, 132, 135 *note*.

Mark, Gospel of, 192, 197.

Marriage, two conceptions of, 121 ff.; in the light of social evolution, 138 ff.; socialist opinion of, 141 *note;* popular discussion of, 144; teaching of Jesus concerning, 151; after divorce, 154; regulation of, 155; only alternative to, 156; rule of, 157 ff.; sanity of teaching concerning, 159 ff.; how Jesus approaches the problem of, 160; selfishness in, 173; commercial spirit in, 175 ff.; Christian, 181.

Marshall, A., 283.

Marx, Karl, 16, 18.

Materialism, 18, 20, 105.

Mathews, Shailer, 68 *note*, 95 *note*, 102 *note*, 148 *note*, 189 *note*.

Matthew, Gospel of, sayings about rich and poor in, 193; in harmony with Paul's epistles, 197.

Maurice, F. D., 21, 37 *note*, 46 *note*.

Mayo-Smith, R., 130 *note*.

Mazzini, Joseph, 14, 42 *note*.

Mehring, F., 17 *note*.

Men, their production the end of society, 310; strengthened by conflict, 313.

Meyer's Commentary, on Jesus' teaching concerning divorce, 152 *note*.

Mommsen, Th., 229 *note*.

Morris, William, 8, 35 *note*.

Mun, A., Comte de, 44.

Münsterberg, E., 256 *note*.

" Musée Social," 39 *note*.

Nash, H. S., 13 *note*.

Nathusius, M. von, 20 *note*, 27 *note*, 41 *note*, 68 *note*.

Nations, mission of, 1 ; retribution upon, 31.

Naumann, F., 17, 52, 61, 140 *note*, 141 *note*, 142 *note*, 189 *note*, 307 *note*.

Neander, J. A. W., 85 *note*.

Newman, J. H., 91 *note*.

Nitti, F. S., 26 *note*, 41 *note*, 42 *note*, 46 *note*, 63.

Nobili-Vitelleschi, F., 14 *note*.

Opportunism, Christian, 36 ff., 104.

Optimism, of Jesus, 300 ff., 308; in industrial agitation, 302.

Outlook, The, 190.

" Parliamentary Report on Elberfeld System," 256 *note*.

Paul, on communism among Christians, 24; his idea of the kingdom of God, 99; on poverty and riches, 195 ff., 201.

Paulsen, F., 13 *note*, 82 *note*, 215 *note*.

Peabody, F. G., 79 *note*, 188, 228 *note*, 233 *note*, 251 *note*, 252 *note*, 256 *note*.

Pearson, Karl, 143 *note*.

Personality, its place in the social order, 102, 104, 127 ; modification of, 110; the aim of Jesus, 111, 126; development of, 112; Mrs. Browning on, 114; its place in organization, 125 ff.; in the industrial order, 282 ff.

Pessimism, in modern socialism, 304 ff.; revolutionary character of, 306; false note of, 306 ff.

Pfleiderer, O., 27 note; 103 note.

Pflüger, Paul, 65 note.

Philanthropy, its ethical note, 10; as an application of the Christian spirit to the social question, 27 ff.; the social question goes beyond, 29; not to rest satisfied with alms, 48; what it needs, 107; work of, 166; found root in Rome, 230; scope of Christian, 231; best form of, 256; mistaken, 339.

Pliny the Younger, 230 note.

Plummer, A., on Ebionism in Luke, 192 note, 194 note.

Political Science Quarterly, 131 note.

Politicus (pseudonym), 32 note.

Poor, the, Jesus' teaching concerning, 226 ff.; Jewish care for, 228; care of, by the church, 232; thought of Jesus for, 238; method of Jesus in dealing with, 248 ff.; different types of, 251; cannot be relieved wholesale, 254; relieved by communicating power, 260 ff.; how power is given to, 263; injudicious efforts for, 330.

Population, concentration of, 163; suburban, 167.

Potter, H. C., 132 note.

Preacher, the, legitimate work for, 30; limitations of, 35; his place in the modern world, 357.

Property, private, its right questioned, 7; open to change, 124; transmission of, 141; its test as an institution, 187; tendency of its possession, 297 note.

Prophet, the, in the social question, 30 ff; criticism of, 35 ff.; of the Old Testament, 87.

Rade, M., 17 note, 65 note, 69 note, 140 note.

Rae, John, 42 note, 48 note.

Ragaz, L., 13 note.

Reformers, weakness of, 319; how they must approach the social problem, 331; enthusiasm of, 332; their first question, 350.

Regeneration, how effected, 90; need of, 115; fundamental, 117; of the world, 309.

Religion, and social discontent, 15; socialist attitude toward, 16; test of, 28; how it meets the social question, 30; social utilization of, 36 ff.; in industrial life, 39; organization of labor by, 43 ff.; Christ's philosophy of, 102; as dependence on God, 103; as solution of the social question, 106; institutionalization of, 109; harmony of, with science, 341; the test of, 356.

Renan, E., on communism in primitive Christianity, 26 note; on social teaching of Jesus, 58; on teaching concerning riches, 191 note.

Repentance, character of, 147.

Réville, A., 229 note.

Ribbe, C. de, 39 note.

Rich, the, 183 ff; teaching of Jesus concerning, 188 ff., 207 ff.; Paul on the duty of, 196; followers of Jesus, 203 ff.; Jewish opinion of, 206; message of Jesus to, 213 ff.; severity of Jesus' demands on, 214; Christian life of, 223 ff.

Riis, J. A., 253 note.

Robertson, J. M., 31 note.

Rogge, Christian, 27 note, 192 note, 194 note, 198 note, 206 note.

Rome, corruption of, 228 ff.

Runze, George, 13 *note*.
Ruskin, 31 *note*, 32 ff., 34 ff., 184, 289, 310 *note*.
Russland, Gustav, 68 *note*.

Sabatier, August, 68 *note*.
Schleiermacher, 102, 103 *note*.
Schmidt, C., 227 *note*.
Schmidt-Warneck, 68 *note*.
Schmoller, Otto, 95 *note*.
Schnedermann, Georg, 93 *note*, 95 *note*.
Schopenhauer, 20.
Schulze-Gävernitz, G. von, 31 *note*.
Schurman, J. G., 134 *note*.
Seneca, 85 *note*.
Shaw, Bernard, 143.
Sin, responsible for social evil, 116; for industrial evil, 296.
Smyth, Newman, 13 *note*.
Social congresses, 37, 55 *note*, 61.
Social democracy, the, programme of, 4, 16 *note*, 44, 295; approves working-men's associations, 42; condemned by Stöcker, 49; rejects Christian socialism, 51.
Social machinery, 108 ff.; dangers in, 113; must be readjusted in each age, 310; must have moral power, 347 ff.
Social question, the, 2 ff.; present characteristics of, 5 ff., 9 ff.; interest of, 11; ethical character, 11, 12 *note*; relation to religion, 14; misinterpretation of, 20; relation of Carlyle and Ruskin to, 31 ff.; ethical rather than economic, 40; teaching of Jesus concerning, 53 ff., 76 ff.; Jesus' view of, 104; all engrossing, 105; how solved, 106; externalism in, 108, 112; how far the fault of the individual, 115 ff.; its root in moral evil, 296; its correlation, 327 ff.; transformations of, 329 ff.; expansion of, 333; fundamentally ethical, 347.

Socialism, attitude toward religion, 14, 16 ff.; Christian, 41 ff., 46 ff., 50 ff.; relation to social democracy, 52, 61; creed of, 109; its end ideal, 122; in the teaching of Jesus, 287; its creed a substitute for religion, 298; misrepresents the world, 308.
Socialists, their philosophy of history, 18, 140; legislation against, 49, 51; Protestant, 51; Christian, 61; attack on the family, 140; on marriage, 141 *note*; on the family, 142 ff.; self-deception of, 180; their distrust of Jesus' teaching, 288 ff.; relation of their ideal and Jesus' ideal, 294 ff.: optimism of, 303; pessimism of, 304 ff.
Söderblom, Nathan, 69 *note*.
Soderini, Count Edward, 46 *note*.
Spectator, 313 *note*.
Spencer, Herbert, 112, 139 *note*, 344.
Starcke, C. N., 134 *note*.
State, the, questioned as an institution, 7; socialism of, in Germany, 48; as a social unit, 140; must relieve destitution, 260; evolution of the socialist, 304 ff.
Stein, Ludwig, 13 *note*, 17 *note*, 28 *note*, 59 *note*, 140 *note*, 297 *note*.
Stevens, G. B., 93 *note*, 101 *note*.
Stimson, F. J., 32 *note*,
Stöcker, A., 48 ff.
Sumner, W. G., 235 *note*.

Taylor, Sedley, on profit-sharing, 314 *note*.
Temperance, sphere of, 333 ff.; economic progress dependent on, 336; method of, 349.
Tenements, model, 166 ff.
Theology, its interest not social, 54 ff.; reaction from, 56 ff.; change of, 69; beginning of, 72; of Jesus, 147.

Thrift, old and new views of, 311 ff.

Tillet, Ben, 6 *note*.

Todt, Rudolf, 26 *note*, 60 ff.

Toy, C. H., 93 *note*, 97 *note*, 98 *note*.

Uhland, Ludwig, 18 *note*.

Uhlhorn, Gerhard, 27 *note*, 29 *note*, 68 *note*, 227 *note*.

Unemployed, the, 184.

United States, criticised by Carlyle and Ruskin, 34; divorce in, 129; charity in, 233.

Van Dyke, Henry, 9, 73, 304 *note*.

Vogüé, E. M., Vicomte de, 46 *note*.

Wagner, A., 2, 3 *note*, 18 *note*, 295 *note*.

Walsh, W., 58 *note*.

Wealth, distribution of, 185 ff.; brought to the test of utility, 187; divergent teaching about, in New Testament, 193 ff., 201;
sayings of Jesus about, 208 ff.; enervating effect of, 211; a trust, 213, 216; how rightly used, 216 ff.; its ministry to happiness, 218; its use in business, 220 ff.

Weiss, Bernhard, 68 *note*, 101 *note*, 192 *note*.

Weiss, J., 95, *note*.

Weizsäcker, Karl von, 27 *note*.

Wendt, H. H., 27 *note*, 68 *note*, 80, 82, 92 *note*, 93 *note*, 95 *note*, 98 *note*, 152 *note*, 191 *note*.

Westcott, B. F., 69 *note*.

Westermarck, E., 134 *note*.

Wichern, J. H., 28.

Willcox, W. F., 130 *note*.

Wilmanns, Gustav, 230 *note*.

Winterstein, A., 46 *note*.

Wright, C. D., 13 *note*, 131 *note*, 164 *note*, 307 *note*.

Wundt, W., 13 *note*.

Yarnall, E., 38 *note*.

Zahn, Th., 198.

Ziegler, Theobald, 12 *note*.

Zinzendorf, N. L., Count von, 87.

New Testament Handbooks

EDITED BY

SHAILER MATHEWS

Professor of New Testament History and Interpretation,
University of Chicago

Arrangements are made for the following volumes, and the publishers will, on request, send notice of the issue of each volume as it appears and each descriptive circular sent out later; such requests for information should state whether address is permanent or not: —

The History of the Textual Criticism of the New Testament

Prof. MARVIN R. VINCENT, Professor of New Testament Exegesis, Union Theological Seminary. [*Now ready.*

Professor Vincent's contributions to the study of the New Testament rank him among the first American exegetes. His most recent publication is " A Critical and Exegetical Commentary on the Epistles to the Philippians and to Philemon " (*International Critical Commentary*), which was preceded by a " Students' New Testament Handbook," " Word Studies in the New Testament," and others.

The History of the Higher Criticism of the New Testament

Prof. HENRY S. NASH, Professor of New Testament Interpretation, Cambridge Divinity School. [*Now ready.*

Of Professor Nash's " Genesis of the Social Conscience," *The Outlook* said: " The results of Professor Nash's ripe thought are presented in a luminous, compact, and often epigrammatic style. The treatment is at once masterful and helpful, and the book ought to be a quickening influence of the highest kind; it surely will establish the fame of its author as a profound thinker, one from whom we have a right to expect future inspiration of a kindred sort."

Introduction to the Books of the New Testament

Prof. B. WISNER BACON, Professor of New Testament Interpretation, Yale University. [*Now ready.*

Professor Bacon's works in the field of Old Testament criticism include " The Triple Tradition of Exodus," and " The Genesis of Genesis," a study of the documentary sources of the books of Moses. In the field of New Testament study he has published a number of brilliant papers, the most recent of which is " The Autobiography of Jesus," in the *American Journal of Theology*.

The History of New Testament Times in Palestine

Prof. SHAILER MATHEWS, Professor of New Testament History and Interpretation, The University of Chicago. [*Now ready.*

The Congregationalist says of Prof. Shailer Mathews's recent work, " The Social Teaching of Jesus " : " Re-reading deepens the impression that the author is scholarly, devout, awake to all modern thought, and yet conservative and pre-eminently sane. If, after reading the chapters dealing with Jesus' attitude toward man, society, the family, the state, and wealth, the reader will not agree with us in this opinion, we greatly err as prophets."

The Life of Paul

Prof. RUSH RHEES, President of the University of Rochester.

Professor Rhees is well known from his series of "Inductive Lessons" contributed to the *Sunday School Times*. His "Outline of the Life of Paul," privately printed, has had a flattering reception from New Testament scholars.

The History of the Apostolic Age

Dr. C. W. VOTAW, Instructor in New Testament Literature, The University of Chicago.

Of Dr. Votaw's "Inductive Study of the Founding of the Christian Church," *Modern Church*, Edinburgh, says: "No fuller analysis of the later books of the New Testament could be desired, and no better programme could be offered for their study, than that afforded in the scheme of fifty lessons on the *Founding of the Christian Church*, by Clyde W. Votaw. It is well adapted alike for practical and more scholarly students of the Bible."

The Teaching of Jesus

Prof. GEORGE B. STEVENS, Professor of Systematic Theology, Yale University. [*Now ready*.

Professor Stevens's volumes upon "The Johannine Theology," "The Pauline Theology," as well as his recent volume on "The Theology of the New Testament," have made him probably the most prominent writer on biblical theology in America. His new volume will be among the most important of his works.

The Biblical Theology of the New Testament

Prof. E. P. GOULD, Professor of New Testament Interpretation, Protestant Episcopal Divinity School, Philadelphia. [*Now ready*.

Professor Gould's Commentaries on the Gospel of Mark (in the *International Critical Commentary*) and the Epistles to the Corinthians (in the *American Commentary*) are critical and exegetical attempts to supply those elements which are lacking in existing works of the same general aim and scope.

The History of Christian Literature until Eusebius

Prof. J. W. PLATNER, Professor of Early Church History, Harvard University.

Professor Platner's work will not only treat the writings of the early Christian writers, but will also treat of the history of the New Testament Canon.

OTHERS TO FOLLOW

"An excellent series of scholarly, yet concise and inexpensive New Testament handbooks." — *Christian Advocate*, New York.

"These books are remarkably well suited in language, style, and price, to all students of the New Testament." — *The Congregationalist*, Boston.

THE MACMILLAN COMPANY

66 FIFTH AVENUE, NEW YORK